MAGNUM OPUS

Library of Congress Cataloging-in-Publication Data
Longhurst, John.

  Magnum opus : the building of the Schoenstein organ at the Conference Center of the Church of Jesus Christ of Latter-day Saints, Salt Lake City / John Longhurst.

            p. cm.

  Includes bibliographical references and index.

  "A symphonic organ for the world's largest theater auditorium" (reprint of article by Jack Bethards in The American organist, Jan. 2004)--P.
  ISBN 978-1-60641-199-5 (hardbound : alk. Paper) 1. Conference Center (Salt Lake City, Utah)--Organs.
2. Organ (Musical instrument)--Construction--Utah--Salt Lake City. 3. Salt Lake City (Utah)--Buildings, Structures, etc. I. Bethards, Jack M. Symphonic organ for the world's largest theater auditorium. II. Title.

  ML594.S2L6 2009

  786.5'19792258--dc22

                          2009025706

Printed in the United States of America
Carr Printing, Bountiful, UT
Blake Palmer, Layout and Design
10 9 8 7 6 5 4 3 2 1

MAGNUM OPUS

THE BUILDING OF
THE SCHOENSTEIN ORGAN
AT THE
CONFERENCE CENTER
OF
THE CHURCH OF JESUS CHRIST OF LATTER-DAY SAINTS
SALT LAKE CITY

BY JOHN LONGHURST

MORMON
TABERNACLE
CHOIR®

CONTENTS

FOREWORD

This Great Work

When I first heard the Salt Lake Tabernacle's brand new Æolian-Skinner organ over the radio in 1949, I never dreamed that I would hear it in person, let alone become a professional organ builder working at Temple Square. I had just become interested in pipe organs, having watched the Schoenstein firm rebuild the organ in our little carpenter-gothic Episcopal church in Northern California. The Tabernacle organ, even over a car radio, gave the impression of being a whale of a lot larger than what I had thought, until then, was a giant and mysterious behemoth in our little church.

Our Sunday morning routine was to listen to what my mother called "The Richard Evans Program" in the car as we drove a fairly good distance from our ranch to church. We would sit in the parking lot until the very last minute and then bolt into the last pew for Morning Prayer. I wanted to stay until I heard Richard Evans say "This is CBS, the Columbia Broadcasting System," but my mother usually won out. What I did hear of that closing theme has stayed in my ears ever since.

I doubt that anything has brought more people into the organ world as players or builders than has the Mormon Tabernacle Choir's broadcast, *Music and the Spoken Word*. I also doubt that anyone could think of making music or building organs at Temple Square as anything less than a singular honor, a unique challenge, and a career high point. My colleagues and I had this pinnacle experience not once, but twice! When we completed the four-year renovation of G. Donald Harrison's Tabernacle masterpiece in 1989, I thought, "Nothing can top this." To learn what that organ had to teach us, and to work on it in collaboration with the Tabernacle organists and technicians, was an opportunity we especially treasured, because we thought it could never be repeated. Somehow, fortune smiled on us again, and we were able to return to Temple Square to build the organ for the new 21,000-seat Conference Center just ten years later.

In deciding whether we should take on this huge project, we were torn by two equally powerful forces. Our desire to get back to Temple Square and enjoy the collegial relationship with people who shared our musical vision was tempered by the chance that we could fall flat on our faces in total failure! Before us was an organ building problem that had never been thought of, let alone solved, in the history of organ building. Giant organs had been built for giant rooms, but never for a theatre-style auditorium with an acoustic designed primarily for speech. We were in completely uncharted territory, with nothing to guide us. There were no pipe scales to copy, not even a stoplist to start our thinking. There was a good probability of an embarrassingly pathetic result that could ruin our firm. Well, I thought, "What's the point of having a company with no board of directors to answer to, if you can't take a risk once in a while?" The Schoenstein family before me took plenty of risks, and our crew was willing to do the same, so we jumped in.

We used every bit of experience we had, studied every source we could think of that would be relevant and, most of all, tried to apply musical and acoustical common sense based on our experience in working in normally sized rooms with dry acoustics. All of that was helpful, but I have now become convinced that something else was at work on this job. You can attribute it to anything you wish, but there surely was some special force at work. I remember clearly one very short phrase that kept recurring in President Hinckley's talks—"This Great Work." He was referring to the work of the Church in all of its phases. Building this Conference Center to bring members of the Church together twice each year was part of This Great Work. When you heard President Hinckley say those three words, it meant volumes more than thirteen letters on this page. He made us realize that we were part of This Great Work—a small part to be sure, but part all the same. I think everyone involved with the Conference Center project felt the same way. You could tell it in the dedication they put into what seemed to be an impossible job. You will read in these pages that the timetable looked unobtainable to even the most heroic of construction workers, but they pulled it off. We thought the acoustic might be unconquerable, but it wasn't. We thought that it would be unthinkable to design an organ case with a large committee of experts, but it wasn't. These are just a few examples of impossible situations that turned around quite mysteriously.

The acoustical questions were magnified, because we had to build the organ before the building was finished. Normally, we design an organ based on an elaborate testing procedure using organ pipes of different scales at each octave to determine the acoustical "curve" of the completed building. We then base our pipe scaling on those findings. In this case, all we had to work with were theoretical projections based on computer modeling provided to us by Paul Scarborough of Jaffe, Holden, Scarborough Acoustics. We have used this system before, but only when the graphs were backed up with lots of prior experience with buildings of a similar size and shape. I had worked with Paul and the Jaffe firm on other projects and had high confidence in their ability, so we plowed ahead.

Scaling was worked out, pipe orders were written, and our usual very detailed voicing instructions were determined for every stop. All this work made us feel good, but the fear of this monster building, with its gaping jaws of acoustical infinity, haunted us constantly. We were not very encouraged when we went to the partially finished auditorium and couldn't even hear a person talking from thirty feet away. On the other hand, loud construction noises echoed on-and-on. The room appeared to combine the deathly quiet of the Arabian Desert and the yodeler's delight of the Swiss Alps. We came back to the shop and kept working with the hope—not the faith—that things would work out!

When we first experienced the finished room, we couldn't believe what we were hearing. It was the sound you'd expect in a very nice modern symphony hall: a pleasant resonance, good sound transmission, and a smooth frequency response. In other words, it turned out to be very much like buildings we had worked in before! At that point, we finally had confidence that our system of designing for this kind of acoustic would work here as well. The main point of that system is placing the center of tonal gravity in the mid-range, where the music is written, concentrating on rich tonal colors that project well such as open and harmonic flutes, strings, and energized diapasons, and depending on reed choruses to furnish the final climax of power, dedicating flue upperwork to providing a distinctive color to the ensemble.

The other miracle of this job was the organ case. The only charge we had from the Church was to bring a bit of the feeling of the Tabernacle organ case to this new building so that people would feel at home. Nothing we came up with seemed to work. What transpired is covered in Chapter Six, which reads like a novel. The process certainly was suspenseful! The case ended up being designed by a very large committee. Generally, that results in a disaster; everyone knows that a camel is a horse designed by a committee! We were nearly as worried about this as we were about the acoustics. When I say that something special was at work here, the results of this committee's work prove it. Despite our misgivings, the process worked with remarkable smoothness. Each person contributed something of value, and the whole was far greater than the sum of its parts.

Looking back on this project, all the mishaps, anxiety, and pressure have faded away in the glow of hearing and seeing the finished result in regular use on Temple Square. Even that regular use is somewhat of a miracle. When the organ was designed, all of us involved in the project thought it would be used just twice a year for general conference and perhaps a few other times for special programs. It has turned out that the Conference Center organ has become a real partner with the Tabernacle organ and has been used regularly for everything from the summer season recitals to Sunday morning broadcasts, for Christmas and Pioneer Day concerts, and for special events far more numerous than were ever expected.

As you read this book, try to imagine the feeling of gratitude that those of us involved with this project have for the honor of being able to participate twice in This Great Work.

Jack M. Bethards
President and Tonal Director, Schoenstein & Co.

PREFACE

The acquisition of a new pipe organ is a major undertaking, requiring consideration of many interrelated questions. How is the proposed organ to be used? What is the nature of the space in which it will be installed? What is the musical tradition of the organization contemplating the purchase? What size instrument is needed? Are sufficient funds available not only to acquire the instrument, but to assure its future maintenance? As the process continues, the questions become more specific, but no less challenging. What tonal style is desired? Who should build the instrument? Should a consultant be involved? Finally, questions regarding stoplist, console layout, mechanical features, pipe display, etc. must be resolved between builder and client. It is a challenging, painstaking process in any circumstance, but when the project involves multiple unknowns and breaks new ground in many respects, the decisions become even more difficult. Such was the situation with the new Conference Center of The Church of Jesus Christ of Latter-day Saints in Salt Lake City.

Throughout its history, the Church has been unable to build edifices fast enough or large enough to keep up with its ever-growing membership. The unique, pioneer-built Salt Lake Tabernacle had served as the principal space for major Church gatherings since 1867. As spacious as it seemed originally, it soon did not meet the demand for seating at Church-wide conferences or major cultural events. In 1996, Church President Gordon B. Hinckley announced plans to build a new structure, occupying an entire ten-acre city block adjacent to Temple Square, that could accommodate 21,000 people.

The process that culminated in the eventual installation of an organ by Schoenstein & Co. mirrored, in microcosm, the complexity of the planning and construction of the building itself. This book details that undertaking from start to finish, providing background and discussing the factors that came into play as options were considered and decisions were made.

Usually it falls to an organ historian, acting as a musical archaeologist, to tell the story of an important instrument decades after its completion. However, the ideal time to undertake such an endeavor is while those who were principally involved are still alive and able to provide firsthand information and while the all-important paper trail is still accessible. It is that belief that provided the impetus for this book.

It is hoped that *Magnum Opus* might be of interest on two levels. First is the fascinating story about how the organ came to be and why it looks and sounds as it does. Second, the knowledgeable organ builder, organist, or connoisseur will be interested in the more detailed documentation of the instrument. For the benefit of readers who may be less familiar with organ jargon, a glossary of some commonly encountered terms is included.

While I found myself quite uncomfortable writing in the first person, for much of the story there was no way to avoid it. I used "we" most of the time, rather than "I," because actions and decisions throughout the entire project were rarely unilateral.

While it was important to include many pertinent dates and facts, I wanted to do so in the context of a readable narrative—a rather uneasy mix of scholarly and more casual writing. The result, I fear, may have turned out to be "neither fish nor fowl," as the saying goes.

Since I still have access to nearly all the major participants in this "drama," I wanted you to "hear" their voices—to get to know them as I do. Therefore, I have quoted liberally, allowing them to "speak" for themselves. When quoting from published sources, I have, as a general rule, retained original spellings, punctuation, grammar and capitalization. Any changes are bracketed.

When one works with others closely for an extended length of time, formalities cease to exist, so first names are used freely throughout the book. The one exception is President Gordon B. Hinckley. Out of respect for him and his position, he is referred to by his title throughout.

Initially, I tried to provide all the background information in a single chapter, but it simply didn't work—the writing raised more questions than it answered. The milieu either needed to be treated in some depth, or not at all. I felt it important to place context around the decision to build such an astonishing edifice as the Conference Center and to review the tradition of musical excellence for which Temple Square is widely known.

Finally, I must acknowledge that this book was a collaborative effort, as was the building of the organ itself. In addition to consulting the documents in my own files, there were many times when it was necessary to ask my fellow Tabernacle organists Clay Christiansen and Richard Elliott to search their memories, their diaries or their files to uncover or corroborate some bit of information. The comments and suggestions from them and all others who read the manuscript were invaluable. Without the cooperation of Schoenstein's president and tonal director, Jack Bethards, and vice-president and plant superintendent, Louis Patterson, this book would not have been possible. Both men spent many hours assembling information and digging through company files. Our in-house organ technicians, Robert Poll and Lamont Anderson, provided information and insight that could only come from skilled and meticulous craftsmen who know the Schoenstein organ from the inside out. Scott Barrick and Nicole Fernley provided generous and much-appreciated assistance with the editing process, and Scott also efficiently coordinated the book's publication. Schoenstein's executive secretary, Ann Bharoocha, facilitated communication and prepared numerous documents. Hailey Walker, paralegal for the Mormon Tabernacle Choir, assisted in obtaining permission to use the creative works contributed by others. The book is greatly enhanced by the photographs freely shared by a number of photographers. My thanks go also to my wife, Nancy, for her support during this past year and for allowing me more than my fair share of time to work at the family computer.

J. L. 5/23/2009

CHAPTER 1

A Growing Church

Even in a day of so-called "mega-churches," a religious edifice seating 21,000 is bound to attract some attention. The Conference Center in Salt Lake City, however, serves quite a different purpose from that of most church buildings. To understand the function of this facility for The Church of Jesus Christ of Latter-day Saints,[1] we need to return to the Church's roots.

The Church of Jesus Christ of Latter-day Saints was officially organized April 6, 1830 in a log farmhouse at Fayette, New York, under the direction of Joseph Smith Jr., its founder, first prophet and president. From that inauspicious beginning, witnessed by just a small gathering of friends, the Church has grown into a major denomination with a worldwide membership of more than 13.5 million.[2] Even as the main body of Latter-day Saints was forced to move westward from New York to Ohio, to Missouri, to Illinois, to Iowa, and finally to the Great Basin in what is now Utah, the Church was simultaneously reaching outward, beyond the borders of the United States into Canada and the British Isles. Later, missionaries were sent to Central and South America, Asia, Africa, the South Pacific and throughout Europe. In an address given October 7, 2007, Church President Gordon B. Hinckley announced that the denomination then had a presence in 176 nations and territories.[3]

Organizationally, the LDS Church is divided into a number of geographical areas,[4] covering virtually the entire world. Each area is comprised of a number of stakes. In turn, each stake encompasses approximately eight wards.[5] A stake is comparable to a diocese, and a ward is similar to a parish. Periodically, in place of regular weekly Sunday services in each ward, conferences are convened, involving these various organizational units. Such conferences are held to bring members together to "sustain," or affirm, support for Church leadership, conduct pertinent business and receive information, instruction, messages and music of encouragement and inspiration. In short, conferences are solemn worship services. Wards hold annual conferences. Stakes meet in conference twice each year. Conferences are conducted periodically on an area-wide basis as well. The entire Church gathers for two-day general conference meetings twice each year on the first Sunday of April and October and the Saturdays immediately preceding.

Regular church meetinghouses are large enough to accommodate ward conferences. Somewhat larger buildings, called stake centers, are built sufficiently large to accommodate stake conferences. When entire areas meet for conference, potentially involving thousands of people, a coliseum or arena must often be used for the occasion. General conferences held at Church headquarters in Salt Lake City, in which the worldwide membership of the Church is invited to participate, require not only a large meeting facility, but also the use of a variety of technologies to reach a diverse and far-flung congregation. Through the Church's history, a number of different edifices have served to house its general conference services.

Kirtland, Ohio

Kirtland Temple.

The first building constructed by the Latter-day Saints to accommodate large gatherings was the temple in Kirtland, Ohio. In contrast to temples today, it was used as a gathering place, as a meetinghouse and as a school. Its cornerstone was laid July 23, 1833. The nearly three-year construction period was one of great hardship for members of the fledgling Church:

The divine command that led to the building of the Kirtland Temple was given to the Prophet Joseph Smith in January 1831 when the Church was beset by poverty and turmoil. At that time, the Saints were to gather to Ohio, where the Lord promised he would endow them "with power from on high." Thus they began to build the first of the Latter-day Saint temples.

The Church then consisted of only a few hundred members, men, women, and children who labored together for the temple and contributed, as Eliza R. Snow wrote, "brain, bone and sinew" and "all living as abstemiously as possible" so that "every cent might be appropriated to the grand object." According to Benjamin F. Johnson, "there was not a scraper and hardly a plow that could be obtained among the Saints," to prepare the ground for the foundation of the temple. As the exact patterns of the Tabernacle of Moses and Solomon's temple had been revealed from on high, so also were the design, measurements, and functions of the Kirtland Temple revealed. Its interior was to be fifty-five feet wide and sixty-five feet long and have a lower and a higher court. The lower part of the inner court was to be dedicated "for your Sacrament offering, and for your preaching, and your fasting, and your praying, and the offering up of your most holy desires unto me, saith your Lord." The higher part of the inner court was to be "dedicated unto me for the school of mine apostles.". . .

The women—who, Joseph once remarked, were "first in temple labors"—did spinning, knitting, and sewing so that temple laborers would have clothes to wear. To give the exterior glaze a sparkling appearance, the women contributed glassware to be broken in bits and applied to the plaster. In his dedicatory prayer, Joseph referred to the sacrifice of the Saints: "For thou knowest that we have done this work through great tribulation, and out of our poverty we have given of our substance to build a house to thy name, that the Son of Man might have a place to manifest himself to his people."

An estimated 1,000 people attended the dedication on March 27, 1836. A repeat dedication ceremony was held on March 31.[6]

Missouri

Even while the Kirtland Temple was being built, a group of "Mormons," as they were then derogatorily called, were settling in Jackson County, Missouri. As early as June 7, 1831, Joseph Smith had received revelation that Missouri was to be "the land of your inheritance, which is now the land of your enemies."[7] A small party of Church leaders, including Joseph Smith, traveled to Missouri in mid-July 1831 to survey the area and designate the place where the Saints would gather. Joseph returned to Kirtland, making periodic visits to Missouri until 1838, when Church headquarters was moved to Far West, a Mormon settlement in Caldwell County, Missouri.

Frequent and often violent confrontations with the Missourians had necessitated the Saints moving from Jackson County to take refuge first in Clay County and later in adjacent counties farther to the north and east. Animosities eventually escalated to the point that on October 27, 1838 Governor Lilburn W. Boggs issued an order stating that, "The Mormons must be treated as enemies and must be exterminated or driven from the state, if necessary for the public peace."[8] Appeals to state officials and the Legislature to revoke Governor Boggs's order were unsuccessful,[9] so the Saints prepared to pack what they could and leave. Joseph Smith and his counselors were imprisoned, so the responsibility for the exodus fell largely to Brigham Young, senior member of the Church's Quorum of the Twelve Apostles. By mid-February 1839, they were on the move across Missouri to the eastern shore of the Mississippi River.

The long journey of more than 150 miles, in the dead of winter, took a tremendous toll in human life and suffering. Finally arriving at Quincy, Illinois and surrounding communities, the refugees were treated kindly and given much needed aid.

Though conferences were convened during the Saints' short time in Missouri, no large meeting facilities were completed during those tumultuous years. Given the constant turmoil, it was all the Saints could manage to build shelters, places of business and small buildings to serve as schools and meeting halls. Yet larger buildings were contemplated. On August 3, 1831, Joseph Smith dedicated a site for a temple to be built in Independence. In a revelation dated April 26, 1838,[10] the Saints were commanded to build a temple at Far West, the cornerstone for which was laid the following July 4. But temples and other large gathering places would have to wait. Survival was the first priority.

Nauvoo, Illinois

Upriver from Quincy, some fifty miles in Hancock County, at a wide bend in the Mississippi River, lay a swampy, sparsely settled community called Commerce. Founded by a pair of speculators in 1834, the site had not proved attractive to other settlers. By the time the Saints arrived in Illinois much of the land was available for purchase. Joseph Smith and his companions had rejoined the main body of Saints, after being allowed to escape custody following a trial in Missouri. The beleaguered Saints procured the mostly vacant land in Commerce and the area surrounding, drained the disease-infested swamps, and began to farm the land and build homes, shops and schools. Even while the Saints seemed to prosper in the city that Joseph Smith renamed Nauvoo,[11] dark clouds loomed on the horizon:

> Nauvoo, the City Beautiful, was a unique place in the history of the Saints, as it was in the history of the American nation as a whole. A people who had arrived on the banks of the Mississippi weak, half-starved, worn-out with persecution, deprived of possessions and means, created a city which, with its surrounding area, by the summer of 1841 housed some eight to nine thousand people, and within another year had "eclipsed every other Illinois city in size, with the possible exception of Chicago. Almost single handedly, the Saints made Hancock County the most populous county in Illinois by the 1845 census." Small businesses were encouraged by an actual Agricultural and Manufacturing Association. There were potteries, tanneries, bakeries, shops, comb and match factories, grist and lumber mills, several brickyards, foundries, a

slaughterhouse—and the river provided easy transportation for the goods the Saints made. Building was one of the largest enterprises. "One visitor reported seeing some two thousand homes, of which 'six hundred of them at least were good brick or frame structures. The number . . . made wholly of brick was about five hundred, a goodly proportion of them large and handsome.'" There was a "common school" system in the city, and public halls for the production of plays and concerts and such public amusements as banquets and dances, lectures and exhibits of art. There were several newspapers, among them the *Wasp*, begun in April of 1842, which was a versatile weekly publication treating a range of subjects from agriculture and trade to science, art and literature. There were also the *Nauvoo Neighbor* and the *Times and Seasons*. There were parades and reviews, festooned by the Nauvoo Legion, and the homey activities of skating and sliding on the ice in winter, picnics, swimming, quilting and husking bees, and competitive racing, pulling sticks, wrestling, and throwing weights in the warmer months.

"When I went to Commerce, I told the people I would build up a city," Joseph reminded his enemies and detractors in January of 1843. ". . . The old inhabitants replied, 'We will be damned if you can.' So I prophesied that I would build up a city, and the inhabitants prophesied that I could not; and we have now about 12,000 inhabitants."

The amazing growth of the Mormon city was threatening to their neighbors, as was the nature of the liberal charter granted by Governor Carlin, certified by the Secretary of State, Steven A. Douglas, and supported by Illinois legislator Abraham Lincoln. The charter provided for the establishment of a university, as well as an independent military unit to be called the Nauvoo Legion. The city mayor and aldermen, members of the city council, were also designated as judges in the municipal court. This feature allowed the Saints to place trusted church leaders in key positions, and provided an avenue of escape from illegal and trumped-up arrest by the issuing of writs of habeas corpus. Of course, enemies of the Church chafed against this power as much as the Saints rejoiced in it.[12]

The crown jewel of Nauvoo was the temple. Located on the crest of a gentle upward slope from the river, the temple was built on the city's most prominent site, visible from miles around:

Built from a high-quality grayish-white to tan limestone, its imposing walls were erected and finished with great skill. The walls were three feet thick at ground level, with some individual stones weighing as much as 4,000 pounds. The building measured 128 feet long and 88 feet wide. The top of the tower stood 158 feet above ground level and was graced by a golden statue of an angel flying in a horizontal position. . . .

Construction of the building began in the fall of 1840. Cornerstones were set with impressive ceremonies during a general conference on April 6, 1841. Financial setbacks and persecution continually interfered with the construction, even up to the days of its completion and dedication. . . .

The call to build so large a structure taxed the resources of a destitute people. The final cost exceeded $1,000,000. Funds came largely from tithes and offerings of Church members, some donating their life savings. Many gave months of physical labor with little or no remuneration, working from early morning until sundown, even during harsh weather.

Original Nauvoo Temple.

Stone for the building was quarried near the city. Wood was brought in from Wisconsin in the form of huge rafts of sawed lumber, which were floated down the Mississippi to Nauvoo. Some British converts contributed a large bell weighing over 1,500 pounds.[13]

In spite of the Saints' relative success in building a thriving community at Nauvoo, tensions mounted, and conflicts with their neighbors became commonplace. Eventually Joseph Smith, his brother Hyrum, and several other Church leaders were imprisoned at nearby Carthage. On June 27, 1844, a large group of armed men stormed the jail, overpowered the guards and murdered both Joseph and Hyrum. Two other Church leaders who remained with the Smiths at the time survived the encounter.

Just a few weeks before his death, Joseph Smith directed that a tabernacle be built in Nauvoo. His proposal was of great interest, not only because of the circumstances that precipitated it, but also due to the manner of construction he suggested. The idea for a tabernacle appears to have come to a head following an experience at a general conference meeting held in Nauvoo on April 7, 1844:

The Lord blessed the Saints with warm, springlike weather on conference Sunday, although it had rained during the Saturday afternoon session. The coming of spring added to the joy of the occasion, and many diarists mentioned the beauty of the Mississippi River Valley, adorned as it was with blossoming trees.

Good weather was a blessing for the Saints because their meetings were held outdoors. In fact, the Mormons did not build any meetinghouses in Nauvoo. Virtually all of their public meetings were held outdoors in areas referred to as "the groves." The Saints held meetings in three different groves located on the edges of the bluff to the northeast, west, and south of the temple. The sloping contours of the bluffs provided a natural amphitheater, to which the Saints added wooden benches and a speaker's rostrum.[14]

On this occasion, the Prophet delivered a major theological address that was said to have lasted more than two hours. The sermon was in response to the accidental death of one of Nauvoo's leading citizens, King Follett.[15] Some contemporary observers estimated the crowd on that occasion to have been as large as 20,000. That may well have been an inflated figure, but undoubtedly it was a very large gathering. With no means of amplification and completely in the open, Joseph certainly would have had great difficulty speaking so that all could hear. As a result, an address he had prepared to give the following day had to be abbreviated, presumably due to vocal fatigue, if not outright hoarseness.[16] At that point Joseph directed that a canvas "tabernacle" be constructed to accommodate future large gatherings; however, it was nearly a year following his death before action was taken relative to that directive. On June 17, 1845, the Quorum of the Twelve Apostles sent a letter to the Saints abroad, which read, in part:

> The walls of our temple are completed and the roof is nearly on. Through the liberality of the brethren that building is in a rapid state of advancement; but it will only accommodate a small portion of our congregation when completed.
>
> Pursuant to the counsel of Joseph Smith given previous to his martyrdom, we now intend to erect a Tabernacle for the congregation made of canvas. It will take about four thousand yards, which, with other fixtures, will cost between one and two thousand dollars.
>
> We have appointed Elder Orson Hyde one of our own quorum, a faithful, trusty and competent man of God, to go forth and raise all the necessary funds for the above purpose, to procure the materials and return with them to this place as soon as possible. Elder Hyde is authorized to

raise the necessary funds by loan, by contribution, or tithing or donation; if by loan, the church here will refund the same in lands at a low rate, or in cash as soon as we can command it, and any contract that he may make in relation to the above, the church will be responsible for.

It is hoped that no brother or sister who has funds that he or she can spare for a season will withhold them from Brother Hyde, for it is the aid that he seeks for us. Also we hope that, the saints will be liberal in their donations, and every other person that wishes well to the Temple of God and to the Tabernacle of the congregation in Zion. May God bless all that feel interested in the matter.[17]

Orson Hyde was successful in raising the necessary funds for the acquisition of the canvas and on September 17, 1845, 4,000 yards of canvas, purchased at a cost of $1,050.56, were shipped to Nauvoo.[18]

Few details concerning the proposed tabernacle are known, but a letter from Orson Pratt (one of the Twelve Apostles) to Reuben Hedlock (president of the British Mission) published in the *New York Messenger* August 30, 1845, gives some idea of its size and proposed location:

It is intended to erect a tabernacle of canvass in front of, and joining the Temple on the west. The form of this tabernacle will be that of an ellipse, its longer axis running north and south, parallel to the front of the Temple. Its height will be 75 feet in the centre, its sides sloping at an angle of 45 degrees. The area of its base will be sufficient to contain eight or ten thousand persons, its seats will gradually rise one above another in the form of an amphitheatre. This will be intended for preaching to the vast congregation; while the temple will be used for the meeting of councils and quorums, and the administrations of ordinances and blessings, and preaching to smaller congregations, &C.[19]

Donald Enders, Senior Curator of Historic Sites in the Church History Department, suggests that with the major and minor axes in a 2:1 ratio that the tabernacle would have been approximately 250 feet in length and 125 feet wide. It would have abutted the front of the temple and perhaps served as an awning over the entrance when not in use.[20]

Though the phrase "Tabernacle of the congregation" may suggest some connection to the Tabernacle built by Moses in the wilderness, in comparing them, Enders has been "unable to find any notable similarities between the two in shape, size, or purpose."[21]

The Nauvoo Tabernacle, however, was never built. In the face of rising hostilities against the Latter-day Saints in Nauvoo, Joseph Smith, in August of 1842, had prophesied that the Saints would be driven to the Rocky Mountains, but that he would not go with them.[22] The following year he took preliminary steps to determine possible locations for the Saints to settle in the West, and to establish a means of organizing the future exodus. Following the death of Joseph Smith, the situation in Nauvoo continued to deteriorate. On September 24, 1845, Brigham Young, in response to pressure from a citizens committee from nearby Quincy, signed a statement declaring the Saints' intention to "leave this country next spring."[23] However, in an attempt to avoid further bloodshed in the face of continuing conflicts, the Saints began leaving Nauvoo two months earlier than planned.

Again in the dead of winter, on February 4, 1846, wagons began to cross the frozen Mississippi River. The Mormon migration to the Rocky Mountains had begun. Even knowing that they would never return to their beloved Nauvoo, some stayed behind to complete the temple. The edifice was finished and dedicated in a private ceremony April 30, 1846, and a public gathering was held the following day, May 1.[24] The remaining Saints were driven from the city on September 17 of that year.[25] In the absence of evidence to the contrary, it is assumed that the 4,000 yards of canvas intended for the tabernacle were used to make tents and wagon covers for the trek west.

Rebuilt Nauvoo Temple, dedicated June 27–30, 2002.

Iowa

Leaving Nauvoo in February, Brigham Young's plan was to reach the Missouri River by spring and for at least one group of Saints to make their way across the mountains to their place of refuge by fall. The rest would stay behind, establishing temporary communities at the Missouri River and at Grand Island to serve as way stations for those who would follow later. Having underestimated the difficulty of crossing Iowa, the Saints did not arrive at the Missouri River until mid-June.

Borrowing a term used by trappers and explorers, they established "Winter Quarters" on the west bank of the Missouri. By the end of 1846 there were nearly 4,000 Saints gathered there. For all intents and purposes, Winter Quarters became the temporary headquarters of the Church. Additional small settlements were begun on the east side of the river, in Pottawattamie County, accommodating still more immigrants.[26]

During 1848, the Saints vacated Winter Quarters upon orders from government officials who were concerned about their settling on Indian lands. Some chose to go west to the Salt Lake Valley, while others went back east across the river where they established the community of Kanesville, Iowa.[27]

A Church conference was to be held in Kanesville December 3–4, 1847, at which the newly organized First Presidency, with Brigham Young as President, were to be sustained:

Reconstructed Kanesville Tabernacle. The statue depicts President Brigham Young, flanked by his counselors Heber C. Kimball and Willard Richards.

The meeting place was so crowded that Brigham Young adjourned the conference until a larger hall could be constructed. He appointed [Henry] Miller, a convert to the LDS Church, to build the structure. With the help of 200 men, Miller constructed a 60-foot by 40-foot building, said to be the largest log cabin in the world, in three weeks. When the conference reconvened, a thousand people crowded into the Kanesville Log Tabernacle, as the building became known, to sustain the new church president. That solemn assembly took place on Dec. 27, 1847.

The tabernacle only lasted about two years. The building was damaged in the spring runoffs of 1848 and 1849. Efforts to repair the structure were not successful, and the building was dismantled in the fall of 1849.[28]

While it was the first, the Kanesville Tabernacle was not the only such structure to be built by the Saints in Iowa. Between 1846 and 1853, at least three other tabernacles were built in the area.[29] One of these, in Big Pigeon, was described as follows:

Another log tabernacle was erected in the Big Pigeon settlement on

Pigeon Creek, Pottawattamie County, Iowa, in the spring of 1849. This temporary building, 53 x 32 feet in size, was constructed of oak logs hewn on the inside with a puncheon floor and a roof of oak lap shingles. In the center of the building on each side was an extension of about 16 x 14 feet, the ground plan thus taking the form of a Greek cross. The Big Pigeon settlement was broken up in 1852, when most of the saints in Pottawattamie County went west to the Rocky Mountains.[30]

Salt Lake City

From the time the Saints fled Nauvoo until the completion of the transcontinental railroad in 1869, it is estimated that some 70,000 individuals, 9,600 wagons and 650 handcarts made the 1,300 mile journey across plains and mountains to Great Salt Lake City, as it was first called.[31] The journey was extremely rigorous, and a significant number of immigrants perished along the way:

> Elder Orson Pratt of the Quorum of the Twelve and Erastus Snow were the first Latter-day Saints to enter the Great Basin, arriving in what is now Salt Lake City on 21 July 1847. They were followed by the advance party that included President Brigham Young. On 24 July, Brigham Young and the rest of the group of 148 saints arrived and on 28 July, President Young selected the site where the Salt Lake Temple would be built. Within a month, the city had been surveyed, 80 acres of land had been planted, 29 log houses had been built, nearby valleys had been explored, a bowery and adobe fort had been constructed, and trade shops had been started. Other pioneer companies followed, starting a flood of immigration into the Great Basin that continued through the turn of the 20th century and afterward.[32]

Apparently the rather crude aforementioned bowery did not rise to a level of construction that the Saints would be proud to call a tabernacle, yet it served the same purpose. A hurriedly built structure, it provided some shade from the sun but little protection in cold or wet weather. Clarissa Young Spencer, a daughter of Brigham Young, provided a rather colorful description of bowery construction:

> It was built by the simple method of putting poles into the ground at short intervals, making the framework of a roof—also of poles—and covering it over with branches, sagebrush, or whatever else might be available. There was never better than a dirt floor, and anything that was handy might be utilized for seats, although after a short time crude benches were built.

I liked to go to meeting in the Bowery, because it was easy to see what was going on outside, and this might be entertaining if the sermon was dry. I suppose it was unsatisfactory to the authorities for the same reason. While the Bowery served fairly well as a meeting place in the summertime, it was quite impossible to hold meeting there during the winter months.[33]

Actually, three separate boweries were constructed on Temple Square, each larger than its predecessor, to better accommodate the burgeoning population of the city. As mentioned, the first was built within a month of the Saints' arrival in the Valley. It was reportedly destroyed by vandals sometime in 1849. The second, sometimes referred to as the "Old Bowery," was erected July 19 to October 6, 1849, and was dismantled December, 1851.

The dismantling of the second bowery allowed for (and provided some recycled material for) construction of a more comfortable and permanent facility that could be used in cold weather. This building, the first of two tabernacles to be built on Temple Square, was begun May 21, 1851, and dedicated April 6, 1852.[34] This structure *was* called a tabernacle by the Saints. After the building of the newer, larger tabernacle in the 1860s, this earlier edifice was referred to as the "Old Tabernacle." Again, Clarissa Young Spencer gives a useful, if somewhat folksy description:

Old Tabernacle and "Big" Bowery.

The "Old Tabernacle" was commenced in 1851 and finished one year later. It was built of adobes and had an arched ceiling which was supported without pillars. The seating capacity was about twenty-five hundred. Father used the co-operative plan of work in making this building, which was so successful in many of his other enterprises. One group of men cut down trees in the canyons, another group worked in the sawmills, while yet other groups were given the tasks of mixing mortar and making adobes. About one half of the building was below the surface of the ground, possibly to help solve the heating problem.

At the door were two huge brass caldrons filled with water, and near by was a dipper, so that the churchgoers might have a refreshing drink upon entering or leaving the building. There were large chandeliers of glass prisms that sparkled in the light of the oil lamps with a fascinating beauty. . . .

On the stand, at the west side, was a funny little door which seemed to me far too small for a man to walk through. A few minutes before the services began this would quietly open and Father would appear followed by his counselors and the twelve Apostles. They would take their seats and then the choir would sing, a beautiful choir of fresh, young voices.[35]

It is worth noting that the choir of "fresh, young voices" to which Mrs. Spencer refers was the beginning of the now world-famous Mormon Tabernacle Choir.

Additional information about that first tabernacle is found in an article in *The Millennial Star:*

The old building [the first tabernacle], with which many pleasant memories of the past are associated, was a somewhat singular structure. The floor was about six or eight feet below the ground level, descending steps being at the entrances to the body of the hall. It was rather low-roofed, long and narrow, and the ceiling was rounded into the walls all around. The speaker's stand was at the north end, and the organ and choir at the extreme south. The acoustic properties were excellent. A voice of ordinary intensity could be heard in every part without the necessity of much effort, notwithstanding the room had a capacity for holding about 3,000 persons.[36]

Glen Leonard, Director of the LDS Museum of Church History and Art, further describes the Old Tabernacle.[37] After stating the dimensions of the building (which he gives as 126 feet by 64 feet), he mentions that "the structure had an acoustical sound shell in the north end" that was undoubtedly included to aid in projecting the spoken word.

While initially the adobe tabernacle provided more comfortable accommodations for meetings, at the rate converts were flooding into the Valley it soon was too small. By 1854, general conferences were again being held in a third bowery, situated just north of the Old Tabernacle:

The [Old] "Tabernacle," however, by the time it was completed, was still inadequate to accommodate the public, and a "bowery," 156 feet long, and 138 feet wide, [the "Big Bowery"] capable of seating an audience of 8,000 was attached on the north, but as this was not roofed in, except by an annual supply of "brush" for shade, it could only be used in the summer season.[38]

Salt Lake Tabernacle ca. 1890.

The solution to the growing need for a larger edifice was announced in General Conference April 1863 by Daniel H. Wells, a counselor to President Brigham Young: "Right here we want to build a tabernacle, to accommodate the Saints at our General Conferences and religious worship, that will comfortably seat some ten thousand people."[39] Such a proposition was indeed amazing:

The construction of so large an auditorium in an isolated territory without railroad access to manufactured building materials was an extraordinary undertaking. Church architect William H. Folsom prepared the first plans under President Young's direction. The design called for a structure 150 feet wide and 250 feet long with semicircular ends and a peaked roof similar to that of the Old Tabernacle. The cornerstone was laid July 26, 1864, and forty-four sandstone piers to support the roof were begun that year.

The next year, President Young appointed an experienced bridge builder, Henry Grow, to superintend the construction. In consultation with the President, Grow modified a type of lattice truss used in bridge construction into huge elliptical arches that spanned the entire width of the structure without intermediate supports, an innovation without parallel for a building of these dimensions. The trusses were constructed of timbers pegged together with wooden dowels that were split and wedged at each end. Cracked timbers were wrapped with green rawhide, which contracted when dry and made a tight binding. When the building was completed, the roof structure was nine feet thick, and the plaster ceiling was 68 feet above the floor.

Truman O. Angell, who replaced Folsom as Church architect early in 1867, designed the exterior cornice and the interior woodwork, including the gallery added in 1869-1870. This 2,000-seat balcony increased the building's seating capacity to approximately 10,000 and improved its acoustics by reducing echoes. Although the Tabernacle was used for the October 1867 conference, it was not formally dedicated until October 1875.[40]

Additional information about the "New" Tabernacle was provided by James E. Talmage (1862–1933), writing in 1912. Elder Talmage, a member of the Quorum of the Twelve Apostles from 1911 until his death, was one of the LDS Church's most respected scholars and theologians. Born in England, Talmage immigrated to Utah in 1876, so he knew the Tabernacle from the year following its dedication until his death:

For it no claim of architectural beauty is asserted; the general appearance is that of a huge inverted bowl resting on pillars. It is in truth a vast elliptical dome supported at the edge by massive sandstone walls and buttresses. The buttresses measure nine feet in width or depth and three feet in thickness. The space between the buttresses is occupied by doors, windows, and walls; the doors open outward, this affording ready means of exit. . . . A capacious gallery, thirty feet wide, extends along the inner walls and is broken at the west end only, where it gives place to the grand organ and the seats reserved for the great choir. In contrast with the usual methods of construction, this enormous gallery is not continuous with the walls. At intervals of twelve to fifteen feet great beams connect the gallery with the wall buttresses, but between these beams the gallery is set forward two and one-half feet from the inside of the walls and the open spaces are guarded by a high railing. It is believed that the surprising acoustic properties of the building are due in part to this feature of construction; the great dome is, in fact, a colossal whispering gallery, as the hundreds of thousands of visitors who have inspected the building know. When it is emptied save for the few, the fall of a pin dropped at the focal point of the ellipse near one end of the building may be heard at the corresponding point near the other end. . . .

At the west end is the rostrum, including the pulpit. The rostrum rises in tiers or terraces, affording accommodations for Church officers of different grades in authority. On either side of the terraced rostrum are platforms for seating other bodies of priesthood or special guests. The rostrum area is so erected that it can be dismantled for placement of a large platform to accommodate such events as symphony concerts, pageants, dramatic offerings, or other public performances in keeping with the spirit of the tabernacle. Behind the rostrum area, rising on either side to the level of the gallery, and occupying the space in front of the great organ, is the choir space, seated to accommodate approximately 375 singers.[41]

While the new tabernacle certainly was (and is) a unique and remarkable structure, it is worth noting that some elements hearken back to ideas realized, or at least considered in earlier tabernacles. The never-built Nauvoo canvas tabernacle was to be elliptical in shape with a raked (though undoubtedly dirt) floor. Regarding the Old Tabernacle on Temple Square, several writers mention its arched ceiling, which was rounded into the walls. Also recorded is the fact that the roof structure had no interior supports, a feature that must have been noteworthy in spans of that distance, particularly in frontier construction. Finally, the rounded ends of the new structure acted as an expansion of the acoustical shell on the north end of the Old Tabernacle. Acoustical considerations must have loomed large in designing the building. With no electronic amplification available at the time, a speaker would need every possible advantage in order to be heard in so vast a space with such large crowds in attendance.

While both the exterior and interior of the Tabernacle were admittedly quite simple and plain, considerable attention was lavished on its interior to give it a less rough-hewn appearance. All of the native pine used in the benches, balcony facing and rostrum railings was painted and faux-grained to give the appearance of oak. Similarly the balcony support pillars were covered with scagliola that yielded a credible simulation of marble.

Soon after arriving in the Salt Lake Valley, Church members began colonizing—establishing settlements in many areas of what is now the western United States, and even in Canada and Mexico. Tabernacles were also built in a number of these communities to serve as meeting places for larger gatherings, and many are still in use. Since these serve the local needs of individual communities rather than the Church as a whole, none approaches the size nor has achieved the fame of the Salt Lake Tabernacle. (Hereinafter, when mention is made of "the Tabernacle," it may be assumed that the reference is to the "new" Salt Lake Tabernacle.)

Following completion of the Tabernacle, Brigham Young saw the need for an additional smaller facility. The large, new tabernacle was difficult to heat in cold weather, and some gatherings did not require so large a space. On August 11, 1877, just eighteen days before his death, President Young proposed that the old adobe tabernacle be razed and a new, more modern structure approximately the same size be built in its place. Work on the new edifice began immediately; the cornerstones were laid about six weeks later. The Gothic-style building is 120 feet by 68 feet., with a central tower rising 130 feet. "Chippings" from the massive blocks used in the construction of the nearby temple were recycled for its walls.

Assembly Hall.

The new building was somewhat more ornate than the Tabernacle. Stained glass adorned its windows. Faux finishes were applied to the benches and balcony support pillars. Its heating system provided adequate warmth. Originally called the Salt Lake Stake Priesthood Assembly Hall, it is now known simply as the Assembly Hall.

As the membership of the Church continued to grow, it became increasingly difficult to accommodate all who wished to attend functions in the Tabernacle, particularly general conference meetings. Over the years, the need to increase accessibility has been met creatively, using a variety of technologies. Audio is broadcast to the grounds of Temple Square where, depending on the weather, hundreds will sit on blankets to listen. Transcriptions of the proceedings are published in Church publications, translated into a number of different languages, and disseminated worldwide. Video is broadcast via a Church-operated satellite system to stake centers worldwide with simultaneous audio translations available in several dozen languages. The services are broadcast in the greater Salt Lake City area on local radio and television stations and on BYU-TV, a broadcast facility at Church-sponsored Brigham Young University, which is available on many commercial cable and satellite systems.   Most recently, general conference has become available over the Internet. Yet in spite of relatively easy access via the media, many wish to experience general conference live, sitting, as it were, face-to-face with the prophet.

Salt Lake Tabernacle following 2005–2006 renovation.

Through the years, the Tabernacle has undergone a number of changes as new technology became available. The conversion to electricity and the addition of central heating greatly expanded the usefulness of the building. The availability of electronic sound transmission was a major breakthrough. Broadcast facilities were added, first for radio and later for television. A basement was excavated underneath the existing structure to provide additional space for offices and other needs. The rostrum was remodeled several times to allow for more seating and provide additional flexibility. A large, removable platform was designed, which provided enough space that the Utah Symphony Orchestra was able to use the Tabernacle as its concert home from 1946 to 1979. Several U.S. presidents and other dignitaries have spoken from its pulpit, along with every Church president, except Joseph Smith. It was named a National Historic Landmark in 1970 and designated a National Civil Engineering Landmark in 1971. Its famous organ was cited by the Organ Historical Society in 1994 as "an instrument of exceptional historic merit, worthy of preservation." Its prestigious choir was awarded the National Medal of Arts in 2003. The venerable building has proven itself adaptable to changing needs and circumstances over the years. It is so rich in history and such an enduring monument to pioneer industry and ingenuity that it has become an icon both within and without the Church. The one thing that could not be changed, however, was its seating capacity, a limitation noted as early as 1880:

> The authorities of the Church have been frequently under the necessity of requesting the Saints residing in the city to give place to those who came from the distant rural districts, that the latter might not be obliged to return home disappointed on account of not being able to participate in the services. The Saints have grown to a community of such proportions that a building sufficient to accommodate all who would gather on a general occasion would have to be of unparalleled magnitude. Unless some yet undeveloped discoveries are made in the department of architectural acoustics, a structure of sufficient dimensions will probably be, before many years, among the impossibilities.[42]

If only the writer of that article could have seen 120 years into the future!

[1]While the Church's full and correct name is The Church of Jesus Christ of Latter-day Saints, because of its length, shortened versions are often used. These include "LDS Church" and "Mormon Church" or sometimes just "the Mormons." Church members are often referred to as "Mormons" or "Latter-day Saints" or sometimes just "Saints."

[2]Church statistical report as of December 31, 2008, as reported in "179th Annual General Conference," *Deseret News*, April 5, 2009.

[3]Gordon B. Hinckley, "The Stone Cut Out of the Mountain," *Ensign 37*, no. 11 (November 2007), 83.

[4]Area Leadership Chart, *LDS Church News* (June 7, 2008). As of August 1, 2008, there were to be twenty-eight areas.

[5]In areas of the world where Church membership is smaller, local congregations form *branches*, rather than wards, and branches are organized into *districts*, rather than stakes.

[6]*Encyclopedia of Mormonism* (New York: Macmillan, 1992), s.v. "Kirtland Temple."

[7]*Doctrine and Covenants of The Church of Jesus Christ of Latter-day Saints*, (Salt Lake City: The Church of Jesus Christ of Latter-day Saints, 1981), section 52, verse 42. This book, regarded as scripture by Latter-day Saints, will hereinafter be referred to as Doctrine and Covenants.

[8]Joseph Smith, *History of The Church of Jesus Christ of Latter-day Saints* 3 (Salt Lake City: Deseret Book Co., 1948), 175.

[9]See R. Scott Lloyd, "The Missouri Era," *2008 Church Almanac*, 167. The extermination order was finally rescinded June 25, 1976 by then Governor Christopher S. Bond. His proclamation read in part that the 1838 order "clearly contravened the rights of life, liberty, property and religious freedom as guaranteed by the Constitution of the United States, as well as the Constitution of the State of Missouri" and further affirmed that "in this Bicentennial year, as we reflect upon our nation's heritage, the exercise of religious freedom is without question one of the basic tenets of our free democratic republic."

[10]See Doctrine and Covenants 115:7–16.

[11]Smith, 4:268. From "A Proclamation of the First Presidency of the Church to the Saints Scattered Abroad," dated January 15, 1841, signed by Joseph Smith, Sidney Rigdon and Hyrum Smith: "The name of our city (Nauvoo) is of Hebrew origin, and signifies a beautiful situation, or place, carrying with it, also, the idea of rest; and is truly descriptive of the most delightful location."

[12]Susan Evans McCloud, *Brigham Young, A Personal Portrait* (American Fork, UT: Covenant Communications, 1996), 100.

[13]*Encyclopedia of Mormonism*, s.v. "Nauvoo Temple." The Nauvoo Temple bell was brought to Salt Lake City and eventually installed in a modest tower on Temple Square between the Tabernacle and Assembly Hall, where it is rung once each hour, on the hour.

[14]Donald Q. Cannon, "The King Follett Discourse: Joseph Smith's Greatest Sermon in Historical Perspective," *BYU Studies*, 18 (Winter 1978): 182.

[15]Ibid., 179. King Follett had played a major part in helping to transform swamp-infested Commerce into a livable and thriving community. He was killed March 9, 1844, when a bucket of rock fell on him while walling up a well. Joseph Smith spoke at his funeral the following day. Prevailed upon by Follett's family, Joseph delivered this additional lengthy sermon at the April general conference in further honor of Follett.

[16]Ibid., 182.

[17]Quoted in Donald L. Enders, "Platting the City Beautiful: A Historical and Archaeological Glimpse of Nauvoo Streets," *BYU Studies*, 19 (Spring 1979): 416.

[18]Ibid., 419–20.

[19]Ibid., 420.

[20]Ibid., 420.

[21]Ibid., 421.

[22]Smith, 5:85.

[23]Joseph Fielding Smith, *Essentials in Church History* (Salt Lake City: Deseret Book Co., 1950), 326.

[24]Andrew Jenson, *Church Chronology: A Record of Important Events Pertaining to the History of The Church of Jesus Christ of Latter-day Saints* (Salt Lake City: Deseret News, 1914), entries for April 30 and May 1, 1846. After the Church was forced to abandon the Temple, an arsonist's fire destroyed all but the stone walls. Later the remaining structure was hit by a tornado and so badly damaged that what little remained had to be razed. The Church later obtained the land upon which the original temple had stood and announced on April 4, 1999, that the temple would be rebuilt. The new structure conforms to the original insofar as was possible and practical. The reconstructed edifice was dedicated in thirteen services June 27–30, 2002, by President Gordon B. Hinckley.

[25]Ibid., entry for September 17, 1846.

[26]*Encyclopedia of Mormonism*, s.v. "Winter Quarters."

[27]Ibid. Kanesville, now called Council Bluffs, was named after Col. Thomas L. Kane, an influential non-Mormon who befriended the Saints.

[28]Dell Van Orden, "Tabernacle of Log Replicated, Dedicated: 'Herculean Task' of First Order," *LDS Church News*, July 20, 1996. In conjunction with the sesquicentennial observance of the Mormon migration, the Kanesville Tabernacle was reconstructed as a joint project of the Pottawattamie County Mormon Trail Association and Kanesville Restoration, Inc. The dedication took place on July 13, 1996.

[29]Ibid.

[30]Andrew Jenson, *Encyclopedic History of The Church of Jesus Christ of Latter-day Saints* (Salt Lake City: Deseret News Publishing Co., 1941), 859.

[31]M. Russell Ballard, "Faith in Every Footstep," *Ensign* 26, no. 11 (November, 1996), 23.

[32]*2008 Church Almanac*, (Salt Lake City: Deseret Morning News, 2008), s.v. "Utah," 273.

[33]Clarissa Young Spencer, *Brigham Young at Home* (Salt Lake City: Deseret Book Co., 1961), 279.

[34]Jenson, *Church Chronology*, entries for May 21, 1851, and April 6, 1852.

[35]Spencer, 279.

[36]"Places of Worship in Salt Lake City," *The Latter-day Saints' Millennial Star*, April 26, 1880, 264. The seating capacity of these meeting halls varies from one account to another. They appear to have been approximations and often seem exaggerated. There were several variables. People 150 years ago were probably of smaller stature than today. When seated on benches, capacity would vary according to how closely together people were crowded. Also, modern fire codes did not exist, so capacity would increase if people were standing. Reports of the capacity of the Old Tabernacle range from 2,200 to 3,000.

[37]Glen Leonard, "Wooden Sunburst from Early Tabernacle Was a Colorful Thing," *LDS Church News* (April 21, 1990).

[38]B. H. Roberts, *A Comprehensive History of The Church of Jesus Christ of Latter-day Saints* (Salt Lake City: Deseret News Press, 1930), 4:23.

[39]"Remarks by President Daniel H. Wells," *Journal of Discourses* (London: Latter-day Saints' Book Depot, 1854–1886), 10:139.

[40]*Encyclopedia of Mormonism*, s.v. "Tabernacle, Salt Lake City."

[41]James E. Talmage, *The House of the Lord* (Salt Lake City: Deseret Book Co., 1968), Appendix 2.

[42]"Places of Worship in Salt Lake City," 265.

A Glimpse at Music in the LDS Church

Religious denominations in western New York State in the early decades of the nineteenth century differed widely in their attitudes toward music. Quakers, followers of George Fox, eschewed all forms of music in their services. Others followed the thinking of John Calvin, allowing vocal music only. Still others freely used both vocal and instrumental music. Similar disagreement existed with regard to dancing. Some denominations viewed dancing as inherently evil, while others were more permissive. However, both music and dancing have played an important role in the lives of Latter-day Saints throughout the Church's history.

Congregational singing in The Church of Jesus Christ of Latter-day Saints has always been viewed as a valid and desirable form of communal worship, as well as a means of teaching and reaffirming the doctrines of the Church. Choral singing has also been highly encouraged and valued. Singing schools were set up in the early days of the Church to help members develop their ability in the vocal art. Church leaders have not subscribed to the Calvinist view that musical instruments are not appropriate in Christian worship, and so organ, piano and various orchestral instruments are also employed in worship services. Secular music and dancing as a part of everyday life have likewise been regarded as wholesome and worthwhile forms of recreation; as viable means of retaining cultural identity as people from many lands are assimilated into the worldwide Church; and for their value in buoying up the human spirit in times of discouragement and adversity.

In 1842, John Wentworth, proprietor of the *Chicago Democrat*, asked Joseph Smith to submit a sketch of his life and of the church that he founded. Joseph responded with a detailed account of events leading to the formation of the Church and the persecution his followers had endured prior to their arrival at Nauvoo. In conclusion, in lieu of a stating a formal creed, the Prophet wrote thirteen brief statements of belief outlining principal tenets of the faith. These were soon codified and have become known as the Articles of Faith. The final one reads:

We believe in being honest, true, chaste, benevolent, virtuous, and in doing good to all men; indeed, we may say that we follow the admonition of Paul—We believe all things, we hope all things, we have endured many things, and hope to be able to endure all things. If there is anything virtuous, lovely, or of good report or praiseworthy, we seek after these things.[1]

Use of the word *anything* in the final sentence implies that in addition to items of a strictly religious nature, the Saints are admonished to appreciate and seek beauty, truth and goodness, wherever they may be found. Wholesome music, both sacred and secular, fits comfortably into Joseph's statement. An editorial in a Church magazine delves further into the comprehensiveness of this concept:

What a glorious statement that is—that whatever is virtuous or lovely or of good report or praiseworthy, is part of the answer as to what religion really is! Anyone who has found ecstatic uplift in the morning wind, who has known the solace of flowers, who has felt the magic of music, and the thrill of patriotism has known something of the religious aspect of things beautiful and praiseworthy; anyone who has experienced the triumph of overcoming temptation, or rising above evil, of crushing unworthy thoughts and ambitions, has known the power of that which is virtuous; one who has patterned a life after a great example, who has sought truth and truths, present and eternal, has glimpsed the spiritual value of seeking things of good report. Perhaps in all doctrinal theological literature there is no more comprehensive, enlightening definition of the uplift of religion and faith than the 13th article in the statement of Latter-day Saint belief, having nothing to do with dogma or creed, nothing to do with ritual or ceremony; having only to do with spiritual values which, when acquired by an individual, would make of him a better person.[2]

Within three months of the Church's founding, Joseph Smith's wife, Emma, was given the responsibility of preparing a hymnal for use in worship. The instruction to Emma also contained assurance of Divine approval of singing in the Saints' worship:

And it shall be given thee, also, to make a selection of sacred hymns, as it shall be given thee, which is pleasing unto me, to be had in my church.

For my soul delighteth in the song of the heart; yea, the song of the righteous is a prayer unto me, and it shall be answered with a blessing upon their heads.[3]

Though the hymnal has been expanded and revised numerous times through the years, a number of hymns found in Emma's early collection are still sung by Latter-day Saints today, along with hymns common to much of Christendom and new indigenous tunes and texts.

Church leaders following Joseph Smith have reaffirmed the value of good music. Though Brigham Young, for example, was the product of a strict upbringing in which instrumental music and dancing were prohibited, he came to value both. In a sermon given in the Old Tabernacle in 1853, he spoke as follows:

> When I was young, I was kept within very strict bounds, and was not allowed to walk more than half an hour on Sunday for exercise. The proper, and necessary gambols of youth having been denied me, makes me want active exercise, and amusement now. I had not a chance to dance when I was young, and never heard the enchanting tones of the violin, until I was eleven years of age; and then I thought I was on the high way to hell, if I suffered myself to linger and listen to it. I shall not subject my little children to such a course of unnatural training, but they shall go to the dance, study music, read novels, and do anything else that will tend to expand their frames, add fire to their spirits, improve their minds, and make them feel free, and untrammeled in body and mind.[4]

President Young had seen to it that the companies of Saints who made their way west to the Salt Lake Valley included musicians to provide leadership for singing and dancing to lift their spirits as they forged the grueling trail. This was in keeping with a revelation given to him at Winter Quarters in January 1847: "If thou art merry, praise the Lord with singing, with music, with dancing, and with a prayer of praise and thanksgiving."[5]

Leona Holbrook provides some interesting insight relative to music and dancing during the westward trek:

> Dancing, during the migrations, kept the people warm in group assembly during cold evenings on the Great Plains. Dancing, combined with prayer and short inspirational talks, kept the emigrants in better accord than long assemblies with no seating provisions. A naturally clear area in a wagon enclosure was selected, a fire lighted and warmed the fringes, and the orchestra was simple in organization. Some emigrant companies were fortunate enough to have a hand organ. Usually, without its being removed from the wagon it formed the basis for the accompaniment. Other instruments used were the fiddle, accordion and flute.[6]

Recreational dancing continued to be a popular social activity after the Saints' arrival in the West. In the twentieth century, the Church's youth auxiliary sponsored recreational and theatrical dance training and exhibitions. Balls were an annual event in the wards and stakes. All-Church and local dance festivals were sponsored. Dancing continues to be a part of Church-sponsored activities for both youth and adults and permeates campus life at Church schools. Many students enroll in classes teaching various types of dance, and student troupes have earned national and even international recognition in competitions.

During the nineteenth century especially, the Saints' musical resources were greatly enhanced by the conversion and subsequent immigration of several well-trained vocal and instrumental musicians from Europe, particularly the British Isles. Prominent bandmasters were converted along with members of their bands, all of whom immigrated together, bringing their instruments and music with them. Instrumental ensembles, especially brass bands, were very popular in Nauvoo and during the early years in the West. The bands performed at important religious or civic occasions and were highly regarded by the populace. Even during the exodus from Nauvoo the bands stayed together and performed a valuable service.

A remarkable account of one band's dedication and skill is provided by the Saints' non-Mormon friend Thomas L. Kane, who visited the Saints in 1846, while they camped at Council Bluffs, Iowa. The occasion was the mustering of some 500 Mormon men into what is known as the Mormon Battalion, in response to a request of the United States government to assist in its war with Mexico:

> Well as I knew the peculiar fondness of the Mormons for music, their orchestra in service on this occasion astonished me by its numbers and fine drill. The story was, that an eloquent Mormon missionary had converted its members in a body at an English town, a stronghold of the sect, and that they took up their trumpets, trombones, drums, and hautboys together, and followed him to America. When the refugees from Nauvoo were hastening to part with their table ware, jewelery, and almost every other fragment of metal wealth they possessed that was not iron, they had never thought of giving up the instruments of this favorite band. And when the battalion was enlisted, though high inducements were offered some of the performers to accompany it, they all refused. Their fortunes were with the camp of the tabernacle. They had led the farewell service in the Nauvoo temple. Their office now was to guide the monster choruses and Sunday hymns; and like the trumpets of silver, made of a whole piece, "for the calling of the assembly, and for the

journeying of the camps," to knoll the people into church. Some of their wind instruments, indeed, were uncommonly full and pure-toned, and in that clear, dry air could be heard to a great distance. It had the strangest effect in the world, to listen to their sweet music winding over the uninhabited country. Something in the style of a Moravian death-tune blown at day-break, but altogether unique. It might be when you were hunting a ford over the great Platte, the dreariest of all wild rivers, perplexed among the far-reaching sand bars, and curlew shallows of its shifting bed—the wind rising would bring you the first faint thought of a melody; and as you listened borne down upon the gust that swept past you a cloud of the dry sifted sands, you recognized it—perhaps a home-loved theme of Henry [Heinrich] Proch or Mendelssohn. Mendelssohn Bartholdy away there in the Indian marshes![7]

Later, as the Church began to establish settlements throughout the west,

> it was part of [Brigham Young's] policy to send out with each colony a music leader to carry on that part of the Sabbath service even if he were a cobbler or a wheel-wright during the week, as many of them were. Good and crowded choirs at all ward meetings were the rule. And Brigham Young never failed to greet the leader and the singers as he came in, nor did he forget his meed of praise when the services were over.[8]

Throughout the 20th century and to the present time, music has remained an integral part of Mormon life, though its uses and applications have evolved, consistent with the changing needs of the Church and with cultural and societal changes.

With the advent of radio and recorded sound, the instrumental groups found in many early Mormon settlements began to disappear. Ad hoc ensembles were formed as needed to play for particular occasions. A standing organization, the Mormon Youth Symphony and Chorus, was formed at Church headquarters in 1969, continuing until 1999. At that time, the chorus was disbanded and the orchestra was replaced with the Orchestra at Temple Square, as an adjunct to the Mormon Tabernacle Choir.

The Church continued its efforts to teach musical skills. During the early years in the West, "the Sunday School and other Church auxiliaries gradually assumed leadership in musical training, providing singing lessons and band memberships for young Latter-day Saints as well as publishing a large amount of newly composed music."[9] A General Music Committee was formed in 1920 which sent professional musicians to teach in wards and stakes and published instruction manuals in conducting and organ playing technique. More recently, the Church's Music and Cultural Arts Division, successor to the General Music Committee, has sent musical missionaries into developing areas of the Church to teach music fundamentals.

A Church-sponsored music school flourished in downtown Salt Lake City between 1920 and 1953. Historian B. H. Roberts records:

> In view of this large interest in sacred music it is not surprising that out of it there has been established a Latter-day Saint School of Music, which may become a distinctive school in the divine art representative of the New Dispensation and reflecting its spirit. This took form first in the autumn of 1920 when the department of music of the L.D.S. University reorganized as the L.D.S. School of Music . . . and became a separate institution, and began its activities with an enlarged enrollment and broader basis. . . . Later this school of music changed its name to the McCune School of Music, and moved its quarters to what had been the palatial residence of Mr. Alfred W. McCune and family at 200 North Main Street. . . . There is a full staff of officers and professors.[10]

Music was an important component of the curriculum at thirty-three academies for secondary education established by the Church between 1875 and 1910 in seven western states, Canada and Mexico.[11] Since the days of the academies there have been flourishing music departments at Church-sponsored Brigham Young University, with campuses now in Provo, Utah; Rexburg, Idaho; and Laie, Hawaii.

Recent decades have witnessed Mormon musicians successfully performing on national and international stages in both popular and classical genres. LDS composers are actively writing in a wide variety of styles and are finding audiences both within and without the Church.

For conferences and other gatherings, the Church assembles temporary choirs to perform only at the specific event. At a general conference session, for example, one might hear a choir of children, youth, missionaries, adult women, or men and boys, all drawn from a particular geographical area.

To the world at large, however, the face of LDS music is the music of the Mormon Tabernacle Choir.[12] The Choir's roots go back to the old adobe tabernacle on Temple Square. As one writer put it, this is "a choir that began singing to sagebrush and is now courted by concert halls in the most sophisticated cities across the globe."[13]

The Choir's first charge, one that is still of highest priority, is to provide inspirational music for Church conferences and other occasions as requested by Church leadership. However in 1893, when the Choir traveled to perform at the *Eisteddfod*[14] being held in conjunction with the Columbian Exposition in Chicago, it took its first tenuous step onto the world stage. Subsequent tours have taken the Choir to all parts of North America and to many other nations worldwide.

The Choir has been heard on recordings since that industry was in its infancy. It has earned a Grammy and several gold and platinum records and now records on its own label. Their recordings are often found high on the *Billboard* charts.

Their radio broadcast, *Music and the Spoken Word*, begun in 1929, has continued uninterrupted to the present. Since 1962, the program has been televised as well. Employing the latest technology, the broadcast is now seen in high definition and heard in 5.1 surround sound. Their recent Christmas programs have been a major part of holiday programming on PBS stations throughout the United States.

When President Ronald Reagan dubbed them "America's Choir," he was acknowledging that although they are a church choir first and foremost, they also have become part of the fabric of the nation where their church took root and eventually found its home. In 2003, President George W. Bush awarded the Choir the National Medal of Arts "for its extraordinary contribution to music and the art of choral singing; for the wide reach and impact of its music; and for inspiring audiences worldwide."[15] They are truly goodwill ambassadors to the world, not only for their church, but for their state and the United States as well.

Through a succession of conductors over the years, the Choir has continued to develop its artistry. Each conductor has built on the strengths of his predecessors. Their repertoire is enormous and diverse. As they attempt to reach the largest possible audience they perform music in a wide variety of genres, always in keeping with the spirit of the Thirteenth Article of Faith, quoted earlier.

Composer and conductor John Williams said of the Mormon Tabernacle Choir, "These are people who are there for the joy of music. It's not a job with them, it's a mission."[16] Mezzo-soprano Frederica von Stade, who has appeared with the Choir on more than one occasion, commented: "There are certain wonderful landmarks that one has in one's career, sort of the brass ring, and I would say one of the top brass rings is to be able to sing with the Mormon Tabernacle Choir."[17]

Brigham Young's daughter, Susa Young Gates, writing a hundred years after the founding of the Church summarized, from her perspective, the high regard in which music was held by the Church and its members to that time:

> No people on earth have appreciated music, or have given more encouragement to the untrammeled expression of this exquisite art, than have [the Latter-day Saints]. It is part of their worship. Their churches have always been crowded with local musicians and splendid choirs, while congregational singing is now, as it ever has been, the predominating feature of religious and social life.[18]

In a contemporary summary of the place of music within the LDS faith, musicologist Michael Hicks posits that Mormons

> have tried to preserve their singularity as a people by singing, playing, and dancing before an onlooking world. The Mormon quest for identity has shaped Mormon musical life for over 150 years.

Mormonism has grown from what seemed to many observers a disreputable adjunct of revivalism to a small, self-contained nation in the Rocky Mountains and thence to a transcultural brotherhood of faith, authority, zeal, and communion. In the process, Mormons have taken pains to cultivate the "divine art" while at the same time cultivating their "Mormon-ness." Consequently, the body of musical work emerging from Mormon culture, be it hymns, folk songs, dance music, or symphonies, has come to have a flesh and bone of its own, an anatomy that is in the image of the religion itself.[19]

NOTES

[1]Articles of Faith 1:13.

[2]Editorial, *The Improvement Era*, September 1933, 672–73.

[3]Doctrine and Covenants 25:12.

[4]Discourse by President Brigham Young, Tabernacle, February 6, 1853, *Deseret News*, weekly edition, July 20, 1854.

[5]Doctrine and Covenants 136:28.

[6]Leona Holbrook, "Dancing as an Aspect of Early Mormon and Utah Culture," *BYU Studies* 18, no. 1 (1975): 128. "Hand" or "Handle" organ was the name used in the United States for the European barrel organ. These devices varied in size, but smaller ones had no keyboard, were usually not chromatic, and could only play whatever music was available on the cylinders their owners might possess. See Sibyl Marcuse, *Musical Instruments: A Comprehensive Dictionary* (New York: W. W. Norton, 1975), s.v. "Hand Organ."

[7]Daniel Tyler, *A Concise History of the Mormon Battalion in the Mexican War*, 1846–47 (Salt Lake City: n. p., 1881), 108.

[8]Susa Young Gates, *The Life Story of Brigham Young* (New York: Macmillan, 1930), 245.

[9]*Encyclopedia of Mormonism* (New York: Macmillan, 1992), s.v. "Music."

[10]B. H. Roberts, *A Comprehensive History of The Church of Jesus Christ of Latter-day Saints* (Salt Lake City: Deseret News Press, 1930), 6:258.

[11]*Encyclopedia of Mormonism*, s.v. "Academies."

[12]While "Mormon Tabernacle Choir" is the Choir's full and correct name, because of its length it will often be shortened to "Tabernacle Choir" or even just "Choir" when the context makes it clear what choir is being referred to.

[13]Heidi S. Swinton, *America's Choir* (Salt Lake City: Shadow Mountain and Mormon Tabernacle Choir, 2004), vii.

[14]*Eisteddfod* is a traditional Welsh cultural festival. Dating as far back as the twelfth century, it serves to promote the Welsh language and the arts.

[15]Photograph of the award certificate, reproduced in Swinton, 8.

[16]Swinton, 3.

[17]Ibid., 110.

[18]Gates, 239.

[19]Michael Hicks, *Mormonism and Music* (Urbana, Illinois: University of Illinois Press, 1989), ix.

CHAPTER 3

The Organs at Temple Square

Joseph Ridges

The colorful history of pipe organs at Salt Lake City's Temple Square begins with Joseph Harris Ridges (1827–1914), one of the several converts from the British Isles who bolstered the Church's musical resources during the nineteenth century. Ridges, a carpenter and cabinetmaker by trade, had grown up near an organ factory in his native London and had a lifelong fascination with organ building, learning what he could by visiting and studying various organs and by observing and talking with the factory workers. However, there is no evidence that Ridges was ever actually employed by the nearby firm. Ridges later related:

> In the spring of the year 1852 I left my home in England for the gold fields of Australia. I was a mechanic and understood organ-building and had filled some rather large contracts in architectural construction, but I tired of this and determined to make my fortune in Australia. On the same boat that I took from England a Mormon elder by the name of Luke Syphus, loaned me some of Orson Pratt's works, in which I became deeply interested, and soon after reaching Australia I was baptized by the president of the mission, Augustus Farnham.
>
> Elder Syphus and myself went into the hills to get timber, mahogany growing there in great abundance. We used to ship it down the river, and thus made a living.[1]

In another account Ridges continues:

> After staying in the bush for some time I returned to the beautiful city of Sydney. Here I picked out a double-storied house, and having a little money coming to me I began to build my first church organ.[2]

Built in 1855–56 and set up in his home, Ridges's instrument was certainly

among the first pipe organs to have been built in Australia, though not the earliest
as he later claimed.[3] He once described the instrument as having "about five stops
outside of two mechanical stops, and perhaps 295 pipes."[4] When Joseph, his wife
Adelaide, and their eldest son subsequently prepared to immigrate to the United
States, the organ was dismantled, and "the various sections of the instrument [were
soldered] up in large tin cases."[5] Family (including a sealed coffin containing the
remains of Joseph's and Adelaide's second son, who had died a few months earlier)
and organ crossed the Pacific together on the barkentine *Jenny Ford*, which carried a
total of 130 Mormon immigrants.[6]

The members of the LDS Church in Australia were financially involved in
some way with Ridges's organ. Whether they helped Ridges with the cost of building
the instrument or perhaps bore the cost of shipping it to the United States is not clear.
In a letter to Brigham Young dated October 30, 1855, President Farnham wrote:

> I have with the aid and assistance of the Saints in these colonies an
> interest to build an Organ, it is got up by free donations with the feeling
> and sanctions of the Saints in these lands, it is to be presented to the
> Church in Zion by the saints in Australia, thus far proves to be a first rate
> instrument for one of its size, when it is finished it will occupy about
> twelve feet in height, by nine, and the face five deep, it is as compact
> as possible. The workmanship is executed by Joseph H. Ridges by this
> means I shall be able to obtain knowledge as we have not got. It being
> the first attempt in the Church of Latter-day Saints I am in hope that it will
> like every other principle increase both in size and tone.[7]

The two-and-a-half-month ocean voyage from Australia to the California
coast was not without incident. President Farnham's journal recorded considerable
sickness and some minor disagreements among the passengers, as well as the ship's
encountering some severe storms, which he described as hurricanes.[8] Just a few
months before the *Jenny Ford* embarked, the *Julia Ann*, carrying fifty-six passengers
of whom twenty-eight were Mormon immigrants, had wrecked on a coral reef near
the Sicily Isles in the Society Island group. Five of the LDS passengers lost their
lives.[9] That surely must have been on the minds of the passengers on the *Jenny Ford*
as they set sail from Sydney May 28, 1856. Josiah W. Fleming, one of those aboard,
recorded:

> Last night the wind was very high and there was a heavy sea, this morning
> it was less, we ran out of the harbor in a quarterly direction by the Island,

and while we were yet in full view of Sydney, the wind ceased to blow so we had no control of the vessel, which was thrown before the waves toward the shore, which was a fearful-looking sight as the waves were beating against the breakers, flying and foaming high in the air, every sail was set and every possible means was used to save the vessel from the approaching danger, but to no purpose. In a short time we discovered a huge rock toward which our vessel was drifting, we saw our fearful danger, without an earthly way to prevent it. Every soul on board was waiting to see the vessel dashed to pieces. At this critical moment I called some of the Elders to come and stand on the side of the vessel nearest the breakers, and by the power of the Priesthood and mighty faith, we might have power with our heavenly Father to turn the vessel in another direction, as it did not seem possible we should come to such a fearful death, yet the vessel continued to drift broadside toward the rock, as one more wave passed, and the vessel lowered within a short distance from the rock, only waiting the next wave to be dashed to pieces. I lifted my eyes to my Father in Heaven for, perhaps, the last time in this life, I felt the power of God immediately rest upon me and I said: "Oh God the eternal Father in the name of Jesus Christ Thy Son, I command this vessel to stand still and go no farther toward this rock." The next wave came rolling along and raised the vessel to the full height, which soon passed and the vessel lowered in the same place. When I saw this, I again lifted my voice to my Father in Heaven and in the name of Jesus commanded the wind to blow and fill the sails, which it did instantly and we were soon out of danger. This power had been placed on my head by Joseph Smith Senior [father of the Prophet], and John Smith Patriarch, who said I should have power over the winds and waves of the sea and they should obey my voice.[10]

The *Jenny Ford* docked at San Pedro August 15. The Ridges family spent the winter in San Bernardino and Los Angeles. "The following spring Brigham Young sent teams and wagons to haul the organ to Salt Lake City, where it arrived in June 1857."[11]

The Old Tabernacle

Ridges's organ was set up in the Old Tabernacle where it was ready for use within a few months following his arrival. As far as can be determined, that was the first of the Latter-day Saints' religious assembly buildings to be equipped with a pipe organ. This is not surprising, given the Saints' relatively impoverished circumstances and the fact that they were frequently relocating under extremely trying conditions.

One researcher finds that "musical instruments in the homes at Nauvoo included several melodeons, three organs and two pianos (two of the latter instruments were brought to Salt Lake Valley with the 1848 migration)."[12] Just what these organs might have been is open to speculation. The American reed organ industry hadn't gotten underway until after the exodus from Nauvoo.[13] Perhaps they were "hand organs" as mentioned in the previous chapter.

There is some confusion regarding the source of wind for Ridges's organ. Brigham Young's daughter Clarissa Young Spencer, writing about the Old Tabernacle states:

> The building was equipped with a fine pipe organ, which was run by water power. My sister Fanny played the organ, and Charley Moore did the pedaling. Poor Charley—he was so in love with Fanny that he would pedal for hours, if need be, just to be near her.[14]

However, speaking at a conference gathering in the Assembly Hall, Junius F. Wells, an Assistant Church Historian, provided different evidence relative to the organ's wind source, and at the same time provided some illuminating detail about the Old Tabernacle:

> Upon the site of this building [the Assembly Hall] there then stood the old adobe tabernacle. It was placed lengthwise, north and south, about 130 feet and was 65 feet wide. On the western side there was a vestry, which had an entrance through the west wall of the temple block. The Presidency of the Church and the Twelve would come in and meet first in that vestry. Rising from it there was the stand, facing the congregation, which was seated facing west, the two broad entrance doors were on the east side of the building. It was soon found that, on account of the length being the other way, the people seated north and south of the stand could not hear, consequently the arrangement was changed and the stand was placed in the north end of the building. The choir was in the south end. The old organ, ten or twelve feet square, I remember very well. Charley Moore used to blow the bellows and we boys would get up there and help him blow.[15]

Mrs. Spencer's recollection of the organ appears to be incorrect. When she describes Charley Moore "pedaling" for Fanny, one wonders whether she means that Charley and Fanny were seated side by side on the organ bench with Charley playing the pedals while Fanny played the manual(s) or, more likely, she meant that Charley was supplying wind for the organ by means of a pedal-operated winding system. There is no evidence that that organ was ever powered by a hydraulic motor; however, the one in the new, larger tabernacle was so powered for some ten years, between 1885[16] and 1895,[17] and that may have been the cause of the confusion. Had the organ in the Old Tabernacle actually employed a water motor, there would have been no reason for Charley to pump the instrument if, in fact, that were the object of his "pedaling." Finally, a hydraulic motor would have required pressure from a water main to operate. Salt Lake City did not have a piped water system until 1876, just a year before the Old Tabernacle was torn down.[18]

Tabernacle interior, showing original Joseph Ridges organ case.

The (New) Tabernacle

The most imposing feature of the Tabernacle is its majestic organ. Since Barbara Owen has thoroughly detailed the organ's history,[19] only a brief synopsis, written by Jack M. Bethards, President and Tonal Director of Schoenstein & Co. is included here:

> Pioneer organ builder Joseph Ridges (1827–1914) installed the first [organ] in 1867. Some pipes and parts from that organ and its successors have been incorporated into the present instrument not only to provide a

link with the past but also to preserve the superb quality of those artifacts. The most notable feature from pioneer days is the central portion of the large organ case. The famous golden pipes, made of wood staves fashioned from Utah timber, still play today. Over the years, the case has been enlarged, but always following the style of the original, which was influenced by the Boston Music Hall organ (Walker, 1863), the most sensational instrument of its day.

Niels Johnson enlarged the organ in 1885. Then an instrument incorporating some of the pioneer pipes and parts was built by the Kimball Company at the turn of the century. Much of that organ was replaced by the Austin Company in 1915. Essentially this is the instrument that was heard on the first radio broadcasts from the Tabernacle in 1930.

Most organ historians consider the present organ to be the most complete and perfect example of the American Classic style. The prime mover in developing the American Classic organ was G. Donald Harrison, who brought this concept to maturity after World War II. [Tabernacle organist] Alexander Schreiner was impressed with this forward-looking approach and felt that an all-American instrument drawing on European and English traditions would be appropriate for the Tabernacle.

The organ presently contains 11,623 individual pipes organized into 147 voices (tone colors) and 206 ranks (rows of pipes). Grouped into 8 divisions, they are controlled from a console with five 61-note manuals (keyboards) and a 32-note pedalboard. All divisions of the organ are located behind the massive casework on the west end of the Tabernacle except the antiphonal division, which is in the lower attic at the east end and speaks through openings behind the center balcony seats. The longest pipe is 32 feet in speaking length; the shortest is three-quarters of an inch. Pipes are made of wood, zinc, and various alloys of tin and lead.
Between 1985 and 1989, Schoenstein & Co. of San Francisco directed a major renovation of the organ, regulating all pipework, rebuilding the console, and installing seventeen ranks of new pipes.[20]

Few organs, anywhere, are as well known and highly regarded. Its fame is the result of several factors. First, is simply its size; with five manuals and 206 ranks it is among the world's larger instruments. Second, it is the product of a master builder. In its present form, it is primarily the work of the Æolian-Skinner Organ Company, whose tonal director was G. Donald Harrison. Many regard it as one of Harrison's greatest achievements and the quintessential example of the American Classic tonal style. It is extremely versatile, successful both in accompanying and solo roles, has a wide dynamic and tonal range, and is convincing in the performance of a wide range of repertoire. Third, credit must be given to the room in which it is housed. The Tabernacle's warm, resonant acoustics are very sympathetic to musical performance, and the organ is placed in the most advantageous position—freestanding in the front of the auditorium, centered on the room's main axis where it is able to take full advantage of the building's architectural "sound shell." Finally, the instrument receives considerable public exposure. A twice-a-week series of free recitals begun in 1901 became a major attraction for residents and tourists in Salt Lake City. By 1909, recitals were presented daily and have continued since that time, with a second performance added Monday through Saturday during the summer tourist season. As a result, the organ has been heard by a large number of people from all parts of the world. The Mormon Tabernacle Choir's weekly network radio broadcast, begun in 1929, continues to the present and is believed to be the longest continuous-running network radio broadcast in the world. Now seen on television as well as heard on radio, the program, in which the organ is heard in both accompanying and solo roles, reaches a wide audience. The Choir and organ have also been heard on recordings since the early days of recording technology, adding still further to the organ's public exposure.

Assembly Hall

Little is known about the Assembly Hall's first organ except that "parts" of Joseph Ridges's Australian-built organ were reused in its construction. Niels Johnson and Shure Olsen, both of whom worked with Ridges on the Tabernacle organ, built the instrument. Barbara Owen observes that "a photograph of the instrument shows a good-sized two-manual organ with an impressive Victorian case."[21] In 1913, that instrument was replaced with a pleasant, though not distinguished, three-manual organ built by the W. W. Kimball Organ Company.

In advance of the commemoration of the Church's 1980 sesquicentennial, a new organ by Robert L. Sipe was commissioned and paid for through private donations. However, a thorough renovation of the Assembly Hall, underway at the time, delayed the organ's installation until 1983. The Sipe organ, with mechanical key action and electric stop action, contains forty-nine stops (sixty-five ranks) over three manuals and pedal. Located front and center in the moderately resonant room, it speaks with sparkling clarity. The stoplist and voicing are in the German classic tradition. Its handsome main and smaller Positiv[22] cases are decorated with various hand-carved elements that have symbolic meaning within the LDS faith. As one decorative feature, the Positiv case bears the date 1830, the year of the Church's founding. Carved into the large main case is the year 1980. The two cases thus symbolize the Church's growth over 150 years.

The Assembly Hall is of a size and acoustical quality that make it the ideal home to the more intimate concerts held on Temple Square.

During the 1980 renovation of the building, a full basement was excavated beneath the main floor. The basement houses three organ studios for use by the Temple Square organ staff. The three modest practice organs are a three-manual electro-pneumatic organ of twelve ranks by Austin Organs (1982), using an Austin console from 1963; an eight-stop, two-manual mechanical action instrument by Casavant Frères (1979); and a three-manual, mechanical action organ of seven stops built by Kenneth Coulter of Eugene, Oregon (1985).

Specifications of all the Temple Square organs may be found at http://www.mormontabernaclechoir.org/organs/.

The Assembly Hall's Robert Sipe organ.

Joseph Smith Memorial Building

In 1987, it was announced that the elegant Church-owned Hotel Utah, originally built in 1909 immediately across Main Street from Temple Square, would be closed, thoroughly renovated, and reopened to provide additional office space for the ever-expanding Church. Also included in the plans were a chapel, a theater, a genealogical research center, two restaurants, and several function rooms available for public use. Following the six-year renovation, the building reopened in 1993 as the Joseph Smith Memorial Building.

As part of the remodeling, an ornate junior ballroom was transformed into a worship space for wards whose members live in the immediate downtown area. The small, recessed stage that had served originally as the ballroom's bandstand became home to a forty-five-rank, electro-pneumatic organ built by Casavant Frères, completed in 1993. Though the room is not particularly "live" acoustically, the organ, with a very complete two-manual French-influenced specification, is very colorful and speaks with authority.

The Casavant organ in the Joseph Smith Memorial Building.

Temple Square panorama. The Conference Center is seen at right. The domed Tabernacle stands behind the six-spired Temple. The top of the Assembly Hall, with its white central tower, is visible left of the Tabernacle. A corner of the white Joseph Smith Memorial Building protrudes at lower left.

The organs in the Assembly Hall and Joseph Smith Memorial Building were consciously selected to provide tonal contrast and variety when compared to the American Classic instrument in the Tabernacle.   With these distinguished and successful instruments just the proverbial "stone's throw" from each other, one is tempted to ask, "What more could an organist possibly want?"

NOTES

[1]Quoted in "Utah's Old Organ Builder, Applauded by 10,000 People," *Salt Lake Daily Herald*, January 2, 1901, 3.

[2]Quoted in "Pioneer Organ Builder's Story," *Deseret Evening News*, February 16, 1901, 9.

[3]See Graeme D. Rushworth, *Historic Organs of New South Wales: The Instruments, Their Makers and Players, 1791–1940* (Sydney: Hale & Iremonger, 1988), 80.

[4]"Utah's Old Organ Builder Applauded by 10,000 People," 3.

[5]"Joseph H. Ridges Is Called Home," *Deseret Evening News*, March 9, 1914, 2. The exact construction of Ridges's shipping crates is not known. Another account states that the organ was "timbered up." It may be that a wooden frame or crate was lined with soldered metal in order to make it waterproof.

[6]Passenger list, *Jenny Ford* 1856, *Mormon Immigration Index*, Salt Lake City: The Church of Jesus Christ of Latter-day Saints. CD-ROM. Several sources incorrectly identify the immigrant ship as the *Jenny Lind*. Also among the passengers were Luke and Christina Syphus and their young daughter, as well as President Farnham, who had completed his missionary service. President Farnham was the leader of this company of immigrants and as such kept a daily journal of the voyage.

[7]John Douglas Hawkes, *A History of The Church of Jesus Christ of Latter-day Saints in Australia to 1900*, unpublished thesis, Brigham Young University, 1965, 48.

[8]Journal of Augustus Farnham Immigrating Company, *Mormon Immigration Index*.

[9]For a detailed account of the dramatic events surrounding the wrecking of the *Julia Ann* and the subsequent heroic rescue of the survivors, see: John Divitry-Smith, "The Wreck of the Julia Ann," *BYU Studies* 29, no. 2 (1989): 5–26.

[10]Letter from Josiah W. Fleming, *Mormon Immigration Index*.

[11]Marjorie B. Newton, "Australian Pioneer Built 'Grand Organ,'" *LDS Church News*, June 25, 1988, 5. Barbara Owen fixes the date of Ridges's arrival at June 12, 1857. See Barbara Owen, *The Mormon Tabernacle Organ: An American Classic* (Salt Lake City: The American Classic Organ Symposium, 1990), 2.

[12]Harold Laycock, "Music Education in The Church of Jesus Christ of Latter-day Saints," *BYU Studies* 4, no. 1 (1961): 109.

[13]Estey Organ Co. began manufacturing reed organs around 1850, and Mason and Hamlin in 1854. See http://www.esteyorgan.com/reed.html and http://www.scripophily.net/mashamorcomw.html (both accessed October 17, 2008).

[14]Clarissa Young Spencer, *Brigham Young at Home* (Salt Lake City: Deseret Book Co., 1961), 279.

[15]Elder Junius F. Wells, Conference Report (April 1924), 112.

[16]"The Tabernacle Organ," *Deseret Evening News*, October 3, 1885. In describing changes to the Tabernacle organ recently made by Niels Johnson, the writer mentions "The wind is supplied by three large bellows, which are operated by two hydraulic motors."

[17]"It Looks Like New: The Great Tabernacle Undergoing Some Necessary Repairs," *Deseret Evening News*, September 28, 1895. As part of an article detailing a number of changes and refinements to the Tabernacle, the author remarks: "A dive down into the basement disclosed the fact that the old water motors have been retired and two electric motors, one of two-horse and the other of three-horse power, substituted to fill the monster lungs of the great organ." Lighting in the building was also converted to electricity at this time. "As has been the case for a long time the use of gas as an illuminator has been discontinued and electricity holds sway; but now the globes have been removed from the jets in all parts of the building, they having been the source of much trouble in the matter of cleanliness."

[18]http://www.slcgov.com/Utilities/NewsEvents/news2007/news4272007.htm (accessed February 27, 2008).

[19]See Barbara Owen, *The Mormon Tabernacle Organ: An American Classic* (Salt Lake City: The American Classic Organ Symposium, 1990).

[20]*Encyclopedia of Mormonism* (New York: Macmillan, 1992), s.v. "Tabernacle Organ." The first Tabernacle Choir broadcast was actually July 15, 1929. Alexander Schreiner (1901–1987), was Tabernacle organist from 1924 through 1977.

[21]Owen, 11.

[22]The lowest manual of the Assembly Hall organ controls an unenclosed division of pipes housed in a separate case, located behind the organist's back. Because of its position, it is technically called Rückpositiv, *rücken* being German for "back."

4

A New Edifice — A New Organ

The Sunday sessions of spring 1996 general conference were held April 7—Easter Sunday. As it happened, I was the organist for the morning session. To conclude the service, President Gordon B. Hinckley stepped to the pulpit to address the congregation:

> Now, my brothers and sisters, if I may say a few words. First, I'd like to say that it's wonderful to see all of you gathered in the Tabernacle this Easter morning. You're a wonderful sight. It is a remarkable thing to contemplate the many more who are assembled in more than 3,000 halls in various parts of the world.

> I regret that many who wish to meet with us in the Tabernacle this morning are unable to get in. There are very many out on the grounds. This unique and remarkable hall, built by our pioneer forebears and dedicated to the worship of the Lord, comfortably seats about 6,000. Some of you seated on those hard benches for two hours may question the word *comfortably*.

> My heart reaches out to those who wish to get in and could not be accommodated. About a year ago I suggested to the Brethren that perhaps the time has come when we should study the feasibility of constructing another dedicated house of worship on a much larger scale that would accommodate three or four times the number who can be seated in this building.

> We recognize, of course, that we can never build a hall large enough to accommodate all the membership of this growing Church. We've been richly blessed with other means of communication, and the availability of satellite transmission makes it possible to carry the proceedings of the conference to hundreds of thousands throughout the world.

But there are still those in large numbers who wish to be seated where they can see in person those who are speaking and participating in other ways. The structure we envision will not be a sports arena. It will be a great hall with fixed seating and excellent acoustics. It will be a dedicated house of worship, and that will be its primary purpose. It will be fashioned in such a way that only a portion or the entire hall may be used, according to need. It will accommodate not only religious services, but will serve other Church purposes, such as the presentation of sacred pageants and things of that kind. It will also accommodate some community cultural events that will be in harmony with its purpose.

The architectural and engineering studies have not gone far enough for us to make a detailed announcement, but the results thus far are encouraging, and we're hopeful that they will materialize.[1]

President Hinckley's announcement made it nearly impossible for me to concentrate on anything else during the Choir's closing hymn, the benediction and my postlude. I was trying to visualize in my mind a room the size he described. If general conference were to be held there, surely an organ would be needed, but what would that organ be? I could not help thinking in terms of the Atlantic City Convention Hall and its monstrous organ. Discussions had been going on for a year, he said; yet no word of it had "leaked" out to the Tabernacle Choir staff. It obviously had been a matter held in strictest confidence among a select few. That realization prompted the next questions. How far had the planning progressed, and had any thought been given to an organ? How were the Tabernacle organists and the rest of the Choir staff to become involved in decisions regarding not only an organ, but configuration of the choir loft and other music-related issues?

The answers began to come soon enough but in a surprisingly informal way! A few days following President Hinckley's announcement as Clay Christiansen and I were eating lunch in the Church Office Building cafeteria, Michael Moody, Director of the Church's Music Division,[2] approached us in company with Church architects Leland (Lee) Gray and Kerry Nielsen. As architect for Church Special Projects, Lee had been asked by President Hinckley some two years earlier to begin studying the feasibility of constructing a large assembly building.[3] About that same time, the Church hired Kerry as a project architect, and he was soon involved as part of the team.[4] The two men had drawings in hand and began to explain plans for the new building as they had progressed to that point. The enormity of the project as a whole became clear very quickly. A few statistics, compiled following the building's completion, will convey a feel for the scale of the endeavor.

The total complex, including both above- and below-ground components, occupies an entire ten-acre city block. In addition to the 21,000-seat main auditorium, there is a 900-seat theater with fully rigged stage house rising seventy-five feet to the grid above. Underground parking provides space for 1,300 vehicles. Some 750,000 cubic yards of dirt were removed from the site, to a depth ranging from twenty-five to seventy-five feet on the sloping lot. Further:

> Twenty-one-thousand-seat, oval-shaped arenas are not uncommon. But arranging this many seats in a fan-shaped configuration with a single focal point, centered on a speaker at the pulpit, is unique in the world. . . .

The congregation stands to sing a hymn at a session of general conference.

. . . [T]he new facility accommodates the latest technology for acoustics, lighting, theatrical systems, telecommunications, broadcast audiovisual, and security. . . .

The total area in the conference center is 1.2 million square feet, (108,000 square meters) with interior volume of 9.43 million cubic feet (267,000 cubic meters).

The structural system for the concrete building . . . includes 10 radial trusses, each up to 287 feet (86 meters) in length and weighing up to 550 tons (500,000 kilograms). The king truss alone weighs 621 tons (560,000 kilograms).

There are a total of 116,000 cubic yards (88,700 cubic meters) of reinforced concrete in the conference center and 27,000 tons (24,300,000 kilograms) of steel, including reinforcing bar, structural steel and miscellaneous pieces. The perimeter walls and shear walls are up to 30 inches (75 centimeters) thick.

The numbers that go with the electrical systems are equally mind-boggling. The building contains 50,000 miles (80,000 kilometers) of wire and 780 miles (1,250 kilometers) of conduit. There are 330 panels for power circuits and more than 300 panels for lighting. . . .

For seating capacity and sheer size, the main auditorium has no peer in the world. It is seven times the size of the Metropolitan Opera House in New York.[5]

Such a monumental building in an inner city setting could easily overpower surrounding

The Conference Center at dusk.

structures and dominate the cityscape. Great care has been taken to avoid that tendency. Much of the structure is below ground level, thus reducing its apparent height. Landscaping at street level, on terraces, and a publicly accessible four-acre garden on the roof, together with fountains and a variety of other water features,

A small stream runs along the front of the Conference Center.

further soften the building's impact. As Clair Enlow puts it, "The entire block now functions as a city park. Church and city collaborated to make it a public amenity and an attractive destination. From its various promontories, visitors take in the sweeping views."[6]

As the architects, Clay, and I began to hone in on the auditorium and its rostrum, it became evident that substantial work needed to be done relative to musical considerations. The choir loft configuration was awkward, but even more disconcerting was the lack of any space whatsoever for a pipe organ. Somewhere along the way, the assumption had been made that the organ would be electronic. The rostrum's rear wall was to be some sort of attractive curtain or grille to be designed

later. They called it a "screen wall." Though no one ever spelled it out, we guessed that the cost of a pipe organ was probably a major consideration. After all, the building itself would require a huge outlay, and certainly every effort would need to be made to control costs. Further, the sheer size of the auditorium dictated that everything that transpired there would likely have to be reinforced electronically, so why not just use electronic organ sound from the outset? Yet, we were convinced that a pipe instrument was tonally superior. Why not start with the best possible sound, even if it did have to be electronically amplified?

Clay and I did not hesitate to express our disappointment in what we had been shown, at which point Lee suggested that we bring on a consultant to work with us. Consultants were being heavily relied upon in every aspect of the project to add their experience and expertise to that of Church employees. The opinion of a respected consultant would add strength and credibility to whatever recommendation we would eventually make relative to the organ.

We immediately reported our encounter with Lee and Kerry to the rest of the Tabernacle Choir's musical and administrative staff and began to consider who might best serve as our consultant. After careful deliberation, we settled on Jack Bethards, President and Tonal Director of Schoenstein & Co. in San Francisco. Jack was highly regarded as a consultant and had been involved in a number of important organ projects. As an organ builder, he had successfully worked in acoustically challenging spaces. We knew he was biased toward pipe organs—a prejudice we all shared—yet any consultant we hired would be biased to some degree. Having worked with Jack over a period of several years during the renovation of the Æolian-Skinner organ in the Tabernacle, we knew him to be meticulous in his thinking and completely open and honest. If a pipe organ had no chance of success in the Conference Center, we knew he would tell us. Certainly, no organ builder would want to risk tarnishing his reputation by attempting to install an instrument in an impossible situation. We submitted Jack's name to Lee Gray in a May 15, 1996, memorandum, and our recommendation was quickly approved. Jack accepted the consulting job, and we sent him an outline of what we felt might be required of the instrument.

At that time, we had little idea of the actual usage to which the organ and building would eventually be put, apart from general conference. General conference services would require the organ to be able to provide suitable accompaniment for choirs up to the size of the Mormon Tabernacle Choir and hymn accompaniment for congregations as large as 21,000. Prelude and postlude music would also be necessary. We assumed, given the size of the auditorium and its anticipated acoustics, that organ recitals would not be held there. The organ would need to be able to hold its own with choir and orchestra, were it to be used for large-scale concerts. To achieve the desired flexibility for staging various types of events, a movable console seemed imperative, thus eliminating any thought of using mechanical action. It also seemed wise to model the console after the Æolian-Skinner console in the Tabernacle. That console is extremely comfortable to play, and having the two similar in layout would facilitate easy adjustment as we moved from one to the other. We felt the safest approach was to build as much tonal flexibility as possible into the instrument, including MIDI[7] capability.

As it turned out, we severely underestimated the uses to which the building would eventually be put. We had no way of knowing, for example, that between 2005 and 2007 the Tabernacle would be closed while undergoing a thorough renovation.[8] During that period, the weekly Tabernacle Choir broadcast would originate from the Conference Center, and the daily organ recitals would be played there as well. The organ we had originally thought to be primarily an accompanying instrument would suddenly become a solo instrument. Nor could we anticipate that during the summer tourist season, crowds attending the Sunday Choir broadcasts would become so large that they could no longer be accommodated in the Tabernacle, and that the broadcasts would soon begin to originate in the Conference Center each year between Memorial Day and Labor Day. We could not foresee the number of regional conferences and other gatherings that would be held there, nor that the Choir would use the Conference Center for all its musical activities during the month of December to accommodate the large crowds attending.

In considering the best solution to the organ question, our initial efforts were focused on the feasibility of a pipe organ. After considerable study and consultation with the architects, acousticians and stage designers, Jack Bethards suggested the following in an October 1996 letter to Project Manager Thomas (Tom) Hanson:[9]

The Church should consider the purchase of an existing instrument. This could save time and money, and, at the same time, yield an outstanding result. The builders of yesteryear specialized in this type of organ construction [using high wind pressures] during the era of large auditorium installations, whereas today's builders do church work predominantly.[10]

Jack had identified several early twentieth century instruments that were rumored to be available or that might become available in the near future. These were installed in various facilities in Memphis, Chicago, Philadelphia, Cleveland and Worcester. Perhaps the most promising was housed at Ellis Auditorium in Memphis. This grand old instrument, installed by W. W. Kimball in 1928–29, was actually two organs installed back-to-back: a four-manual, forty-one-rank organ speaking into the building's South Hall and a seventy-four-rank, five-manual organ speaking into the North Hall. The two organs could be played simultaneously from the larger console. Lee Gray, Tom Hanson, Jack Bethards and I flew to Memphis to inspect the instruments and consider their possible use.

There was a great amount of justifiable civic pride attached to these instruments. Those involved were having difficulty deciding whether the organs should be sold or put into storage. That indecision, in addition to the difficulty of removal, having to deal with the asbestos in the building, and the need to thoroughly renovate and rebuild the instrument for our purpose, led us to the conclusion that this was not a viable solution.[11] The use of other existing instruments posed many of the same challenges.

The decision as to whether a pipe organ might even be considered clearly lay with President Hinckley. Mormon Tabernacle Choir President, Wendell Smoot,[12] arranged for the two of us to meet with the President to discuss the matter. President Hinckley also invited Ted Simmons, Managing Director of the Church's Physical Facilities Department.[13] The meeting was cordial, efficient and businesslike.

I had prepared a two-page summary of what I felt were the major points to be considered in the meeting. The document first addressed the Church's mission, image and musical tradition:

> There has been a long and respected tradition of fine music emanating from Temple Square. The many who look to us for musical leadership are watching this project with intense interest, expecting a continuation of that tradition.

One distinguishing feature of monumental Christian houses of worship is a fitting pipe organ. The Tabernacle has earned recognition as one of those great religious edifices. For 130 years that building's majestic pipe organ, generally considered one of the world's premiere instruments, has supported and inspired choirs and congregations with its vibrant, clear tone. Our new structure undoubtedly has the potential to become one of the world's most imposing religious edifices. Might not the absence of an appropriate pipe organ detract from its credibility as such?

The Tabernacle organ's imposing façade has always been a dominant feature of the building and is widely recognized as one of the Church's most visible and identifiable symbols. Except for its console, an electronic instrument would eliminate any visible evidence of an organ from the room.[14]

The document continued by discussing our perception of the tonal limitations of electronic organs and our experience when using electronic instruments to accompany the Tabernacle Choir on tour. While an electronic organ, used alone, certainly added color and breadth of sound, as compared to a piano, its tone seemed quite sterile against the richness of the Choir's opulent sound. Electronic organs fared better when used in conjunction with an ensemble of acoustic instruments, and best when used as an adjunct to the entire Orchestra at Temple Square. Issues of obsolescence, longevity, and serviceability were also mentioned. The final point was, "Once the building is built without space for a pipe organ, the decision is irreversible."

President Hinckley, then 86, listened intently as we presented our concerns. He then asked Ted Simmons how much it would cost to put a pipe organ in the building. Ted estimated five million dollars! I don't know how he arrived at that figure—whether he thought the organ itself would cost that much, or whether he had included the ancillary costs for rethinking and redrawing the entire front of the auditorium, along with additional construction costs. My heart sank when I heard his reply. Surely, if cost were the deciding factor, a five million dollar price tag would drive the final nail into the coffin, and our dream of a pipe organ would come to an abrupt end. To my great surprise, President Hinckley was unfazed, and agreed that we should study the matter further and then return to report our findings and make a recommendation.

It was felt by all involved that in order to continue our study and begin the process of exercising "due diligence," we needed to familiarize ourselves with some large, custom-designed electronic organs. In early May 1997, Tom Hanson, Lee Gray, Wendell Smoot and I flew to Southern California, where we were joined by Jack Bethards. On this trip, we evaluated one all-electronic and two combination pipe/electronic instruments. The hybrid organs, if successful, were of interest as a possible compromise. The inclusion of pipes not only strengthened the instruments tonally, but also added the possibility of an attractive pipe display. The use of electronics conserved space and funds. In each organ, the pipes were voiced to be cohesive with the electronics. Even in the case of expanding an existing pipe organ, some re-voicing of pipes was done to facilitate their combining optimally with the electronics.

Our time in California also afforded the opportunity to meet with one of the architects from the Portland, Oregon firm[15] responsible for the new building's design, along with one of the acousticians[16] working on the project. The meeting was beneficial as the impact of the organ was discussed from the various perspectives represented by the participants.

Later that month, Tom, Lee, Jack and I met again in Southern California. This time the Salt Lake contingent also included then Tabernacle Choir Associate Conductor, Craig Jessop, and Tabernacle organists Clay Christiansen and Richard Elliott. The object of this trip was to inspect a particularly large electronic organ, perhaps even bigger than would be required for the new Assembly Building. It was built by a highly respected firm and installed in a relatively "dry," moderate-sized worship space.

As a result of these two excursions, we returned to Salt Lake City having made some important observations:

1. The builders of electronic organs have made significant progress through the years. As they continue to improve their product, however, obsolescence becomes inevitable.

2. The size of an organ, be it pipe or electronic, needs to be in correct proportion to the space in which it is housed.

3. Quantity and quality of sound are not necessarily synonymous.

4. Electronic organ tone fares much better in a reverberant space.

5. The pleasantness of electronic sound is inversely proportional to the extent to which it is amplified.

6. Single electronic stops can be quite convincing, but ensembles and choruses are less so.

7. Principal stops, which are the backbone of the organ, seem to be the most difficult to replicate electronically.

8. If the addition of some pipes contributes substantially to an organ's success, then wouldn't all pipes yield the best possible result, assuming sufficient space and funds were available?

An additional question surfaced with regard to maintenance of an electronic instrument. Would it be necessary to involve outside technicians who would have access to proprietary parts? If it were necessary to call in outside personnel in an emergency, how quickly could they respond? The need for immediate service, on occasion, is one of the justifications for our having a full-time, in-house technical staff.

Our experiences in California had not convinced us that an electronic organ would best meet our needs. In the meantime, Jack Bethards, having continued to study the evolving building plans and having maintained an ongoing dialogue with the architects and acousticians, had offered encouragement about the feasibility of a pipe organ in the space. In a report dated May 22, 1997, Mr. Bethards wrote:

> As someone outside the Church, I can assure you that the Tabernacle Choir and organ represent the Church to the public more clearly and forcefully than does any other symbol. I was introduced to the sound of an organ, as were thousands of others in my profession, by your Sunday broadcasts and recordings. People will be watching this project with intense interest and, in many cases, will use whatever example you set as a model. Like it or not, you are looked upon by most of the Christian world for musical leadership.
>
> By the same token, as your consultant, I will be watched carefully and my reputation is on the line. I can assure you, therefore, that I have approached this work with caution. Although I bring a natural preference for pipe organs, I have kept an open mind toward electronics. The last thing that the pipe organ industry needs is a failure in this brightest of all spotlights. No builder would attempt this project without assurance of success. I believe all of us in the field would rather see an electronic here than an inadequate pipe organ.[17]

In his summary, Jack asserted that, "a pipe organ will work in the auditorium as presently designed, without compromise to itself or to other architectural or performance elements." He further wrote in his concluding recommendation:

> A pipe organ should be [the] musical backbone of the new assembly building. To be successful and practical it should be as small as possible to get the job done. This will promote good layout and efficient maintenance. Only the sounds needed to back up the activities planned for the building should be included. This organ does not need to be an all purpose recital instrument. Its success will depend upon excellent custom design to fit the hall's acoustic—not on its size or complexity.

> I suggest a budget of $3,500,000.00 for the organ.[18]

We determined, therefore, to recommend a pipe organ to the First Presidency and declared our intention in a memorandum addressed to those principally involved. That memo, signed by both Wendell Smoot and myself, summarized our experiences in California with electronic organs as well as touring with an electronic instrument to accompany the Tabernacle Choir. The concluding recommendation read, "Considering tonal quality, maintenance, and obsolescence, along with visual and artistic impact, we feel strongly that the question of an organ for the Assembly Building is best answered with a pipe instrument."[19] Wendell made the appointment to meet again with President Hinckley.

Besides Wendell Smoot and me, all three members of the First Presidency[20] were present at the meeting, along with Ted Simmons. We reported our findings and made our case as best we could. Ted Simmons presented a summary that he had prepared giving the pros and cons of pipes vs. electronics from his perspective. His document pointed out the advantages of electronics over pipes based on cost, flexibility and acoustics. His conclusion read:

> The existing Tabernacle organ is a world recognized instrument. The new instrument perhaps should not compete with the existing instrument and is basically for choir accompaniment. Significant advances have been made in electronic organ sound, but to trained ears the pure pipe organ sound is still unmatched.[21]

While both Ted and I had tried to be objective in our presentations, it seemed apparent that we favored opposing sides of the issue. At that point, Wendell suggested that since the Tabernacle Choir would be one of the major beneficiaries of a pipe organ, he would be prepared to contribute substantially toward the cost of the organ out of Choir funds. I was overwhelmed by Wendell's offer. I had no idea he was considering such a gesture. It demonstrated to me how much confidence he had in the judgment of his staff. The meeting ended with President Hinckley promising to further consider the matter and to give us a decision later.

Several suspenseful and prayer-filled days passed before word came down that our recommendation had been approved by the First Presidency. There would indeed be a pipe organ in the new assembly building! We never learned what factor(s) weighed most heavily in their decision.

President Gordon B. Hinckley addresses those gathered at the Conference Center groundbreaking ceremony.

The groundbreaking ceremony for the still unnamed building was held July 24, 1997—the 150th anniversary of the entry of the Mormon pioneers into the Salt Lake Valley. The platform that was erected to seat the dignitaries was a miniature bowery, reminiscent of those built on Temple Square by the early settlers. In his remarks on that occasion, President Hinckley said:

> This will be a magnificent structure. It will cost a lot of money. I'm grateful to say that through the great faith of the Latter-day Saints, we have the means with which to build it. I hope we will not waste a single penny. I hope we will be prudent and wise and careful and that the outcome of all this will be a structure of which we can be proud and of which I believe the Lord will be proud. His name will be spoken frequently within this hall. His name will be worshiped as will the name of his Beloved Son, our Savior and our Redeemer, and the voices which speak in this hall . . . will be carried across the world to the nations of the earth as this Church goes on and continues to grow from its present membership of 10 million, scattered in more than 160 nations, to numbers beyond our ability to calculate and to places beyond our ability to guess at this time. . . .
>
> . . . This will be a place for general conference. This will be a place for other meetings. This will be a place of the arts. . . .It will be built as well as we know how to build in this season of the history of the world and I hope that it will stand for as long as the earth lasts and serve the purpose of the kingdom of God.[22]

He further remarked, with tongue somewhat in cheek:

The Tabernacle Choir has made the Tabernacle its home. That Tabernacle will continue to be the home of the Tabernacle Choir for its broadcasts, recordings and other undertakings. But this hall will be much used also by the Tabernacle Choir, and to accommodate their desires and their wishes the building will contain a fine pipe organ. And just to make sure that they do something toward that, we've asked them to contribute about a million and a half dollars out of their private funds, to not travel so much, to stay home and make that money available to us for this great building.[23]

President Hinckley's goal was to have the building finished in time for the April 2000 general conference. Now it remained for the contractors to complete the building on schedule and for us to produce a pipe organ that could do everything expected of it. Both would prove to be formidable tasks!

NOTES

[1]*Discourses of President Gordon B. Hinckley* (Salt Lake City: The Church of Jesus Christ of Latter-day Saints, 2004), 1:97–98.

[2]Since that time the Music Division has been renamed Music and Cultural Arts Division.

[3]W. Dee Halverson, *The Conference Center: The Story of Its Construction* (Salt Lake City: Legacy Constructors, 2000), 26.

[4]Ibid., 32.

[5]Clair Enlow, "LDS Conference Center Welcomes the Faithful," *Architecture Week*, February 7, 2001, D1.1–3. This is an excellent article that addresses both the physical and aesthetic aspects of the Conference Center.

[6]Ibid., D1.2.

[7]See the Glossary for explanations of this and other technical terms encountered in the text.

[8]The Tabernacle was closed at the end of December 2004 and was reopened and rededicated by President Gordon B. Hinckley at the Saturday afternoon session of general conference, March 31, 2007.

[9]Tom later recalled, "I was working on a project for the Bechtel Company in India about the time that the announcement in general conference was made by President Hinckley that the Church was going to build this particular project. I wrote to the Church saying that we were ready to do this for them, and I received a much more cordial phone call back saying, 'We're not interested in Bechtel, but we want to see your resume.' So I sent my resume and a couple of months later in 1996, I was employed by the Church as the project manager on the Conference Center." See Halverson, 23.

[10]Draft of letter from Jack Bethards to Thomas Hanson, October 16, 1996. Copy in possession of the author.

[11]The South Hall organ was purchased by, restored and installed at Bartlett United Methodist Church in nearby Bartlett, Tennessee, in 2002. The North Hall instrument apparently remains in storage.

[12]The office of President of the Mormon Tabernacle Choir is an unpaid, church-service position. While having responsibility for the entire Choir operation, the President primarily concentrates on business and personnel matters, leaving musical considerations to the music staff. Professionally, Wendell Smoot headed a highly respected money management firm in Salt Lake City. As Choir President, he reported directly to President Hinckley, meeting him with some regularity to discuss Choir affairs. With the growth of the Choir organization, the position has evolved into a full-time, though still unpaid, Church calling.

[13]The Physical Facilities Department is responsible to oversee the planning, construction and maintenance of all Church-owned buildings worldwide. Ted Simmons passed away in September 1998.

[14]John Longhurst, "Considerations for the Assembly Building Organ," undated. Document in possession of the author.

[15]Zimmer Gunsul Frasca Architects was the firm entrusted with the design of the building. Robert Frasca, a senior partner in the firm, was the Partner in Charge of Design for the Conference Center. William (Bill) Williams represented the firm on this occasion.

[16]Paul Scarborough of Jaffe, Holden, Scarborough Acoustics of Norwalk, CT.

[17]Jack M. Bethards, "Assembly Building—Consultant's Organ Status Report," May 22, 1997. Copy in possession of the author.

[18]Ibid.

[19]Memorandum from Wendell Smoot and John Longhurst to Ted Simmons, Tom Hanson, et al., May 22, 1997. Copy in possession of the author.

[20]Thomas S. Monson and James E. Faust served as counselors to President Hinckley during this period. The group of three leaders is collectively called the "First Presidency."

[21]Ted Simmons, "Organ Choices for the Assembly Building," undated. Copy in possession of the author.

[22]"Pioneer Sesquicentennial Celebration Footage 1996–97," Videocassette #AV2098–89 in the Church History Library of The Church of Jesus Christ of Latter-day Saints.

[23]Ibid.

In Search of a Builder

Prior to the July 24, 1997, groundbreaking, our efforts relative to the organ had focused primarily on the question of electronics vs. pipes. Now that the decision had been made to purchase a pipe organ, we could begin to consider, in greater detail, the characteristics of the instrument and possible builders.

There was general agreement on several points. A mechanical action instrument would not provide the flexibility needed to accommodate the anticipated varied uses of the organ. The builder would need to be one who employed nonmechanical action proudly, rather than condescendingly. The sound should be noble, even heroic, to complement the size of the room. We desired a rich, warm, colorful yet clear tone, firmly grounded at eight-foot pitch in the manual divisions and sixteen-foot pitch in the pedal. We would look for a builder who was meticulous in his attention to both tonal and mechanical details.

In spite of our busy schedules at Temple Square, all the organists make time, on occasion, to play recitals away from Salt Lake City. As a result, we had considerable collective firsthand experience with the work of a fairly large number of organ builders. Based on that experience we listed several firms whose work we wished to consider further. Hearing of the proposed project, one representative contacted us requesting that his firm be considered. Some of the builders on our list had not installed organs in our immediate area. Others had, but their instruments were either very small or did not represent their current work. Therefore, we scheduled a third trip to Southern California. Our entourage included Richard Elliott, Clay Christiansen and me, along with our lead organ technician, Robert Poll.[1] We organists would focus primarily on the sound and "feel" of the instruments; Robert would focus on evaluating quality of materials and workmanship.

We felt the need to make our evaluations as fair and objective as possible and at the same time have notes that we could refer to at some future date. To meet those needs, Richard Elliott devised a form for each organist to complete for each organ. Robert made a comparable form for himself that listed pertinent technical considerations. We scored each item on a scale ranging from one to five, five being the highest mark. The various elements of the evaluation were weighted differently according to their relative importance. The average of the organists' marks plus the technician's marks could total a maximum of 100 points.

On this trip, we visited four organs over a period of two days, August 26–27, allowing ourselves two to three hours with each instrument. The scores of the four organs ranged from 50.5 to 91.6 points.

Temple Square organ technicians Robert Poll (behind) and Lamont Anderson.

The organ that scored highest made quite an impression on us. Murray M. Harris originally built it for St. Paul's Procathedral in Los Angeles in 1910–11. (Earlier, in 1904, the company had built an organ for the St. Louis World's Fair—the organ that was to become the nucleus of the instrument in the John Wanamaker store in Philadelphia, one of the largest and most storied organs currently in existence.) The three-manual, forty-one-stop St. Paul's organ moved with the congregation to a new, larger church in 1924, where it remained until 1980. St. James' Episcopal Church, on Wilshire Boulevard in Los Angeles, subsequently acquired the organ, where it was installed in 1995. The organ, as we heard it, had been thoroughly renovated in a collaborative effort involving H. L. Schlicker Co., Austin Organs, Inc., and Rosales Organ Builders. Writing about the renovated organ, Manuel Rosales states:

> The plan included adding sixteen stops in the Murray Harris style. The instrument would also require new slider wind chests, expression boxes and a state-of-the-art console. Although this would result in essentially a new working mechanism for the organ, the tonal character of the Murray Harris organ would be retained and enhanced.[2]

Speaking about Harris's work in general, Rosales explains:

> The craftsmanship exhibited extraordinary attention to detail, and the voicing produced an ensemble in step with the orchestrally-inspired tastes of the day, but with an energy and drama all too rarely encountered. Murray M. Harris himself imparted a coveted tonal signature.[3]

Summarizing the tonal qualities of the renovated organ at St. James', Rosales continues:

> The organ possesses clear and unforced Diapason tone with a bountiful collection of unison colors. The Great chorus is bold and well defined.

The Swell and Choir chorus[es] are each appropriately softer and make excellent accompaniment divisions. The chorus reeds are likewise varied in strength also making beautiful solo stops. The stops created by Austin Organs were designed and voiced using examples and scales from other Harris instruments, except for the Cornet V, which is appropriately patterned after a stop in the Metropolitan Cathedral, Mexico City. The entire ensemble is underpinned by the original 32' Contra Bombarde whose low CCCC pipe is two feet across![4]

Our assessment of the instrument agreed with Rosales's one hundred percent. Here were the warmth, color and nobility we felt were needed for our organ!

During the months I was working closely with Jack Bethards, I had asked him on more than one occasion if he felt that Schoenstein & Co. could take on a project of this size and, if so, whether he wished us to consider his firm along with others that were "on our radar." Apart from his work at the Tabernacle, I had played several of his smaller organs. During one of our trips to Los Angeles in May, while we still had electronic organ sounds in our ears, Jack had taken us to Our Mother of Good Counsel Roman Catholic Church to hear a relatively small two-manual Schoenstein. The idea had been to allow us to compare the impact of just a modest number of pipe ranks with that of larger electronic instruments. While in Dallas to perform at the Meyerson Symphony Center, I was able to see Jack's creative and very successful instrument at Highland Park Presbyterian Church. During 1997, Schoenstein & Co. was installing and finishing the imposing instrument at First-Plymouth Congregational Church in Lincoln, Nebraska. To this point, Jack had always been noncommittal in his reply to my query. I could tell that he had reservations about taking on the project. Toward the end of August, I received a letter from Jack in which he detailed three areas that had concerned him relative to his firm's being considered as a possible builder for our organ. First was the question of a possible conflict of interest, as viewed either by the Church or by his competitors, because of his work as our consultant. His second concern was whether his firm could realistically complete a project of this size given our timetable and the work to which Schoenstein was already committed. Finally, he questioned whether this job would "preserve and enhance" Schoenstein's reputation as one of America's finest organ builders.

He felt that if the Church sensed no conflict of interest between his work as consultant and his being considered as a possible builder, and if his dual status were fully disclosed to other firms being evaluated, that the first issue could be resolved. Relative to the second point, he felt that Schoenstein & Co. could undertake the job if other firms and individuals were involved in what he called a "consortium." Finally, he addressed the third point:

> The assignment ahead of us is unprecedented in the entire history of the organ! There is a greater chance of stubbing one's toe than becoming a hero. The challenge from a tonal director's point of view is unimaginably tantalizing, however, the danger from a president's point of view must be considered. I have had to weigh the balance of these two points quite seriously. Given the direction that the design concept has taken, I have finally resolved all my doubts and am convinced that this instrument has every chance of success. What will be required is boldness and common sense combined with the cooperation and enthusiastic support of architect, acoustician, sound equipment contractor and (most of all) client. Having worked on this project for quite a while now, I have confidence that all of these will be in place.[5]

We added Schoenstein & Co. to our list of potential builders.

The next step in our selection of a builder was one that I took alone. Prior to undertaking a tour, members of the Tabernacle Choir's administrative, technical and musical staff traverse the tour route, visiting venues and hotels, confirming arrangements, doing whatever is necessary to assure a smooth-running tour. Traveling with an entourage of some 500 people obviously requires careful planning and extreme attention to detail. Such was the case in September 1997. I was scheduled to be part of the group to leave September 4 to go to Europe in advance of the Choir's tour the following summer. London was to be the first stop, providing an opportunity that was too fortuitous to pass up. Having felt that our organ should have a rich, warm "English" sound (a feeling that was reinforced by our recent visit to St. James' Episcopal Church), I arranged to leave on Labor Day, September 1, ahead of the rest of the touring party.[6] I had previously contacted organ builders N. P. Mander Ltd. and Harrison & Harrison Ltd. to see if I could arrange to spend time with each firm to discuss our project. Both were most gracious in accommodating my request. Accordingly, I spent Wednesday with John Mander, managing director of N.P. Mander, and Thursday with Mark Venning, managing director of Harrison & Harrison. During those two days I was able to see a variety of organs in a number of churches, including St. Paul's, Winchester and Westminster Cathedrals. The instruments were wonderful; they exhibited the color and breadth of sound that I felt were needed in our new building.

In a letter following my visit, Mark Venning confirmed many of the same conclusions that our consultant, Jack Bethards, had reached:

> The scale of the project is certainly unique in organbuilding terms. An organ of commanding quality will certainly be needed: virtually a massed choir of organ voices! Vigour, colour, richness and drama will all be needed on a large scale. Loud, forced tone would defeat the object— sheer decibel power soon becomes oppressive. As with any good organ, the prime requirements are eloquence and cohesion, with convincing and well-proportioned choruses as the backbone of the instrument.
>
> In such a large space, the task for an organ is tremendous. I would normally shun all forms of sound reinforcement for organs, but I think it is clear in this case that some assistance will be required, especially in the more distant parts of the Hall. This will have to be done with great subtlety, and with excellent equipment: considerable experimentation will be needed. Much will, of course, depend upon the acoustic properties of the room.
>
> The question may then be asked whether it would not be better to rely entirely on an electronic sound source: however, I strongly agree with you that the true sound of a pipe organ will be an inestimable advantage in musical terms. That must be the best way to achieve successful results in these unique circumstances.
>
> Construction of such an organ would be a heroic undertaking.[7]

Both firms expressed an interest in the project, and I have no doubt that either would have achieved a wonderful result. An unfavorable currency exchange rate was discouraging. Of even more concern was the availability of time in the new building for installation and tonal finishing. As it turned out, unfettered access for installation and total quiet for tonal work were commodities in very short supply prior to and following the dedication of the building. Organ work had to be completed in numerous short trips over an extended period of time, a situation that would have been very awkward and expensive with crews traveling from England.

October 27 saw us on the road again, this time to Colorado Springs to see the work of yet another American builder. This time, we three organists and Robert Poll, our lead technician, were joined by Craig Passey, from the Church's Purchasing Department.[8] The organ we saw had much to recommend it, and we were pleased to consider its builder along with the others on our list.

It was now time to narrow the field. Richard, Clay and I, along with Robert Poll, thoroughly discussed our findings from trips taken over the past three months and recommended three builders to be given further consideration. With Tom Hanson's approval, we invited each of those three firms to submit a proposal. The packet we sent included information about the building, with drawings of the auditorium and organ space. We listed the uses to which we felt the organ would be put and gave a description of our vision of the instrument tonally and mechanically. Jack Bethards's role as consultant was fully disclosed, and we proposed a date to visit each firm's place of business.

In mid-November, Tom Hanson, Craig Passey, Robert Poll and I took a two-day trip east to visit the shops of two of our three potential builders. We made a similar trip to San Francisco in early December to visit Schoenstein & Co. The purpose of these visits was for us to meet the men and women who would be principally involved in our project, to tour their shops and to view their construction procedures firsthand, and for Craig to inquire as to their business practices. Having satisfied ourselves that all three companies were solid on all counts, we asked each to suggest an organ they had recently completed that they felt best represented their current work. Accordingly, Clay, Richard, Robert and I planned one final trip that would take us to Pittsburgh, Washington, D. C. and Omaha to see and play these recommended instruments.

In the meantime, we received the three firms' proposals. Each had prepared an intriguing and exciting set of specifications that carefully addressed the points we had asked to be considered. We studied them carefully and compared them in every imaginable way. Though they represented contrasting approaches, they all seemed viable!

Our two-day trip east to inspect the builders' recommended organs was scheduled for January 5–6, 1998. Each of the three instruments was impressive, to say the least, but our encounter with the sixty-four-rank, four-manual Schoenstein at St. Paul's Episcopal Church on "K" Street in Washington was very much akin to our experience with the Murray M. Harris organ in Los Angeles a few months earlier. Here were warmth, suavity, color, fire, delicacy, nobility and versatility in one very beautiful instrument. In retrospect, perhaps we were hearing vestiges of the interest Jack Bethards had in the organs of Harris early in his career, as noted by organ historian Orpha Ochse.[9] Though not installed in the most desirable location, it still created a thrilling impact throughout the room. The feeling among all four of us was that Schoenstein & Co. should build the organ for the Assembly Building. While I am confident that either of the other builders would have furnished us with a wonderful instrument as well, the Schoenstein came closer to the tonal ideal that we felt was optimal for this new organ on Temple Square.

We wasted no time communicating our recommendation. In a memorandum dated the day after our return, I wrote, in part:

> The [Schoenstein] sound is warm, expressive, and rich, and will be readily accepted by those accustomed to hearing the Tabernacle organ. . . .
>
> Happily the price quoted in the Schoenstein proposal is comfortably under our estimated cost. . . .
>
> There are three additional points relative to cost. First, since the exact nature of the pipe display has not been determined, the cost for any special decorative or structural elements relating thereto could not be included in the proposal. Second, any support or reinforcement beyond normal organ building practice that may arise out of seismic considerations would be additional. Third, as we consider the proposal in minute detail, it is likely that some modifications may be desired, either for musical or technical reasons, that could affect the cost in a relatively minor way.
>
> It is critical that we proceed without delay if we expect timely delivery and installation of the organ. We are already about three months behind our schedule for the job. I suggest that we send Schoenstein & Co. a letter of intent immediately so that they can begin the preliminary stages of the project, even while the final details of the contract are being determined.[10]

The three points mentioned above relative to cost all became relevant to the project. Salt Lake City lies near the Wasatch Fault and is considered to be in what the Disaster Center classified as Seismic Zone 3.[11] The Conference Center was designed structurally, however, to meet the more stringent requirements for Zone 4 "plus an importance factor."[12] Additional bracing of the organ's structural framework did become necessary. Costs involved with the casework and façade would be considerable, and changes to the specification would likewise affect the final cost.

The contract with Schoenstein & Co. was finally signed by Craig W. Passey on January 26, 1999, a full year after we had recommended them to build the organ. Even though the suggested letter of intent was never sent, Schoenstein began some preliminary work on the project while awaiting the signed contract. Work on the façade design and refinement of the specification—the next topics to be discussed—continued throughout 1998.

[1]Robert Poll and his associate, Lamont Anderson, maintain not only the eight (nine, if a small demonstration organ is included) pipe organs at Church headquarters but also our two harpsichords. In addition, they oversee the maintenance of the numerous pianos in the various buildings, contracting much of that work to outside piano technicians. Robert has been employed by the Church since 1982. He had previously been employed by his brother's firm, H. Ronald Poll and Associates, a Salt Lake City-based organ building and service company. Lamont has been in Church employ since 1986. These two men are extremely skilled and take great pride in their work.

[2]Manuel Rosales, "The 1911 Murray M. Harris Organ at St. James' Episcopal Church, Los Angeles, California," (excerpts from an unpublished article, prepared for the Long Beach and Los Angeles Chapters of the American Guild of Organists, February 11, 1996), 4.

[3]Ibid., 1.

[4]Ibid., 4. CCCC is the pitch designation for the lowest note of a 32' stop, sounding four octaves below middle C.

[5]Letter from Jack Bethards to the author, dated August 25, 1997.

[6]England's Princess Diana died tragically on August 31, the day before I left Salt Lake City. I arrived in London to find the country in shock and mourning, a mood very similar to that to be found later in the United States following the tragedy of September 11, 2001. I stayed at a hotel in London's Kensington district, near Royal Albert Hall where the Choir would be performing. Kensington Palace, the Princess's residence, was very near my hotel. I walked to the Palace several times during my short stay and was deeply moved by what seemed to be acres of flowers left by grieving admirers who formed long queues to enter the grounds.

[7]Letter from Mark Venning to the author, dated October 10, 1997.

[8]Craig Passey, CPM (Certified Purchasing Manager), had responsibility for the purchase of fixtures and furnishings for the Conference Center, including the organ. He was a wonderful ally throughout the entire enterprise, with a keen eye for value and quality. Craig was not hesitant to "stick his neck out" a bit to acquire a particular product if he felt it was the best choice. His approach was very much "hands on." He didn't know much about pipe organs at the outset, but he did a great deal of research and became quite knowledgeable very quickly.

Having a little extra time in Colorado Springs before our return flight, we made an unannounced visit to the Air Force Academy in hopes of seeing the organ there but were unsuccessful.

[9]Orpha Ochse, *Schoenstein & Co.* (Richmond, Virginia: OHS Press [the publishing arm of the Organ Historical Society], 2008), 10.

[10]Memorandum from the author to "Those Involved with the Assembly Building Organ," January 7, 1998.

[11]http://www.disastercenter.com/build/seismic.htm, accessed April 9, 2009. In 2008, the United States Geological Survey updated its Seismic Hazard Maps, no longer using Seismic Zones. See http://pubs.usgs.gov/fs/2008/3018/pdf/FS08-3018_508.pdf, accessed April 9, 2009.

[12]W. Dee Halverson, *The Conference Center: The Story of Its Construction* (Salt Lake City: Legacy Constructors, 2000), 131.

The Façade

An organ is a work of art not only sonically, but visually as well. Whenever pipes are exposed to view, there is an opportunity to arrange them in an attractive manner, using their overall lengths and the shape and arrangement of their mouths to create attractive lines across the case. A variety of finishes can be applied to the pipes to further increase the visual possibilities. The wood case that houses the pipes offers additional decorative options. Just as an artistic presentation can heighten one's enjoyment of a meal, a dramatic and beautifully designed and executed display of pipes in a handsome case seems to enhance the sound of an organ. Jack Bethards weighs in on this point:

> They say that an organ sounds the way it looks. The façade sets up a certain expectation of what the organ will sound like. It is as much a signature of the instrument as is the sound. It must be inspiring.
>
> No matter who designs and builds an organ case the public ascribes it to the organ builder. As unfair as it may seem, the reputation of an instrument and its builder is made (or broken) as much by its case as by its sound.[1]

Often, the all-important designs for the case and pipe display, as well as the appearance of the console, are predetermined and included in the contract. In the case of the Conference Center organ, they were not. The project architects wanted to participate in the development of the visual design of the instrument to be certain that the result complemented other elements in the room. However, the contract needed to be executed as quickly as possible in order for the engineering and construction of chests and pipes to begin if there were to be any hope of a timely installation. As a result, the contract was written to exclude the casework and any special treatment of the display pipes, including decorative finishes, mouth styles, extra-length feet or bodies as well as nonstandard racking.

Initially, both the project architects and Schoenstein's designers drew some preliminary concepts independently. Each was working at a disadvantage. The architects had little or no prior experience with organ cases and no realistic idea of the possibilities or practical requirements for using pipes in a display. The Schoenstein designers did not have a clear idea of what the architects felt would best enhance the design features of the room. While these early drawings were not particularly fruitful in determining the final design of the case, they did make it clear that the mechanics and aesthetics of the case design needed to be considered simultaneously.

Jack Bethards felt it wise to involve Steuart Goodwin as consultant and point man in the case design. In his proposal to build the Conference Center organ, as part of the consortium[2] needed to assist Schoenstein & Co. with the project, Jack had specifically mentioned using Steuart as a design consultant, voicer and tonal finisher. Steuart operates his own firm, Steuart Goodwin Pipe Organs, in San Bernardino, California. Though he has built a number of new instruments and rebuilt several more, in recent years Steuart has become increasingly well known as a design consultant and tonal finisher. He has an affinity for E. M. Skinner and Æolian-Skinner instruments. His work with Schoenstein & Co. on the Tabernacle organ renovation in the 1980s had convinced us of his consummate skill as a tonal finisher, and we were pleased to know that he would be involved in the Conference Center project.

Another firm heavily involved in the organ case design and execution was Fetzers' Inc., a Salt Lake City architectural woodworking enterprise in business since 1909.[3] Fetzers' was no stranger to the organs at Temple Square. They added the wings on either side of Joseph Ridges's original Tabernacle organ case in the second decade of the twentieth century to accommodate Austin's rebuilding of that instrument. When the new organ was installed in the Assembly Hall in the early 1980s, Fetzers' added pipe shades, moldings and other decorative elements, including carvings by Richard McDonald, to an otherwise unadorned case. Jack Bethards, knowing that the Conference Center project would stretch the capacity of Schoenstein's woodworking shop beyond reasonable limits, agreed that Fetzers' should build the organ case. They had the expertise, the most sophisticated equipment available anywhere and a strong interest in being part of an artistic venture such as this. In addition, they were located in Salt Lake City, thus reducing shipping costs and facilitating installation. They also had the contract for the other woodwork in the rostrum area. Paul Fetzer, Vice President for Design, became a vital part of the operation, contributing a wealth of experience, creativity and practicality to the process. He later recalled, "My role at first was to coordinate the woodwork of the organ and that grew into interpreting and reinterpreting the woodwork to its form as it stands today."[4]

The façade design team was complete: Steuart Goodwin represented the organ builder; Paul Fetzer represented the firm who would build the massive case; Lee Gray and his colleague, Scott Bleak, looked after the Church's interests; and Bill Williams served as liaison from Zimmer Gunsul Frasca Architects. We organists were kept informed at every stage of development, and Jack Bethards monitored the process very closely.

The starting point for the design process was a desire expressed by Church leadership that the new building should not feel foreign to those accustomed to the Tabernacle. They wanted people to feel as comfortable as possible in these new surroundings. That desire would be reflected in the overall plan of the rostrum area. For the organ, it meant a symmetrical pipe layout with two large towers like the familiar façade of the Tabernacle organ, rather than a single central tower as is often seen. A second concern, voiced by the architects, was the danger of the case appearing flat when viewed from the long distances inherent in the huge room.

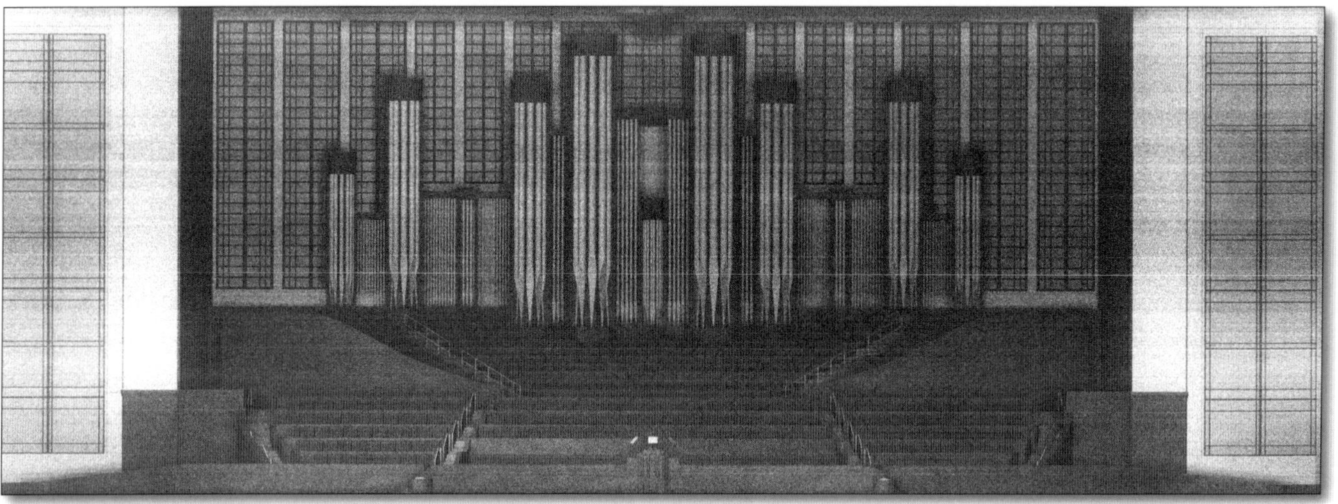

Figure 6.1

Dozens of drawings were produced during the several months of the design process. The few selected for inclusion here represent some of the major stages of development in that endeavor. The very early computer rendering shown in figure 6.1 gives some idea of the beginning point for the case design. The relationship to the Tabernacle organ's façade is evident with two large central towers, a massive center portion and wide wings on either side. It covers the entire width of the choir loft, a distance of some ninety feet. There is no attempt to depict detail in the case, nor is there any concern over whether pipes might actually be available to fill the towers and flats as depicted. This is simply a study in size, shape and proportion. The case is shown in front of an interpretation of the screen wall, mentioned earlier. Originally conceived before the decision to include a pipe organ, the concept of the screen wall seems to have been to create the illusion that there was no wall behind the rostrum—that a person seated in the auditorium was peering through a window, as it were, into an infinite space beyond. As the case design developed into a powerful artistic entity, it became evident that the screen wall would compete with rather than complement the case, and it was finally abandoned.

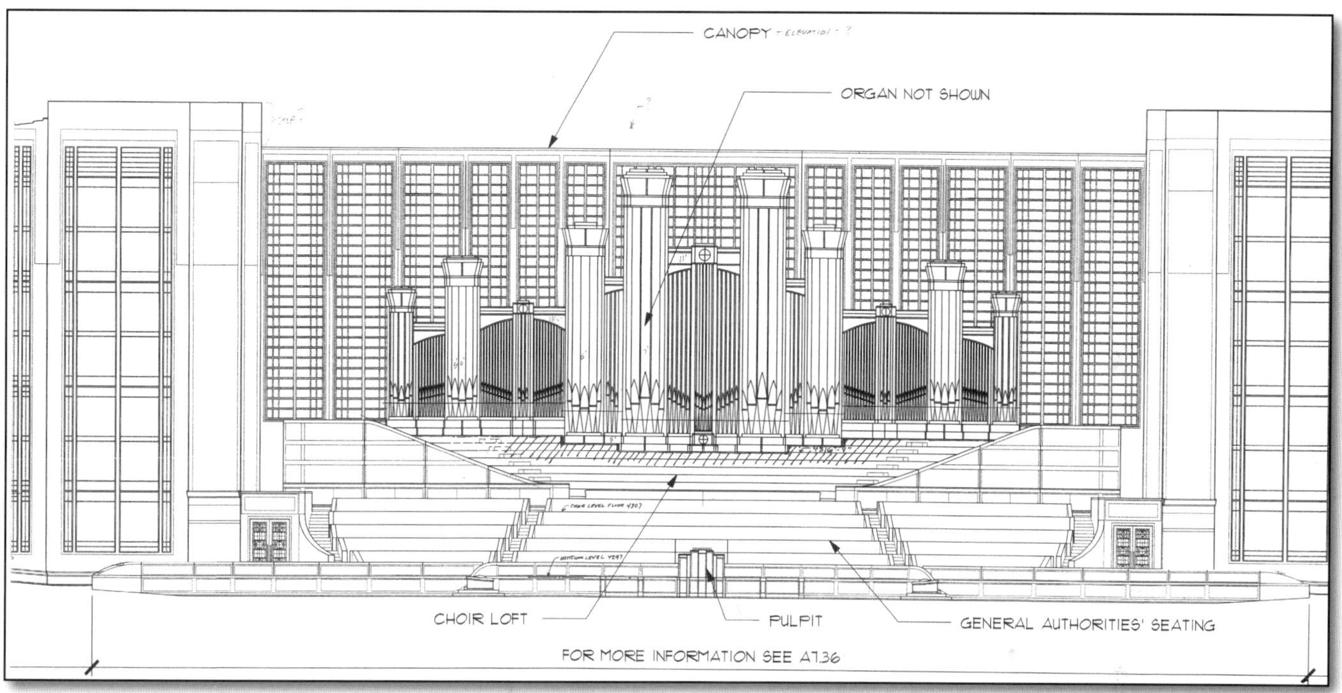

Figure 6.2

In figure 6.2, the height of some of the towers has been modified somewhat, but basically it is an elaboration of the shape shown in figure 6.1. Some additional interest is introduced by virtue of the angular lines of the pipe mouths and the tower crowns. The first introduction of curved elements can be seen at the top of the pipe flats.

Figure 6.3

The freehand sketch in figure 6.3 shows further refinement of the concepts shown in the earlier drawings. The spacing of the towers has been adjusted and the central portion of the case has been reworked. The plan view shows an intent to mimic the concave line of the choir loft. This drawing, presumably by Bill Williams, was sent to Steuart Goodwin by fax shortly after Steuart was brought onto the project and was the point of departure for his work.

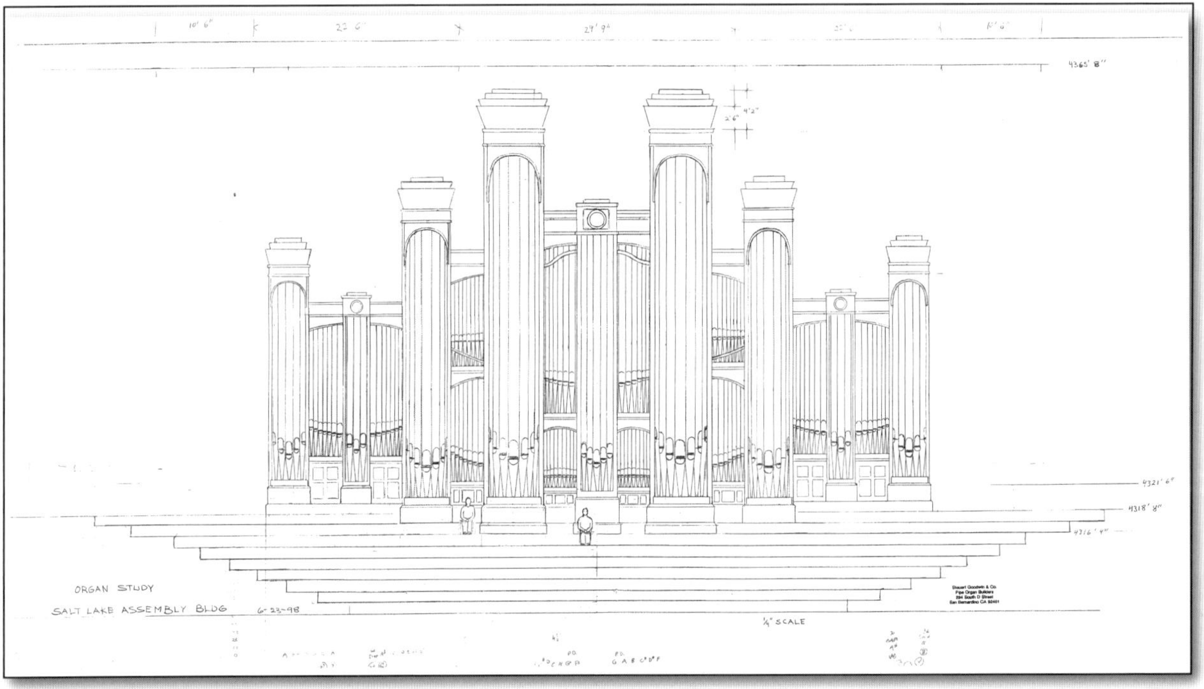

Figure 6.4

Steuart Goodwin's study drawing dated June 23, 1998 (figure 6.4) again shows minor adjustments in the spacing of the towers and reworking of the central portion of the case. Additional curved elements are introduced, and for the first time we see double stacking of pipes. Steuart says of this drawing:

MAGNUM OPUS

I presented this sketch at a meeting of the architects and consultants who were working on details of the design and appearance of the front platform area of the auditorium. The initial concept shows a ninety-foot wide pipe backdrop across the entire choir seating area [figure 6.3]. I recommended eliminating the fifteen-foot sections on either end. They would have been only decorative and had to be removable. I also felt that the design ought to include both large and smaller pipes with as many actual speaking pipes as possible. I chose to use string-toned pipes in the largest towers, feeling that their slimness would help create a sense of verticality to counteract the extreme width of the design.[5]

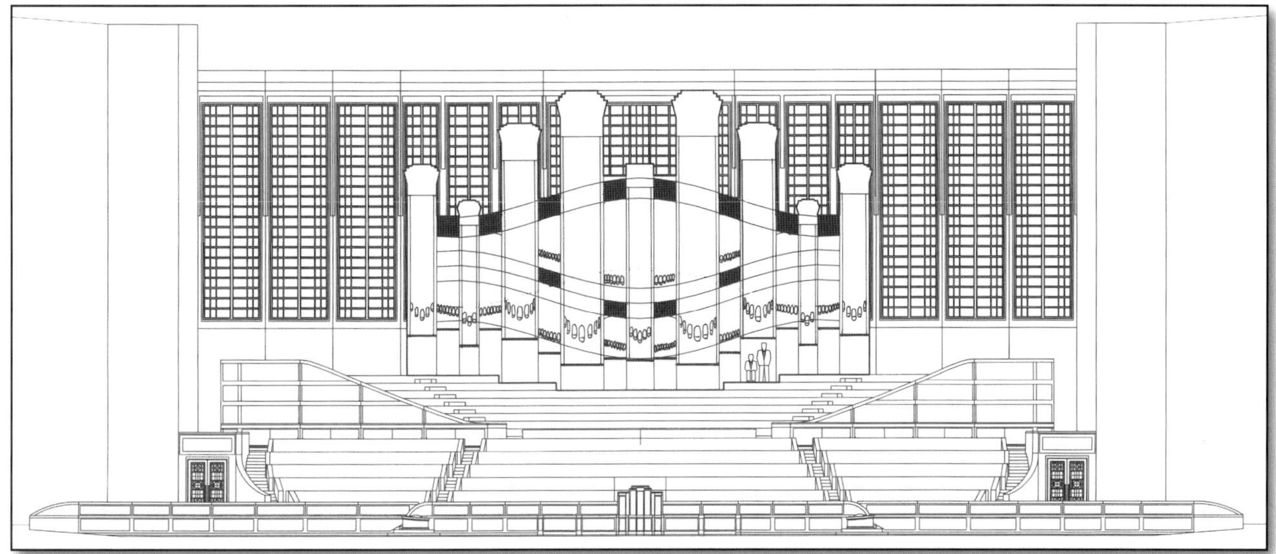

Figure 6.5

Scott Bleak, who worked with Lee Gray in the Architecture and Engineering Division of the Church's Physical Facilities Department, generated numerous drawings of the organ case, contributing a number of his own ideas to the project. In figure 6.5, Scott begins to study the application of sweeping curves across the width of the case. That concept is fleshed out in figure 6.6. The curve of the mouths of the pipes in the flats is mirrored by the woodwork at the tops of the flats. The woodwork dividing the stacked pipes in the center of the case has been raised to form another broad curve with the woodwork in the adjacent double-stacked flats. Note that the plan view now shows the line of the façade being straight, rather than curved.

Figure 6.6

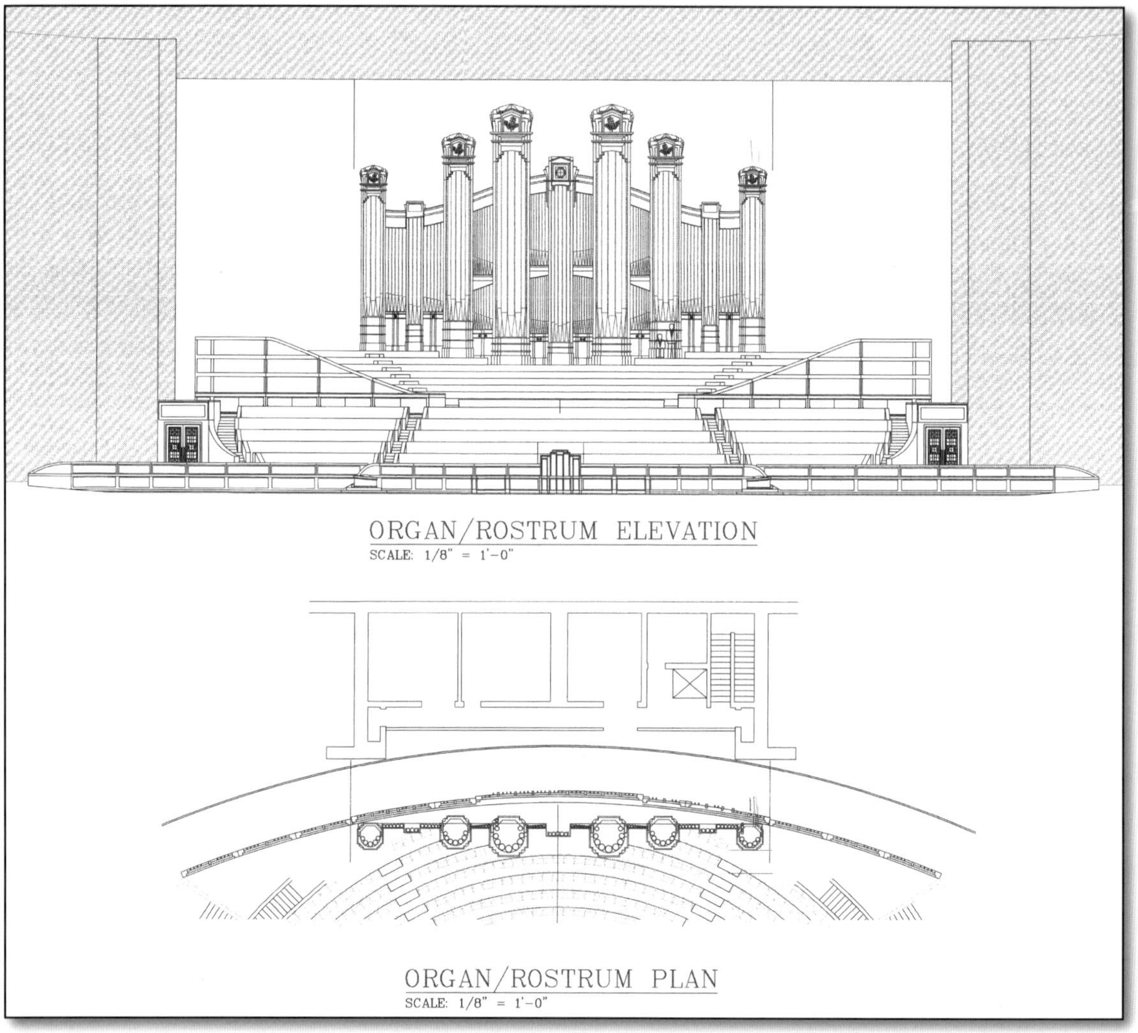

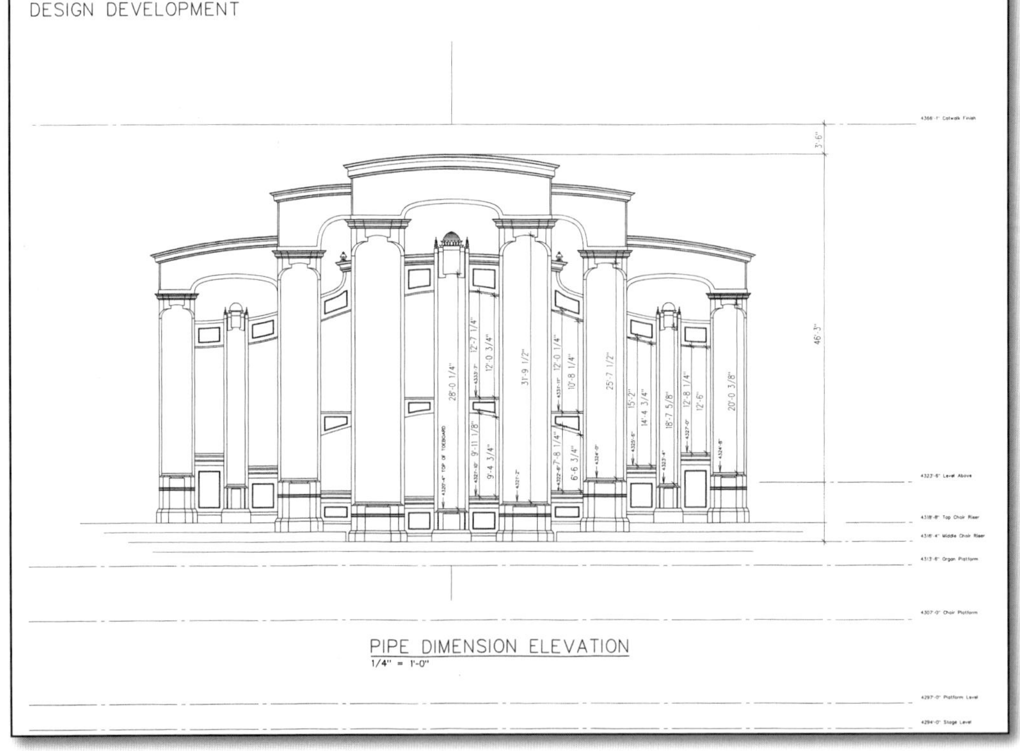

ORGAN/ROSTRUM ELEVATION
SCALE: 1/8" = 1'-0"
ORGAN/ROSTRUM PLAN
SCALE: 1/8" = 1'-0"

Figure 6.7

DESIGN DEVELOPMENT
PIPE DIMENSION ELEVATION
1/4" = 1'-0"

The next major innovation came near the end of the design process and is shown in figure 6.7, dated November 11, 1998. Paul Fetzer speaks of this important new element as well as the need for an acoustical shell over the top of the organ:

> The idea of the large towers was originally to mimic somewhat the shape of the Tabernacle organ. But on further review we found that it was looking too much like the Tabernacle organ and Lee Gray's staff came up with the idea of putting arches over the organ. Simultaneously, Steuart Goodwin expressed the need to put a roof to capture the sound within the organ so it was not lost in the vast ceiling of the new Conference Center. He wanted the sound moved forward into . . . the rest of the hall. This was accomplished by putting a roof structure from the façade of the organ to the back wall, at such an angle as would express the sound forward through the pipes and through the organ structure itself. Everything on the organ either became transparent to sound or reflective to the sound being produced in the organ itself.[6]

The roof structure that Steuart envisioned over the interior portion of the organ was designed and built. It is a tiered A-frame design, the tiers corresponding to the arches of the façade. The structure slopes downward toward the rear of the chamber in horn-like fashion. The surface consists of a layer of three-quarter-inch medium-density fiberboard with seams caulked. It is "glued and screwed" to a layer of three-quarter-inch plywood that, in turn, is attached to an elaborate steel framework.

The arches as first drawn (figure 6.7) were quite massive and drew a sharp reaction from Jack Bethards:

> As we do with all of our in-house case designs, we have shown this design to many people whose judgment we trust and to just plain folks. I must say that I was quite stunned by the number and force of the negative reactions. Thus, when we put all the comments together, it is clear that a good deal of refinement is required. . . .
>
> I hasten to add at this point that we are confident that this concept can work. We are not against the arch, in fact we are intrigued by it. In order to make it work from an organ building perspective, however, it needs work.
>
> The massive arch structure needs to appear as though it is physically well supported. Letting it appear as though the organ pipes are the only means of support won't work. . . .
>
> The arch could be a serious sound trap for the top of the display pipes and, possibly, for the pipes behind. (On the other hand it could be a positive sound reflector. This depends on how clever we are with the design.)

The arch is so massive that it tends to make the gigantic 32-foot organ pipes look puny. This collection of pipes is a monumental array and it would be a terrible shame to diminish it by optical illusion.[7]

Steuart seized the opportunity for further refinement:

I proposed that the arch should be slimmed down and given an acoustical function by curving the underside to reflect sound into the room. I also saw the opportunity to place some of the largest 32' pipes in a second row façade with their tops visible in the window-like spaces created by the arch. Then I eliminated the vertical crowns and pipe shades allowing the tower pipes to be seen full length.[8]

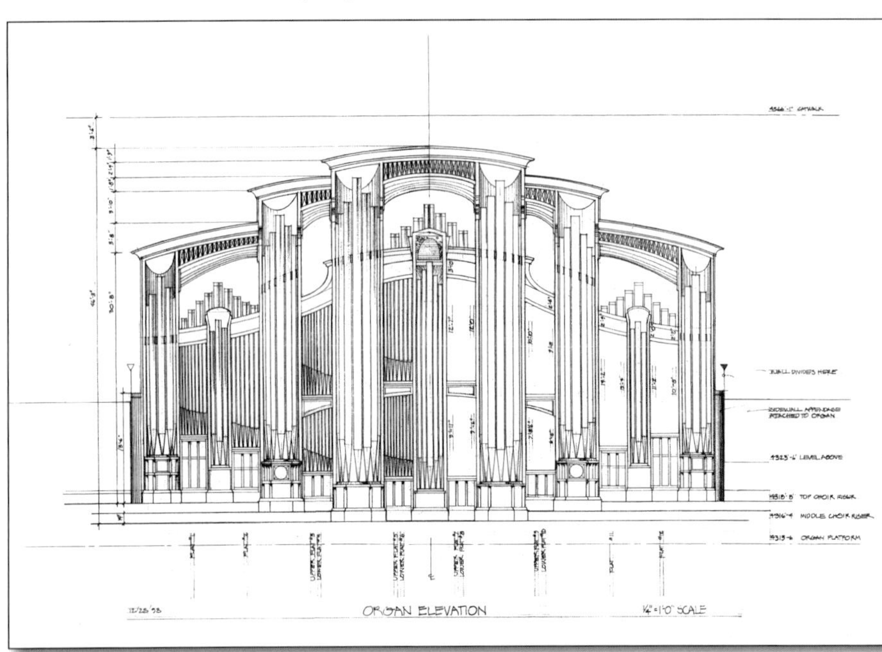

Figure 6.8

Steuart's ideas are reflected in the drawing shown in figure 6.8. Paul Fetzer also speaks of this new concept for the functionality of the arches:

One of the interesting structures of the organ is the underside of the arches, which express the sound forward. Mr. Goodwin made the suggestion that we should express the sound the way it leaves the mouth of a bugle or a horn. One Saturday as I was working independently of Mr. Goodwin, we both came up with the same idea, to make larger reflective structures on the underside of the organ arches. We called each other on Monday morning and said, "Hey I've got this idea." We were both very enthused to hear each other confirm the fact that the sound needed to be expressed forward and out, not focused such as a cone or round structure might do. We decided to create large curved structures which would mimic the mouth of a horn.[9]

The way in which the acoustical arches were eventually built is a story within a story. Paul Fetzer relates it best:

MAGNUM OPUS

It so happened that I was investigating boat building at that particular time and got in contact with a boat lumber supply company in Anacortes, Washington, who referred me to the Northwestern School of Wooden Boat Building in Port Townsend, Washington. . . . Those folks were very helpful in instructing us on how we might be able to build structures that were stout enough to act as arches which would hold the cornices up. At the same time they must be thick enough to be reflectors for the sound of the organ pipes below. Justin Losee of our firm . . . got together with some contractors in the area and finally contracted with Ed Louchard of Louchard Yacht Restoration Company to build these five huge magnificent arches. The center arch is 14 feet long, 6 feet deep and 3½ feet high, made out of inch-and-a-quarter-thick solid cherry wood. The other arches are of similar construction. We originally conceived those to look like the belly of [a] harp or the back of a lute. In other words, bring a musical connotation as well as an actual physical reflective structure.

People came from all around the peninsula to see these being built, and the . . . *Peninsula [Daily] News* ran an article on the boat structures. There is a little sign attached to the back of the largest boat structure, and everyone who worked on them has his signature attached. They'll be immortalized there.[10]

None of the individual boat-building firms in the area had the manpower to be able to produce the arches as quickly as they would be needed, so workers from several firms worked cooperatively at the Louchard shop in order to complete the work on time.[11]

The arches and the second row of façade pipes

The underside of one of the arches of the organ case at the Fetzers' Inc. plant. Paul Fetzer is seen at the side.

also worked advantageously in helping to express a sense of depth to the case. As Steuart Goodwin explains:

The second row of pipes gave us the sense of depth the architects were after as well as a logical place to locate these pipes where their tones could get into the room well. The curving "boat bottoms" serve to lead the eye into the interior, so as to furnish a depth perspective for the distant viewer. I believe their visual aspect is more important than their sonic benefit since, acoustically speaking, they are not nearly deep enough to function like the acoustic clouds used in symphony halls (or the exponential curve of a trumpet bell for that matter). I felt the important thing was to visually suggest that function. This is related to my inclusion of pipes of widely varying size in the façade; I wanted to state that this is a functioning musical instrument.[12]

With just a few more refinements, the design was complete. The finished case is depicted in Lee Gray's freehand drawing (figure 6.9).

A large and very substantial framework was required to support the 26,400-pound weight of the massive case and the estimated 17,150 pounds of zinc pipes contained in it.[13] KPFF Consulting Engineers of Portland, Oregon, the same firm that provided the structural engineering for the rest of the building, designed the steel structure. Allen Steel Company of Salt Lake City fabricated and installed it. These firms also designed and erected the steel structure that supports the ceiling over the

Figure 6.9

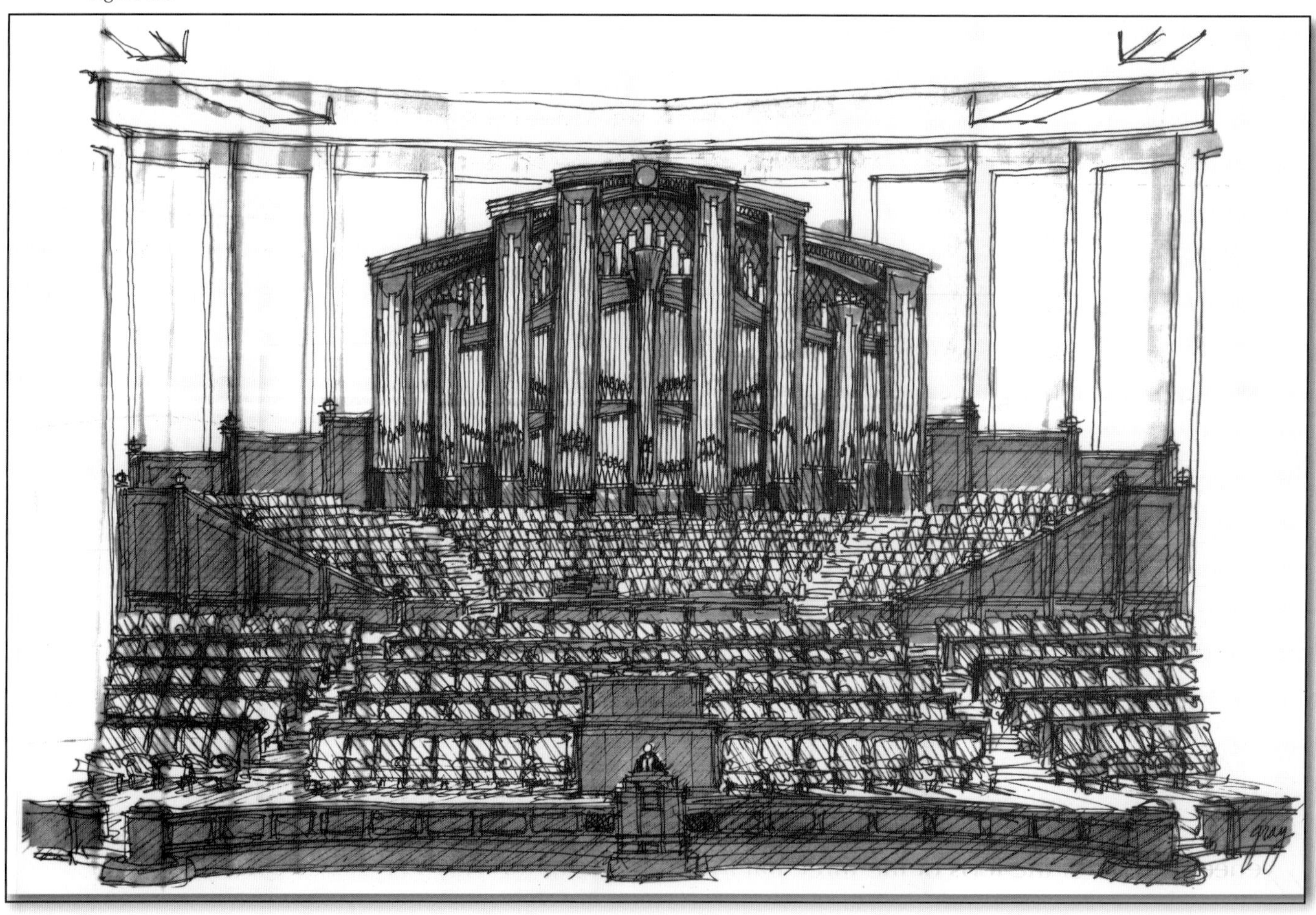

interior of the organ chamber.

The wood used in building the casework is remarkably beautiful. Paul Fetzer speaks of the very special veneer that was found:

> The wood veneer on the organ case is very interesting and beautiful. The veneer is from a really astounding cherry wood log that was found by Lee Gray and my brother Wallace [Fetzer] as they made trips to veneer mills in the East. The wooden organ case veneer is put together in such a way to accentuate the beautiful grain of that cherry log. This particular cherry tree was grown in northern Pennsylvania, not far from the village of Harmony and the Susquehanna River. It grew to more than forty inches in diameter and we call it a one-in-a-million veneer log.[14]

Lee Gray provides additional detail about how the veneer was acquired:

> I traveled to the veneer plant in Michigan to look at dozens of cherry logs, to find ones that could be mixed together to make the veneer. There were none that impressed me. At the end of the row of veneer logs there was a pile of movers' blankets. I asked what was under the blankets. The response was "nothing." "There must be something under those, what is it," I asked. Again, the response was "nothing." Finally, the man said it was some very select veneer. I asked what kind of veneer, and he said it was cherry. I said that I wanted to look at it, and he said I couldn't. When I asked why, he said because if I were to look at that veneer I wouldn't want any of the others, and added that it was already sold. As he walked away, I pulled the blankets back and saw that the log that was there was gigantic compared to the small logs I had been looking at before. He finally brought out the owner of the veneer plant, who told me that the log was sold to a friend of his in Japan for use in his executive boardroom. I said that I wanted the log. He asked why he should sell it to the Church. I said that if it was sold to his friend it would be seen by a few Japanese businessmen, but if I bought it for the Church it would be seen by millions of people for hundreds of years. He then said, "It's very expensive." He then told me how much. It was less costly than the Swiss pear veneer we had already purchased for the lobby spaces, so I purchased the log. And the rest is history.[15]

That single log yielded sufficient veneer to complete not only the organ case and console but most of the rostrum woodwork as well. A contrasting light-colored veneer is used at the tops of the three flat towers—one in the very center of the case containing five pipes, and matching towers just in from the extreme sides of the case, containing three pipes each. To distinguish these from the rounded towers, Steuart Goodwin coined the term "clock towers." Paul Fetzer continues:

> We have three structures which [Steuart] called "clock towers.". . .Those three structures have ornaments on them which are in sort of a sun burst shape. They consist of a rippled sycamore veneer and cherry veneer, and they are also expressive in that they reflect the sound produced by the pipe[s] below.[16]

The decision as to the finish on the zinc façade pipes did not come easily or quickly. By mid-November 1998, that issue had still not been resolved. Jack Bethards, in a letter to Tom Hanson, emphasized that "if the façade pipes are not ordered by mid-December, there will be no hope of getting them to Salt Lake in time for gold leafing (if

that is the desired finish)."[17] President Hinckley had told Lee Gray that he did not want silver-colored pipes in the display, so that limited the options somewhat. When gold leaf was being considered, I prepared a spreadsheet to estimate the amount of gold leaf needed to cover the visible portions of the front pipes. The figure was in excess of 2,700 square feet! Samples of pipe metals, including plain and flamed copper were examined, and a variety of paint finishes was considered. Finally, with time closing in, Lee Gray consulted with Robert Evans of the Salt Lake City firm Architectural Metal Restoration. The result was the creation of a custom, proprietary finish, used only for this job. Mr. Evans, a colleague, and Metro Foti, proprietor of New Image Body and Paint in nearby Bountiful, Utah, devised the formula. The four-step process, applied at Mr. Foti's shop, involved coating the pipes with a gold leaf flux and finishing with a satin finish clear coat. In keeping with the architects' wish that the paint finish be unique to this project, those involved are obligated not to divulge

One of the three sound-reflective "clock tower" ornaments being assembled at Fetzers' Inc.

details beyond that. Close up, the finish has a subtle "orange peel" texture. From a distance, it is luminous and chameleon-like under the Conference Center's sophisticated theatrical lighting. Who would have thought to paint organ pipes in an automobile body shop? On second thought, however, both automobiles and pipes do involve the skillful application of a paint product to sheet metal.

The finished case is seventy-three feet wide and forty-five feet high. The largest display pipe is the middle one seen through the center "window," which plays the lowest note (CCCC) of the Pedal 32-foot Diapason.[18] It is thirty-six feet six inches tall, with a diameter of eighteen inches. Of the 170 pipes in the display (including the 27 pipes whose tops are seen through the "windows"), 148 are actual "speaking" pipes. The remaining twenty-two are silent dummies. The pipes that comprise the front display are identified in figure 6.10. The speaking pipes behind the arch windows consist of notes 1–12 of the Pedal Diapason 32-foot and notes 1–6 of the Great Dulciana 32-foot. Coincidentally, the number of pipes visible in the façade equals the number of years between the LDS Church's founding in 1830 and the completion of the Conference Center in 2000.

Lee Gray enjoys telling that the mold for the gilded medallion atop the case was created from a snow saucer. The convex surface of the saucer was covered with clay to a thickness of about half an inch, smoothed, and then dimpled using an egg-shaped pantyhose container. After curing, the clay was covered with a liquid silicone rubber compound, which was then used to create the "master" mold. The disc, 38½

Left: The lowest note (and largest pipe) of the Pedal 32' Diapason, ready for shipment from the plant of A.R. Schopp's Sons Inc. in Alliance, Ohio. Pictured left to right, back row: Larry Hively, Cye Proctor, Brian Rudolph, Mark Trainer, Robert Schopp. Front row: Ron Miller, David Schopp.
Right: Terry Johnson points to that same pipe following its installation.

A view of the tops of "Haskelled" pipes (see note 18).

Figure 6.10

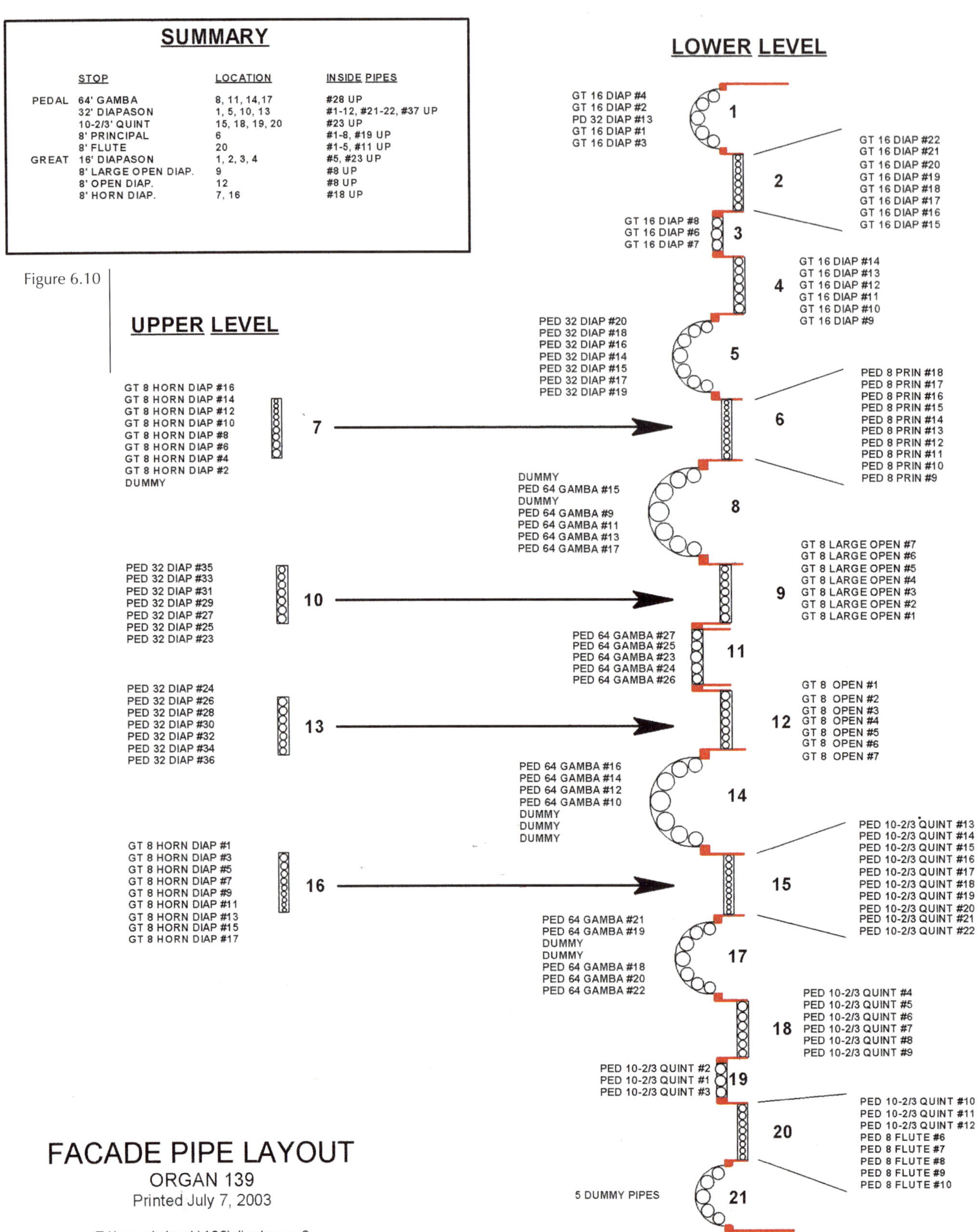

FACADE PIPE LAYOUT

ORGAN 139

Printed July 7, 2003

F:\home\chuck\139\display.vc6

inches in diameter, was cast using a phenolic resin and gilded with twenty-three-carat gold leaf. The orb (which some have referred to as an "oculus") was created by Lavar Walgren of 3 D Art, Inc. in Salt Lake City.[19] Its glowing appearance is the result of being lighted by a single, dedicated spotlight.

The interior of the casework has been signed by many of the craftsmen who worked on it, not just the workers at Louchard's, but Fetzers' artisans as well.[20] All who participated seemed to sense the uniqueness and grandeur of the project, and their autographs symbolize the pride they took in their work and their desire to be remembered for their part in such a monumental artistic endeavor.

NOTES

[1]Letter from Jack Bethards to Thomas Hanson, dated November 19, 1998.

[2]The various firms and individuals participating in the project are identified throughout the text. Jack Bethards also lists the principal collaborators at the end of an article he wrote for _The American Organist_ that is reproduced as Appendix 4.

[3]In 2005 Fetzers' Inc. moved into a new and expanded facility in the western part of the Salt Lake Valley. The firm is now known as Fetzer Architectural Woodwork. Following their work at the Conference Center, Fetzers' Inc. teamed once again with Schoenstein & Co. to provide the casework for the 64-rank Martin Foundation concert organ in Nashville's Schermerhorn Symphony Center. In 2008, they completed the interior woodwork during the renovation of Alice Tully Hall at New York City's Lincoln Center.

[4]W. Dee Halverson, _The Conference Center: The Story of Its Construction_ (Salt Lake City: Legacy Constructors, 2000), 144.

[5]http://www.goodwinorgans.com/ConfCentCase.htm (accessed December 1, 2008).

[6]Halverson, 144–45. Dedicated organ microphones, the need for which was assumed at the beginning of the project, turned out to be unnecessary. While organ sound is picked up by the choir microphones and reinforced along with the choir, for organ recitals with an audience of several thousand seated in the center portion of the pie-shaped space, no amplification is needed.

[7]Letter from Jack Bethards to Thomas Hanson, dated November 19, 1998.

[8]http://www.goodwinorgans.com/ConfCentCase.htm (accessed December 1, 2008).

[9]Halverson, 145.

[10]Ibid., 145–46.

[11]Interview by the author with Paul Fetzer, January 23, 2009.

[12]Steuart Goodwin, e-mail message to author, December 9, 2008.

[13]Interview by the author with Paul Fetzer, January 23, 2009.

[14]Halverson, 146. A typical cherry log yields 10,000 to 15,000 square feet of veneer. The log referred to here provided some 31,000 square feet of veneer.

[15]E-mail from Leland Gray to John Longhurst, March 5, 2009.

[16]Halverson, 146.

[17]Letter from Jack Bethards to Thomas Hanson, dated November 19, 1998.

[18]Looking at the organ façade, one might think that the two largest towers contain pipes longer than the 32-foot Diapason. This is an illusion. The unseen windchest on which the Diapason pipes are placed is lower than the toes of the pipes in the façade towers. Also it should be mentioned that all nine of the speaking pipes in the largest façade towers have been "Haskelled." This is a treatment developed by William Haskell in the early twentieth century, wherein an open pipe is made to sound lower than its visible length by suspending a canister in the top of the pipe, with its closed end up. The pipe then sounds as though it were the length of the outside pipe and the inside canister combined. Were it not Haskelled, the GGGGG# Gamba, the center pipe in the large tower just to the left of center, would need to have a speaking length of some forty feet. The resonators of the four pipes in the 64-foot octave of the Pedal Trombone are full length, the longest one reaching the necessary forty-foot length. They are located against the back wall of the organ chamber and are not part of the display being discussed. Also, they are mitered for added structural strength and so that they will fit within the available height to the ceiling.

[19]Telephone conversation with Leland Gray, January 20, 2009.

[20]See Appendix 3.

Refining the Stoplist

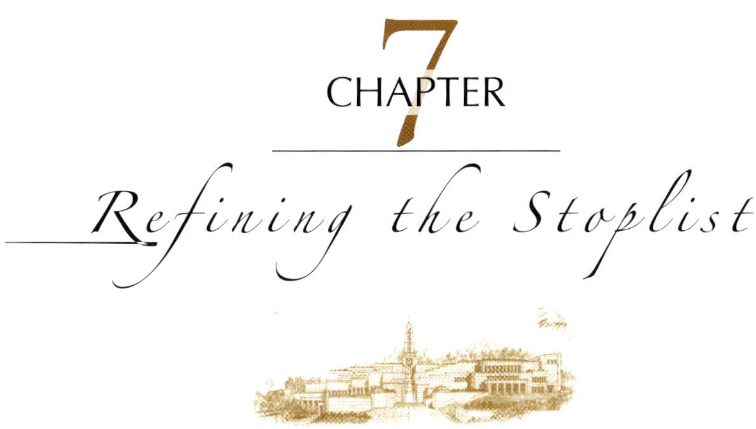

Buying an organ is analogous to purchasing a new automobile. Similar features and accessories can be found in a variety of price ranges from different manufacturers. While a careful inspection of competing vehicles and a test drive are necessary before one can make an intelligent choice based on comparative cost and quality, the window sticker on a vehicle provides a beginning point. From it, the buyer learns the mechanical and safety features of the vehicle along with warranty information, and the included accessories are listed. The "window sticker" for a new organ is called a *stoplist*. The stoplist—or *specification*, as it is often called—identifies the various sets of pipes in an organ, lists couplers and accessories to be included, and may contain construction information that the builder wishes to call to a client's attention. Unlike automobiles, however, pipe organs are not mass-produced. Each is custom designed to satisfy the requirements of a particular client and to provide the finest result possible for the space in which it is to be housed.

Arriving at the final stoplist for an instrument requires considerable exchange of ideas between builder and client. The larger and more complex the instrument, the longer it may take to achieve consensus. The starting point for such discussion occurs when the builder is first contacted about a prospective project and is given a general idea of the client's vision for the instrument. The builder, after careful thought, study and further interaction with the client, then responds with a proposed specification.

In our November 10, 1997 letter to the three builders who were invited to submit a proposal, we offered the following guidelines:

> We solicit your proposal for an organ of four or five manuals and pedal for the new building's main auditorium. Its primary use will be in religious services and large-scale concerts. During services it will accompany the singing of a congregation of 21,000 and choirs up to 400 voices (often the Mormon Tabernacle Choir). Concerts will often include large choral forces with or without a symphony orchestra. The instrument should be capable of holding its own with an orchestra in performances of oratorios,

etc. The organ will need to be capable of rendering solo repertoire during services, broadcasts, and concerts, although it is not anticipated that the facility will be a regular venue for solo organ recitals.

Given the size of the room and its acoustical treatment, it is expected that both choral and organ music, as well as speech, will need some reinforcement in order to be heard comfortably throughout the space. Acoustically, the room will be moderately dry and optimized for speech. Theater-type seating will be installed, the floor will be carpeted, and wall and ceiling surfaces may receive some acoustical treatment. A sophisticated sound system will offer the option of additional electronic reverberation when desired. It is our intention that the organ be scaled and voiced to balance with the choir, and that no attempt be made to design an organ of sufficient power to fill the room with sound unaided.

Tonally, it is felt that the organ should be firmly centered at 8' pitch, with breadth, richness, and nobility in keeping with the scale of the room. The instrument should be eclectic, so as to facilitate the accompaniment of the Tabernacle Choir's diverse repertoire (Bach to Broadway). In addition to fully developed principal choruses, telling chorus reeds, and colorful flutes at a variety of pitches, a strong orchestral component is desired, including several string stops along with a wide variety of solo colors, both flue and reed. It would be advantageous to have solo voices distributed over at least two manuals (with independent expression). . . .

It appears that the provided space will accommodate a large-scale instrument of about 125 ranks, and budget should be available to fund an instrument of that size. We desire a comprehensive instrument, but do not wish to compromise accessibility for tuning and service for the sake of size.

Our desire for solo stops on multiple manuals results from many years of experience at the Tabernacle. The Tabernacle Choir's organists are often called upon to realize accompaniments originally written for orchestra. In order to perform these scores more authentically, we sometimes play them as duets, with two organists on the bench. In such scores, there are often multiple solo lines sounding simultaneously. The Tabernacle organ's fifth manual (Antiphonal) was not particularly useful in this regard until the renovation in the 1980s when two stops from the main organ (the

Great Cornet and the Tuba Mirabilis) were made available there. The frequency with which we found ourselves using these two stops on a second "solo" manual, convinced us of the desirability of having a variety of solo colors spread across two different manuals.

Appropriate drawings were included with our letter showing the size of the auditorium and the space available for the organ. The builders were invited to contact us with any questions they might have. The response from Schoenstein & Co. was dated December 11, 1997, and included a proposed stoplist dated that same day.

The proposed specification was carefully considered along with those submitted by the other two prospective builders. As soon as the decision was made to award the contract to Schoenstein, we immediately focused on that proposal in minute detail, paying particular attention to the stoplist. In doing so, we kept in mind our many years of experience with the Tabernacle organ, looking for ways to achieve maximum flexibility, color and impact from approximately two-thirds as many pipes. While the Tabernacle organ contains 206 ranks, Schoenstein's original proposal for the Conference Center organ called for 128 ranks. The size was determined by the available space for the instrument, along with Jack Bethards's assurance that an organ of that size, carefully designed, could meet our needs.

There were numerous telephone calls, faxes and letters back and forth between Jack Bethards and us as we considered many ideas, some suggested by us and some by him. Over the next five months, the specification was revised four times, the fourth iteration, dated May 18, 1998, being the one that was eventually submitted as part of the contract. The changes, of course, altered the cost, which was reflected in a new contract price, vis-à-vis the original proposal.

Compared to the stoplist given in the proposal, the fourth revision added two new speaking stops to the Great, the organ's main division: Dulciana 32-foot and Doppelflöte 8-foot. The Tabernacle organ was originally to have included a 32-foot flue on the Great, but whether for economic reasons or lack of space, it was never installed. I suggested to Jack Bethards that we consider including one on this organ, but I thought we might do it electronically to conserve both space and budget. At the same time, I suggested the inclusion of an electronic 64-foot stop in the Pedal. Jack, whose strong preference is to avoid electronic substitutes for pipe voices, proposed using pipes for the Great 32-foot stop and making it available in the Pedal. He further suggested that rather than use an electronic 64-foot stop in the Pedal, we extend both the existing Gamba 32-foot and Trombone 32-foot ranks just four notes each into the 64-foot octave. We also preferred using pipes over electronics, and since

Jack assured us adequate space would be available, we agreed. The Doppelflöte is a lovely and distinctive flute stop that we wanted to include on the organ, and the Great seemed the logical place. We also added a Tremulant that does not affect the windchests containing the principal chorus and reeds. Finally, we elected to make the two high-pressure reeds available on the Great.

The double enclosure that was originally planned to create the Swell's Ethereal section was moved to the Solo. The later revision of the Swell contains two reed choruses at 16-, 8-, and 4-foot pitches, one French and the other English in character.

Manual I, originally called Orchestral, was renamed Choir. Manual V, originally labeled Celestial, was renamed Orchestral. The new, doubly enclosed portion of the Solo was called Grand Solo.

In the Choir, a new Violin 8-foot and Celeste 8-foot were added, and the original Voix Sérénissime 4-foot and Celeste 4-foot were changed to 8-foot stops. A Rohr Schalmei 4-foot was added to complete a petit reed chorus at 16-, 8-, and 4-foot pitches.

Three changes were made to the Solo division. The tubas were placed under double expression as mentioned above, a Tierce Mixture was added to crown the Tuba chorus, and the Harmonic Trumpet (originally on Manual V) and Tuba Mirabilis exchanged places to correspond with their placement on the Tabernacle organ. Tuben III, a Schoenstein innovation, is an interesting stop. When drawn, it plays the Bass Tuba 16-foot an octave higher (at 8-foot pitch) together with the Tuba Clarion 4-foot an octave lower (at 8-foot pitch) and the Tuba 8-foot rank, producing the stentorian sonority of three 8-foot tuba stops playing in unison.

The only change to the newly named Orchestral division, other than the exchange of the Tuba Mirabilis for the Harmonic Trumpet, was the addition of a Variable Tremulant. When drawn, the Variable Tremulant defeats the nominal function of the Crescendo pedal, which is then used to control the speed of the Tremulant in that division. (The Clarinetti III would function in the same manner as the Tuben III explained above.)

In addition to the two 64-foot extensions and the new Dulciana 32-foot stop borrowed from the Great, a Quint 10²/₃-foot rank was added to the Pedal for yet more reinforcement to the 32-foot line. An independent Flute 8-foot was added, along with 8- and 4-foot strings under expression, borrowed from the Choir. The original Mixture V was separated into two stops, a Mixture II and a Mixture III. Finally, the Great Trumpet 8-foot was borrowed into the Pedal at both 8- and 4-foot pitches.

Five digital percussion stops, to be supplied by Walker Technical Co. of Zionsville, Pennsylvania, were added to provide additional variety.

Intramanual couplers remained the same, but sub- and super-couplers were added from the fourth and fifth manuals to the Great manual for added flexibility. A Solo to Orchestral coupler was added so that the fourth and fifth manuals could, in effect, be reversed.

A Pedal Tutti to Choir was added, again to enhance flexibility. The Pedal Tutti couplers to Swell and Choir are extremely useful when realizing florid orchestral bass lines at the organ or for four-hand performances. Two additional divide points were added for the Pedal Divide.

The combinations remained essentially the same, except that all Pedal combinations were made available under Manual I, and functions of the programmable piston sequencer were defined.

Additional reversibles were added to control the new 64-foot stops and Cymbelstern, and the decision was made that coupler reversibles would turn off sub- and super-couplers, if they happened to be on, as well as 8-foot couplers.

The options for the functions of the five balanced pedals were reconsidered, and it was decided to use small drawknobs on the nameboard, controlled by a separate combination action, to assign those functions. Preparations for the MIDI interface were specified in more detail.

Some additional controls and connectors were added to the console to provide functions that are useful on the Tabernacle organ console for the benefit of the technicians as well as the organists.

To facilitate comparison, the stoplist proposed initially and the one submitted as part of the contract are shown side by side.

PROPOSED STOPLIST
December 11, 1997
5 Manual and Pedal Organ
98 Voices—128 Ranks

<u>GREAT</u> II   Pipes

16'	Diapason	61
16'	Bourdon (Wood & Metal)	61
8'	Diapason (Large)	61
8'	Diapason (Medium)	61
8'	Diapason (Small)	61
8'	Gamba	61
8'	Harmonic Flute	61
8'	Stopped Diapason	61
4'	Principal	61
4'	Octave	61
4'	Gemshorn	61
4'	Forest Flute	61
2⅔'	Twelfth	61
2'	Fifteenth	61
1³⁄₅'	Seventeenth	61
2'	Mixture (V) *ff*	305
1⅓'	Mixture (IV) *f*	244
1'	Mixture (III) *mf*	183
16'	Bass Trumpet	61
8'	Trumpet	61
4'	Clarion	61

CONTRACT STOPLIST
Revision 4
May 18, 1998
5 Manual and Pedal Organ
103 Voices—130 Ranks

<u>GREAT</u> II   Pipes

32'	Dulciana	61
16'	Diapason	61
16'	Bourdon (Wood & Metal)	61
8'	Diapason (Large)	61
8'	Diapason (Medium)	61
8'	Diapason (Small)	61
8'	Gamba	61
8'	Harmonic Flute	61
8'	Doppelflöte	61
8'	Stopped Diapason	61
4'	Principal	61
4'	Octave	61
4'	Gemshorn	61
4'	Forest Flute	61
2⅔'	Twelfth	61
2'	Fifteenth	61
1³⁄₅'	Seventeenth	61
2'	Mixture (V) *ff*	305
1⅓'	Mixture (IV) *f*	244
1'	Mixture (III) *mf*	183
16'	Bass Trumpet	61
8'	Trumpet	61
4'	Clarion	61
	Tremulant	
8'	Tuba Mirabilis (Orchestral)	
8'	Harmonic Trumpet (Solo)	

<u>SWELL</u> (Enclosed) III

16'	Diapason	68
16'	Bourdon (Wood)	68
8'	Diapason	68
8'	Claribel Flute	68
8'	Lieblich Gedeckt	68
8'	Viole de Gambe	68
8'	Viole Celeste	68
8'	Flauto Dolce	68
8'	Flute Celeste (TC)	56
4'	Octave	68
4'	Harmonic Flute	68
2'	Fifteenth	61
2'	Tierce Mixture (III) *mf*	183
2'	Quint Mixture (V) *f*	305
32'	Contra Fagotto	68
16'	Fagotto	12
8'	Trumpet	68
8'	Oboe	68
8'	Vox Humana (w/Tremulant)	61
4'	Clarion	68
	Tremulant	

Inner Box—Ethereal

16'	Bombarde	61
8'	Trompette Harmonique	61
4'	Clarion Harmonique	61
4'	Principal	61
2'	Plein Jeu (VIII)	488

<u>SWELL</u> (Enclosed) III

16'	Diapason	68
16'	Bourdon (Wood)	68
8'	Diapason	68
8'	Claribel Flute	68
8'	Lieblich Gedeckt	68
8'	Viole de Gambe	68
8'	Viole Celeste	68
8'	Flauto Dolce	68
8'	Flute Celeste (TC)	56
4'	Octave	68
4'	Harmonic Flute	68
2'	Fifteenth	61
2'	Tierce Mixture (III)	183
2'	Quint Mixture (V)	305
32'	Contra Fagotto	68
16'	Bombarde	68
16'	Fagotto	12
8'	Trompette	68
8'	Cornopean	68
8'	Oboe	68
8'	Vox Humana (w/Tremulant)	61
4'	Clairon Harmonique	68
4'	Clarion	68
	Tremulant	

ORCHESTRAL (Enclosed) I

Stops shown by tonal family

16'	Bass Viol	68
8'	Viola Pomposa	68
8'	Celeste	68
8'	Echo Gamba	68
8'	Celeste	68
4'	Voix Sérénissime	68
4'	Celeste	68
16'	Lieblich Bourdon (Wood and Metal)	68
8'	Chimney Flute	12
8'	Concert Flute (Wood)	68
4'	Nachthorn	68
2⅔'	Nazard	61
2'	Harmonic Piccolo	61
1³⁄₅'	Tierce	61
8'	Echo Diapason	68
4'	Fugara	68
2⅔'	Twelfth	61
2'	Fifteenth	61
1⅓'	Nineteenth	61
1'	Twentysecond	61
16'	Bass Horn	12
8'	Trumpet	68
8'	Flügel Horn	68
8'	Cromorne	68
	Tremulant	
8'	Tuba Mirabilis (Solo)	
8'	Harmonic Trumpet (Celestial)	

SOLO (Enclosed) IV

8'	Diapason	61
8'	Symphonic Flute	61
4'	Principal	61
2'	Mixture (V)	305
8'	French Horn	61
	Tremulant	
	Variable Tremulant	
16'	Bass Tuba	61
8'	Tuba	61
4'	Tuba Clarion	61
8'	Tuben (III)	
8'	Tuba Mirabilis *(Unenclosed)*	61

CELESTIAL (Enclosed) V

16'	Major Flute (Wood)	12
8'	Major Flute (Wood)	61
8'	Stentor Gamba	61
8'	Celeste	61
4'	Flute Octave	12
2⅔'	Flute Twelfth	
2'	Flute Piccolo	12
1³⁄₅'	Flute Seventeenth	
16'	Bass Clarinet	61
8'	Clarinet	61
4'	Sopranino	61
8'	Clarinetti (III)	
8'	English Horn	61
	Tremulant	
	Flute Tremulant	
8'	Harmonic Trumpet *(Unenclosed)*	61

CHOIR (Enclosed) I

Stops shown by tonal family

16'	Bass Viol	68
8'	Viola Pomposa	68
8'	Celeste	68
8'	Violin	68
8'	Celeste	68
8'	Echo Gamba	68
8'	Celeste	68
8'	Voix Sérénissime (Dulcet type)	68
8'	Celeste (Dulcet type)	68
16'	Lieblich Bourdon (Wood and Metal)	68
8'	Chimney Flute	12
8'	Concert Flute (Wood)	68
4'	Nachthorn	68
2⅔'	Nazard	61
2'	Harmonic Piccolo	61
1³⁄₅'	Tierce	61
8'	Echo Diapason	68
4'	Fugara	68
2⅔'	Twelfth	61
2'	Fifteenth	61
1⅓'	Nineteenth	61
1'	Twentysecond	61
16'	Bass Horn	12
8'	Trumpet	68
8'	Flügel Horn	68
8'	Cromorne	68
4'	Rohr Schalmei	68
	Tremulant	
8'	Tuba Mirabilis (Orchestral)	
8'	Harmonic Trumpet (Solo)	

SOLO (Enclosed) IV

8'	Diapason	61
8'	Symphonic Flute	61
4'	Principal	61
2'	Mixture (V)	305
8'	French Horn	61
	Tremulant	
	Variable Tremulant	
	Inner Box—Grand Solo	
16'	Bass Tuba	61
8'	Tuba	61
4'	Tuba Clarion	61
8'	Tuben (III)	
2'	Tierce Mixture (III-VI)	294
8'	Harmonic Trumpet *(Unenclosed)*	61

ORCHESTRAL (Enclosed) V

16'	Major Flute (Wood)	12
8'	Major Flute (Wood)	61
8'	Stentor Gamba	61
8'	Celeste	61
4'	Flute Octave	12
2⅔'	Flute Twelfth	
2'	Flute Piccolo	12
1³⁄₅'	Flute Seventeenth	
16'	Bass Clarinet	61
8'	Clarinet	61
4'	Sopranino	61
8'	Clarinetti (III)	
8'	English Horn	61
	Tremulant	
	Variable Tremulant	
	Flute Tremulant	
8'	Tuba Mirabilis *(Unenclosed)*	61

32'	Diaphone (Wood)	12
32'	Diapason	12
32'	Gamba	12
32'	Sub Bass (Wood)	12
16'	Diaphone (Wood)	32
16'	Open Wood	32
16'	Diapason	32
16'	Diapason (Great)	
16'	Violone (Wood)	32
16'	Gamba	32
16'	Bass Viol (Orchestral)	
16'	Sub Bass (Wood)	32
16'	Major Flute (Celestial)	
16'	Bourdon (Swell)	
16'	Lieblich Bourdon (Orchestral)	
8'	Open Bass (Wood)	
8'	Principal	32
8'	Gamba	12
8'	Stopped Bass (Wood)	12
8'	Bourdon (Swell)	
8'	Lieblich Bourdon (Orchestral)	
4'	Fifteenth	32
4'	Flute	32
2⅔'	Mixture (V)	160
32'	Trombone	12
32'	Fagotto (Swell)	
16'	Trombone	32
16'	Bass Tuba (Solo)	
16'	Bombarde (Swell)	
16'	Bass Trumpet (Great)	
16'	Fagotto (Swell)	
16'	Bass Horn (Orchestral)	
16'	Bass Clarinet (Celestial)	
8'	Tromba	32
8'	Tuba (Solo)	
8'	Fagotto (Swell)	
8'	Clarinet (Celestial)	
4'	Octave Tromba	12
4'	Clarinet (Celestial)	
	Pizzicato Bass (Plays 16' Open Wood at 8' pitch through Pizzicato relay)	

Harp on Orchestral	61 Generators
Celesta on Orchestral	61 Generators
Harp on Solo	61 Notes
Celesta on Solo	61 Notes
Chimes on Solo	32 Generators
Chimes on Great	32 Notes
Chimes on Pedal	32 Notes

64'	Gamba (GGGGG#)	4
32'	Diaphone (Wood)	12
32'	Diapason	12
32'	Gamba	12
32'	Dulciana (Great)	
32'	Sub Bass (Wood)	12
16'	Diaphone (Wood)	32
16'	Open Wood	32
16'	Diapason	32
16'	Diapason (Great)	
16'	Violone (Wood)	32
16'	Gamba	32
16'	Bass Viol (Choir)	
16'	Sub Bass (Wood)	32
16'	Major Flute (Orchestral)	
16'	Bourdon (Swell)	
16'	Lieblich Bourdon (Choir)	
10⅔'	Quint	32
8'	Open Bass (Wood)	
8'	Principal	32
8'	Gamba	12
8'	Flute	32
8'	'Cello (Choir)	
8'	Stopped Bass (Wood)	12
8'	Bourdon (Swell)	
8'	Lieblich Bourdon (Choir)	
4'	Fifteenth	32
4'	Flute	32
4'	Viola (Choir)	
2⅔'	Mixture (II)	64
1⅓'	Mixture (III)	96
64'	Contra Trombone (GGGGG#)	4
32'	Trombone	12
32'	Fagotto (Swell)	
16'	Trombone	32
16'	Bass Tuba (Solo)	
16'	Bombarde (Swell)	
16'	Bass Trumpet (Great)	
16'	Fagotto (Swell)	
16'	Bass Horn (Choir)	
16'	Bass Clarinet (Orchestral)	
8'	Tromba	32
8'	Tuba (Solo)	
8'	Trumpet (Great)	
8'	Fagotto (Swell)	
8'	Clarinet (Orchestral)	
4'	Octave Tromba	12
4'	Trumpet (Great)	
4'	Clarinet (Orchestral)	
	Pizzicato Bass (Plays 16' Open Wood at 8' pitch through Pizzicato relay)	

Harp on Choir	61 Generators
Celesta on Choir	61 Generators
Orchestral Harp on Solo	61 Generators
Orchestral Bells on Solo	61 Generators
Celestial Chimes on Solo	61 Generators
Chimes on Great	32 Generators
Tower Chimes on Pedal	32 Generators
Cymbelstern	

<u>COUPLERS</u>
Intramanual

Swell	16', Unison Off, 4'
Orchestral	16', Unison Off, 4'
Solo	16', Unison Off, 4'
Celestial	16', Unison Off, 4'

Intermanual

Great to Pedal	8'
Swell to Pedal	8', 4'
Orchestral to Pedal	8', 4'
Solo to Pedal	8', 4'
Celestial to Pedal	8', 4'
Swell to Great	16', 8', 4'
Orchestral to Great	16', 8', 4'
Solo to Great	8'
Celestial to Great	8'
Swell to Orchestral	16', 8', 4'
Solo to Orchestral	8'
Celestial to Orchestral	8'
Celestial to Solo	8'

<u>SPECIAL COUPLERS</u>
Pedal Tutti to Swell

Great Tutti to Solo
Pedal Divide*
Swell to Great Sforzando**
Solo to Great Sforzando**
*Pedal Divide deactivates Pedal couplers notes 1–12 and
Pedal stops notes 13–32.

**Sforzando couplers activated by toe lever.

<u>COMBINATIONS</u> (99 Memory Levels)

General	0, 1–20

1–5 and 11–15 duplicated by toe studs
1–3, 5–7, and 13–15 duplicated on right side of keyboards

Great	0, 1–8
Swell	0, 1–8
Orchestral	0, 1–8
Solo	0, 1–8
Celestial	0, 1–8
Pedal	0, 1–8

6–8 duplicated on thumb pistons under Manual I
Programmable piston sequencer

<u>REVERSIBLES</u>
Great to Pedal (thumb and toe)
Swell to Pedal (thumb and toe)
Orchestral to Pedal (thumb)
Solo to Pedal (thumb)
Celestial to Pedal (thumb)
Solo to Great (toe)

32' Trombone (toe)
32' Diaphone (toe)
32' Fagotto (toe)
32' Sub Bass (toe)

<u>COUPLERS</u>
Intramanual

Swell	16', Unison Off, 4'
Choir	16', Unison Off, 4'
Solo	16', Unison Off, 4'
Orchestral	16', Unison Off, 4'

Intermanual

Great to Pedal	8'
Swell to Pedal	8', 4'
Choir to Pedal	8', 4'
Solo to Pedal	8', 4'
Orchestral to Pedal	8', 4'
Swell to Great	16', 8', 4'
Choir to Great	16', 8', 4'
Solo to Great	16', 8', 4'
Orchestral to Great	16', 8', 4'
Swell to Choir	16', 8', 4'
Solo to Choir	8'
Orchestral to Choir	8'
Orchestral to Solo	8'
Solo to Orchestral	8'

<u>SPECIAL COUPLERS</u>
Pedal Tutti to Swell
Pedal Tutti to Choir
Great Tutti to Solo
Pedal Divide*
Swell to Great Sforzando**
Solo to Great Sforzando**
*Pedal Divide deactivates Pedal couplers notes 1–12 and
Pedal stops notes 13–32. Two optional divide
points to be selected by client.
**Sforzando couplers activated by toe lever.

<u>COMBINATIONS</u> (99 Memory Levels)

General	0, 1–20

1–5 and 11–15 duplicated by toe studs
1–3, 5–7, and 13–15 duplicated on right side of keyboards

Great	0, 1–8
Swell	0, 1–8
Choir	0, 1–8
Solo	0, 1–8
Orchestral	0, 1–8
Pedal	0, 1–8

1–8 duplicated on thumb pistons under Manual I
Programmable piston sequencer. *Next* and *Review* thumb
pistons. *Next* and *Review* functions also can be
programmed to operate on any piston or group of
pistons. Indicator light to show piston sequencer in
operation.
Pedal combinations on manual pistons optional.

<u>REVERSIBLES</u>
Great to Pedal (thumb and toe)
Swell to Pedal (thumb and toe)
Choir to Pedal (thumb)
Solo to Pedal (thumb)
Orchestral to Pedal (thumb)
Solo to Great (toe)
64' Contra Trombone (toe)
64' Gamba (toe)
32' Trombone (toe)
32' Diaphone (toe)
32' Fagotto (toe)
32' Sub Bass (toe)
Cymbelstern (thumb and toe)

Manual I/II (thumb) with indicator lights
 Full Organ (thumb and toe) with indicator lights (4 memory
  levels)

MECHANICALS
1. Five Balanced Pedals with selector knobs on nameboard to
   assign functions as follows:
    A. Celestial/Ethereal
    B. Orchestral/Ethereal/Celestial
    C. Swell/Ethereal/Celest./Orch.
    D. Solo/Ethereal/Celest./Orch.
    E. Cresc./Ether./Celest./Trem.
Reversible piston with indicator light for expression adjust on

Notes: In normal expression mode each of the balanced
    pedals performs its nominal (first) function. The
    alternate expression shades default to full open.
      In adjust expression mode, for shades to operate
    they must be assigned to a shoe. Any shades left
    unassigned will default to full open.
      In adjust expression mode, the Crescendo shoe
    will perform its nominal function unless an alternate
    function is assigned to that shoe. The expression
    shade selections will defeat the Crescendo function.
    The Tremulant selection defeats both the Crescendo
    and expression shade functions.
      Expression adjust will revert to normal when the
    organ is turned off.
2. Crescendo (4 memory levels)

3. Crescendo bar graph indicator
4. MIDI Interface—In/Out (Appropriate controls provided for
   access to MIDI from each keyboard and for MIDI
   expression.)

5. Record/Playback Sequencer

CONSOLE
1. Five manual and pedal open American-style case with
   adjustable bench and adjustable music rack all of
   oak and walnut or other hardwood to suit the
   auditorium décor.
2. Bone and ebony covered manual keys with articulated
   touch.
3. Polished ebony drawknobs with ivory resin faces and brass
   shanks.
4. Console platform with rollers.

7. Nontraditional controls located in drawers under the key
   desk.

6. Multiplex system with multiple plug points.

REVERSIBLES (cont'd)
Manual I/II (thumb) with indicator light
 Full Organ (thumb and toe) with indicator light (4 memory
  levels or one for each combination memory)
 Note: Coupler reversibles affect sub and super couplers in off
  mode.

MECHANICALS
1. Five Balanced Pedals with selector knobs on nameboard to
   assign functions as follows:
    A. Orch./Grand Solo/Solo
    B. Choir/Grand Solo/Orch.
    C. Swell/Grand Solo/Orch./Ch.
    D. Solo/Grand Solo/Orch./Ch.
    E. Cresc./Tremulants/Grand Solo
Reversible piston with indicator light for expression adjust on
Pedal selector to have separate combination action with 6
pistons.
Notes: In normal expression mode each of the balanced
    pedals performs its nominal (first) function. The
    alternate expression shades default to full open.
      In adjust expression mode, for shades to operate
    they must be assigned to a shoe. Any shades left
    unassigned will default to full open.
      In adjust expression mode, the Crescendo shoe
    will perform its nominal function unless one of the
    Variable Tremulant knobs is drawn or Grand Solo
    expression is selected. Grand Solo expression will
    defeat Crescendo. Variable Tremulant defeats both
    Crescendo and Grand Solo expression.
      Expression adjust will revert to normal when the
    organ is turned off.
2. Crescendo (4 memory levels). Circuit to cancel percussion,
   celestes and tremulants when crescendo is on.)
3. Crescendo bar graph indicator
4. MIDI Interface—In/Out (Appropriate controls provided for
   access to MIDI from each keyboard (6) and for MIDI
   expression on Balanced Pedal A for all six channels.
   MIDI sound modules to be in console.)
5. Prepared for touch-sensitive top manual.
6. Record/Playback Sequencer prepared for remote control
   operation.

CONSOLE
1. Five manual and pedal open American-style case with
   adjustable bench and adjustable music rack all of
   oak and walnut or other hardwood to suit the
   auditorium décor.
2. Bone and ebony covered manual keys with articulated
   touch.
3. Polished ebony drawknobs with ivory resin faces and brass
   shanks.
4. Console platform with rollers and position lock.
5. Special master indicator light operating parallel with the
   most important individual indicator lights.
6. Nontraditional controls located in drawers under the key
   desk.
7. "Console power only on" switch for silent practice with
   combination action.
8. Technician call button.
9. Multiplex system with multiple plug points on platform and
   in rehearsal/storage area.

CONSOLE (cont'd)
8. Pedal light.

5. Clock/timer similar to that at the Tabernacle.

CONSOLE (cont'd)
10. Pedal light.
11. Music light in music rack base.
12. Coupler light.
13. Radio Broadcast "Stand By" and "On Air" lights.
14. Clock/Timer system similar to that at the Tabernacle. ("Broadcast Timer")
15. Air fan.
16. Temperature monitoring recording system for all divisions, blower and console.
17. Prepared for intercom stations for auditorium/choir system and organ tuning system.
18. Prepared for Auditorium system P.A. speaker in console.
19. Prepared for T V monitor.

Normally the contract specification (in this case dated May 18, 1998) would be the final word with regard to the stops and accessories. In the case of the Conference Center organ, it was not. All involved were continually looking for ways to add tonal color and flexibility to the instrument as well as ease of control from the large console. In February 1999, a month following the signing of the contract, Jack, in consultation with Steuart Goodwin, proposed a rather dramatic change to the Orchestral division. The idea, suggested in a February 24 telephone call, was to include several theater organ stops for the characteristic colors they would add to the fifth manual. To accomplish this without financial impact, we would give up the Choir Violin 8-foot and its accompanying Celeste, plus the Orchestral Clarinet 8-foot and Sopranino 4-foot stops. We studied the proposal carefully and, after discussing it the next day in a conference call including Jack, Richard, Clay and myself, agreed to the rather unexpected and adventuresome departure from traditional church organ design. The remodeled Orchestral division is shown side by side with the stoplist from the contract specification.

CONTRACT STOPLIST
May 18, 1998

REVISED STOPLIST
FEBRUARY 24, 1999

ORCHESTRAL		Pipes	ORCHESTRAL		Pipes
16'	Major Flute	12	16'	Major Flute	12
			8'	Phonon Diapason	61
8'	Major Flute	61	8'	Major Flute	61
8'	Stentor Gamba	61	8'	Stentor Gamba	61
8'	Celeste	61	8'	Celeste	61
			4'	Diapason Octave	12
4'	Flute Octave	12	4'	Flute Octave	12
2⅔'	Flute Twelfth		2⅔'	Flute Twelfth	
2'	Flute Piccolo	12	2'	Flute Piccolo	12
1³/₅'	Flute Seventeenth		1³/₅'	Flute Seventeenth	
16'	Bass Clarinet	61	16'	Bass Clarinet	61
			8'	Tuba Horn	61
8'	Clarinet	61	8'	Clarinet	12
4'	Sopranino	61			
8'	Clarinetti (III)				
8'	English Horn	61	8'	English Horn	61
			8'	Orchestral Oboe	61
			8'	Vox Humana	61
	Tremulant			Tremulant	
	Variable Tremulant			Variable Tremulant	
	Flute Tremulant			Flute Tremulant	
8'	Tuba Mirabilis (*Unenclosed*)	61	8'	Tuba Mirabilis (*Unenclosed*)	61

The next modifications to the stoplist came in May 1999. With just a few exceptions, these were not tonal changes, but simply name changes on the drawknobs. As an illustration, the Pedal Stopped Bass 8-foot shown in the contract stoplist (revision 4) is actually a 12-note extension of the Sub Bass 16-foot. The new revision makes that clear by renaming the stop Sub Bass 8-foot. One tonal change was necessitated by the elimination of the Sopranino 4-foot in the Orchestral division. It was replaced in the Pedal by the Choir Cromorne 8-foot, sounding at 4-foot pitch. The composition of two mixture stops was also altered. Jack Bethards explained those alterations in a cover letter dated May 24, 1999, that accompanied what he labeled "Final Stoplist."

> The changes relate to actual pipe construction after scaling and to what I see as a need for simplicity on such a large console. For example, I have tried to make very explicit which stops are straight and which ones involve borrows. This is particularly important in the Pedal. Although the different names for different pitches are more pleasing on paper, I am convinced that using the identical name at every pitch will make it much easier to identify exactly what sound is to be expected from the borrowed stop. Steuart [Goodwin] also convinced me that we might as well come right out and call the "theatre" style stops exactly what they are, so I have followed Wurlitzer nomenclature on these.

We organists asked for a few changes even beyond Schoenstein's Final Stoplist. Some changes were made to make it easier to discriminate among stops with identical names when glancing quickly at them. On the Great, for example, three stops were labeled "Mixture." To facilitate quick visual identification we suggested they be renamed "Full Mixture," "Mixture" and "Sharp Mixture." Other names were chosen to give the nomenclature a bit more cachet. "Harmonic Trumpet" was renamed "Millennial Trumpet" in honor of the year 2000, which would mark the completion of the Conference Center. The Great "Chimes" were renamed "Les Cloches de Hinckley," a double entendre referring to the composition by Louis Vierne as well as to honor President Gordon B. Hinckley, whose vision was responsible not only for the Conference Center itself but for the organ as well. While "Fifteenth" is technically correct for the 4-foot principal stop in the 16-foot series, we opted to call it "Choral Bass," which is the nomenclature used on the Tabernacle organ. As tonal details were being worked out, some changes in mixture composition were made that are shown in the Final Stoplist. Two additional stops are borrowed into the Pedal: the Swell Diapason 16-foot and the Great Dulciana 32-foot, borrowed at 16-foot pitch.

The table below identifies the stops involved in these changes.

CONTRACT STOPLIST		"FINAL" STOPLIST		MODIFIED FINAL STOPLIST	
GREAT		GREAT		GREAT	
16'	Diapason	16'	Double Open Diapason		unchanged
8'	Diapason (Large)	8'	Large Open Diapason		"
8'	Diapason (Medium)	8'	Open Diapason		"
8'	Diapason (Small)	8'	Small Open Diapason	8'	Horn Diapason
8'	Stopped Diapason	8'	Chimney Flute		unchanged
		4'	Gemshorn	4'	Octave Gemshorn
2'	Mixture (V)	2'	Mixture (IV–V)	2'	Full Mixture (IV–V)
		1⅓'	Mixture (III)	1⅓'	Sharp Mixture (III)
		8'	Harmonic Trumpet	8'	Millennial Trumpet
SWELL		SWELL		SWELL	
8'	Diapason	8'	Open Diapason		unchanged
8'	Lieblich Gedeckt	8'	Stopped Diapason		"
4'	Octave	4'	Principal		"
2'	Tierce Mixture (III)	2⅔'	Tierce Mixture (III)	2⅔'	Cornet (III)
		2'	Quint Mixture (V)	2'	Plein Jeu (V)
CHOIR		CHOIR		CHOIR	
8'	Celeste	8'	Viola Celeste		unchanged
8'	Celeste	8'	Gamba Celeste		"
8'	Voix Sérénissime	8'	Viol d'orchestre		"
8'	Celeste	8'	Viol Celeste		"
8'	Chimney Flute	8'	Lieblich Bourdon		"
16'	Bass Horn	16'	Flügel Horn		"
		8'	Harmonic Trumpet	8'	Millennial Trumpet
SOLO		SOLO		SOLO	
2'	Tierce Mixture (III–VI)	2'	Tierce Mixture (IV–VI)		unchanged
		8'	Harmonic Trumpet	8'	Millennial Trumpet
ORCHESTRAL		ORCHESTRAL		ORCHESTRAL	
16'	Major Flute	16'	Tibia Clausa		unchanged
8'	Major Flute	8'	Tibia Clausa		"
4'	Flute Octave	4'	Tibia Clausa		"
2⅔'	Flute Twelfth	2⅔'	Tibia Twelfth		"
2'	Flute Piccolo	2'	Tibia Piccolo		"
1⅗'	Flute Seventeenth	1⅗'	Tibia Tierce		"
		8'	English Horn	8'	Cor Anglais
PEDAL		PEDAL		PEDAL	
		16'	Diapason (Great)	16'	Great Diapason
		16'	Diapason (Swell)	16'	Swell Diapason
16'	Major Flute (Orchestral)	16'	Tibia Clausa (Orchestral)		unchanged
8'	Open Bass (Wood)	8'	Open Wood		"
8'	'Cello (Choir)	8'	Bass Viole (Choir)		"
8'	Stopped Bass (Wood)	8'	Sub Bass (Wood)		"
		4'	Fifteenth	4'	Choral Bass
4'	Flute	4'	Octave Flute		unchanged
4'	Viola (Choir)	4'	Bass Viole (Choir)		"
		2⅔'	Mixture (II)	2⅔'	Rauschquinte (II)
4'	Clarinet (Orchestral)	4'	Cromorne (Choir)		unchanged
PERCUSSION		PERCUSSION		PERCUSSION	
			Chimes (on Great)		Les Cloches de Hinckley (on Great)

One more change came very late in the process. The July 2000 issue of *The American Organist* featured, on its cover and in an article, a new organ built by C. B. Fisk Organbuilders for the Minato Mirai Hall in Yokohama, Japan. Clay mentioned the article to me before I received my copy of the magazine. His mentioning it piqued my interest, so when my copy arrived I went immediately to the article. In studying the specification I noticed its enclosed, floating Tuba division and immediately wondered whether we might not have been wise to float the Grand Solo division on the Schoenstein organ. I mentioned it to Clay, and he thought the idea had merit. I did not act immediately on the notion, but finally on July 13, I broached the subject during a telephone call to Jack Bethards.

Jack was a bit hesitant at first, but as we talked further, he could see the advantage of the concept. The biggest difficulty would be modifying the relay, which was nearing completion and due to be shipped within days. Jack said he would explore the possibility with Peterson Electro-Musical Products, Inc., who were supplying the organ's electrical systems, and asked that we organists discuss the matter over the weekend to be certain we were of one mind on the issue.

Clay, Richard and I spoke shortly thereafter and found that we were in agreement. On July 14, I left a voicemail message for Jack detailing our proposal. On July 19, Jack phoned me at home, late in the day, saying that it would be possible to modify the relay. As it turned out the delay in shipping the modified components was only a matter of hours. The modification required the addition of four drawknobs among the Special Couplers: Grand Solo off Solo, Grand Solo on Great, Grand Solo on Swell, and Grand Solo on Choir.

Because of the heavy use of the Conference Center following its opening, installation and tonal finishing of the organ took some five years to complete. While it was frustrating to wait so long for the finished instrument, that time provided an opportunity for the organists to use each stop, as it became available, in a variety of contexts. In so doing, we were able to suggest a few minor modifications to Jack Bethards to refine the tonal palette. Some of those suggestions involved the loudening or softening of certain stops or perhaps the touching up of an isolated pipe here and there. In a few cases, Jack felt it wise to make scaling adjustments.

In two instances, ranks were completely changed in order to facilitate smoother build-ups in the Great and Swell divisions. Jack Bethards speaks of these changes:

> We knew at the outset that normal stopped flutes were not terribly effective in large buildings so we included only a few. The results proved the point and caused us to eliminate two more and replace them with diapasons! The straight 8' Stopped Diapason in the Swell was replaced with the 8' Small Open Diapason. The 8' Chimney Flute in the Great gave way to an 8' tapered principal (Gemshorn). These aided greatly the dynamic buildup in these divisions.

With the removal of the Swell Stopped Diapason, the Bourdon 16-foot was extended to provide a suitable 8-foot flute for the Swell. With the addition of the Small Diapason 8-foot in the Swell, the Small Open Diapason 8-foot on the Great was renamed Horn Diapason 8-foot to avoid possible confusion. The original Great Gemshorn 4-foot was renamed Octave Gemshorn 4-foot to indicate that it was not an extension of the new Gemshorn 8-foot.

While experimenting one day, Steuart Goodwin and his associate, Wendell Ballantyne, discovered that the Pedal Open Wood 8-foot made a wonderfully rich and powerful solo stop. The addition of twenty-nine pipes made it available as a manual stop. Named Stentor Diapason, it was made available on both the Solo and Great. It works wonderfully well, not only as a lustrous solo flue, but also as a firm underpinning for the rest of the organ.

One additional change was made very late in the finishing process. The organists felt that the Orchestral Clarinet 8-foot, a Wurlitzer rank, would be more useful if it were louder. Attempts to louden the existing pipes were unsuccessful, and it was decided to replace the entire rank.

The separate Tibia Tremulant in the Orchestral division was removed; the general Tremulant and Variable Tremulant proved adequate for the Tibias. The space made available by the removal of that drawknob was filled by duplexing the Choir Cromorne 8-foot on the Orchestral manual.

The inner set of Grand Solo swell shades was removed. This allowed the tubas to speak with even greater impact, and their dynamic range, as controlled by the remaining outer set of shades, proved perfectly adequate in the vast space of the auditorium. The pipes of the Grand Solo are contained in a separate enclosure above the rest of the Solo division pipes. It was a simple matter to rewire the outer swell shades of the upper enclosure to operate independently from the shades below.

Finally, with the heavy usage given the Conference Center organ during the renovation of the Tabernacle, it was found that the original ninety-nine levels of combination action memory were used up very quickly with five staff organists plus guest organists constantly preparing for daily recitals, weekly Choir broadcasts plus conferences and other special events. As a result, in 2008 a duplicate set of memories was added, effectively doubling the organ's original memory capacity. The organist switches between the two systems by means of a thumb piston located under the fifth manual. Two LEDs, one in the key slip beside the thumb piston and another in the name board, indicate which of the two systems is currently in use.

The organ's stoplist, current through 2009, is shown below, including mixture compositions and the provenance of reused pipes. Pipe scaling data are given in Appendix 1.

CONFERENCE CENTER
THE CHURCH OF JESUS CHRIST OF LATTER-DAY SAINTS
Salt Lake City, Utah

SCHOENSTEIN & CO.
San Francisco, California
Opus 139, 103 Voices—130 Ranks

GREAT (II) (5½" wind)

32'	Dulciana	61
16'	Double Open Diapason	61
16'	Bourdon (wood)	61
8'	Stentor Diapason (Solo)	
8'	Large Open Diapason (7½" wind)	61
8'	Open Diapason	61
8'	Horn Diapason	61
8'	Gamba	61
8'	Gemshorn	61
8'	Harmonic Flute	61
8'	Doppelflöte (wood)	61
4'	Principal (7½" wind)	61
4'	Octave	61
4'	Octave Gemshorn	61
4'	Forest Flute	61
2⅔'	Twelfth	61
2'	Fifteenth	61
1⅗'	Seventeenth	61
2'	Full Mixture (IV–V) (*ff* –7½" wind)	266
2'	Mixture (IV) (*f*)	215
1⅓'	Sharp Mixture (III) (*mf*)	175
16'	Bass Trumpet (7½" wind)	61
8'	Trumpet (7½" wind)	61
4'	Clarion (7½" wind)	61
8'	Tuba Mirabilis (Orchestral)	
8'	Millennial Trumpet (Solo)	
	Tremulant	

SWELL (Enclosed—III) (5½" wind)

16'	Double Open Diapason	68
16'	Bourdon (wood)	68
8'	Open Diapason	68
8'	Small Open Diapason	68
8'	Silver Flute	68
8'	Bourdon	12
8'	Viole de gambe	68
8'	Viole céleste	68
8'	Flauto Dolce	68
8'	Flute Celeste (TC)	56
4'	Principal	68
4'	Harmonic Flute	68
2'	Fifteenth	61
2⅔'	Cornet (III) (*mf*)	183
2'	Plein Jeu (V) (*f*)	276
32'	Contra Fagotto (10" wind)	68
16'	Bombarde	68
16'	Fagotto (10" wind)	12
8'	Trompette	68
8'	Cornopean (10" wind)	68
8'	Oboe	68
8'	† Voix humaine	61
4'	Clairon harmonique	68
4'	Clarion (10" wind)	68
	Tremulant	
	† Separate tremulant	

CHOIR (Enclosed—I) (5½" wind)

16'	Bass Viol	68
8'	Viola Pomposa	68
8'	Viola Celeste	68
8'	Echo Gamba	68
8'	Gamba Celeste	68
8'	Viole d'orchestre	68
8'	Viole céleste	68
16'	Lieblich Bourdon (metal)	68
8'	Lieblich Bourdon	12
8'	Concert Flute (wood)	68
4'	Nachthorn	68
2⅔'	Nazard	61
2'	Harmonic Piccolo	61
1⅗'	Tierce	61
8'	Echo Diapason	68
4'	Fugara	68
2⅔'	Twelfth	61
2'	Fifteenth	61
1⅓'	Nineteenth	61
1'	Twenty-second	61
16'	Flügel Horn	12
8'	Trumpet	68
8'	Flügel Horn	68
8'	Cromorne	68
4'	Rohr Schalmei	68
8'	Tuba Mirabilis (Orchestral)	
8'	Millennial Trumpet (Solo)	
	Tremulant	

SOLO (enclosed—IV) (11½" wind)

8'	Open Diapason	61
8'	Phonon Diapason (Orchestral)	
8'	Symphonic Flute	61
4'	Principal	61
4'	Octave (Orchestral)	
2⅔'	Quint Mixture (V)	288
8'	French Horn	61
8'	Cor Anglais (Orchestral)	
8'	Clarinet (Orchestral)	
	Tremulant	
	Variable Tremulant	

Separate Shades — Grand Solo (17½" wind)

16'	Bass Tuba	61
8'	Tuba	61
4'	Tuba Clarion	61
8'	† Tuben (III)	
2'	Tierce Mixture (IV–VI)	309

Unenclosed

8'	†† Stentor Diapason (25" wind)	29
8'	Millennial Trumpet (15" wind)	61

† Draws Bass Tuba, Tuba, and Tuba
  Clarion, all at 8' pitch

†† Extends Pedal Open Wood

MAGNUM OPUS

ORCHESTRAL (enclosed—V) (10" wind)

16'	Tibia Clausa (wood)	12
8'	Phonon Diapason	61
8'	Tibia Clausa	61
8'	Stentor Gamba	61
8'	Celeste	61
4'	Octave	12
4'	Tibia Clausa	12
2⅔'	Tibia Twelfth	
2'	Tibia Piccolo	12
1⅗'	Tibia Tierce	
16'	Clarinet	61
8'	Tuba Horn (15" wind)	61
8'	Clarinet	12
8'	Cromorne (Choir)	
8'	Cor Anglais	61
8'	Orchestral Oboe	61
8'	† Vox Humana (5½" wind)	61
	Tremulant	
	Variable Tremulant	
	Unenclosed	
8'	Tuba Mirabilis (20" wind)	61

† Separate Tremulant

PEDAL (5½" wind)

64'	Gamba (GGGGG#)(10" wind)	4
32'	Diaphone (wood) (25" wind)	12
32'	Diapason (10" wind)	12
32'	Gamba	12
32'	Dulciana (Great)	
32'	Sub Bass (wood) (10" wind)	12
16'	Diaphone (wood)	32
16'	Open Wood (10" wind)	32
16'	Diapason	32
16'	Great Diapason (Great)	
16'	Swell diapason (Swell)	
16'	Violone (wood) (7½" wind)	32
16'	Gamba	32
16'	Bass Viol (Choir)	
16'	Dulciana (Great)	
16'	Sub Bass	32
16'	Tibia Clausa (Orchestral)	
16'	Bourdon (Swell)	
16'	Lieblich Bourdon (Choir)	
10⅔'	Quint	32
8'	Open Wood	12
8'	Principal	32
8'	Gamba	12
8'	Flute	32
8'	Bass Viol (Choir)	
8'	Sub Bass	12
8'	Bourdon (Swell)	
8'	Lieblich Bourdon (Choir)	
4'	Choral Bass	32
4'	Octave Flute	32
4'	Bass Viol (Choir)	
2⅔'	Rauschquinte (II)	64
1⅓'	Mixture (III)	96
64'	Trombone (GGGGG#) (20" wind)	4
32'	Trombone	12
32'	Contra Fagotto (Swell)	
16'	Trombone	32
16'	Bass Tuba (Solo)	
16'	Bombarde (Swell)	
16'	Bass Trumpet (Great)	
16'	Fagotto (Swell)	
16'	Flügel Horn (Choir)	
16'	Clarinet (Orchestral)	
8'	Tromba (15" wind)	32
8'	Bass Tuba (Solo)	
8'	Bass Trumpet (Great)	
8'	Bombarde (Swell)	
8'	Fagotto (Swell)	
8'	Clarinet (Orchestral)	
8'	Flügel Horn (Choir)	
4'	Tromba	12
4'	Bass Trumpet (Great)	
4'	Cromorne (Choir)	
	† Pizzicato Bass	

† Plays 16' Open Wood at 8' pitch
through pizzicato relay

PERCUSSIONS (Walker Digital)

Harp (Choir)	61
Celesta (Choir)	61
Orchestral Harp (Solo)	61
Orchestral Bells (Choir)	37
Celestial Chimes (Solo)	32
Les cloches de Hinckley (Great)	32
Tower Chimes (Pedal)	32
Cymbelstern (Great)	

COUPLERS

Intramanual

Swell	16', Unison Off, 4'
Choir	16', Unison Off, 4'
Solo	16', Unison Off, 4'
Orchestral	16', Unison Off, 4'

Intermanual

Great to Pedal	8'
Swell to Pedal	8', 4'
Choir to Pedal	8', 4'
Solo to Pedal	8', 4'
Orchestral to Pedal	8', 4'
Swell to Great	16', 8', 4'
Choir to Great	16', 8', 4'
Solo to Great	16', 8', 4'
Orchestral to Great	16', 8', 4'
Swell to Choir	16', 8', 4'
Solo to Choir	8'
Orchestral to Choir	8'
Orchestral to Solo	8'
Solo to Orchestral	8'

SPECIAL COUPLERS

Pedal Tutti to Swell
Pedal Tutti to Choir
Great Tutti to Solo
Pedal Divide 12/13*
Pedal Divide 17/18
Pedal Divide 20/21
Swell to Great Sforzando**
Solo to Great Sforzando
Grand Solo off Solo
Grand Solo on Great
Grand Solo on Swell
Grand Solo on Choir
MIDI coupler to each keyboard

SPECIAL COUPLERS (cont'd)
*Pedal Divide deactivates Pedal coupler notes 1-12 and Pedal
stop notes 13-32, etc.
**Sforzando couplers activated by toe lever

MECHANICALS
- Solid State Capture Combination Action with:
    99 memories x 2
    104 pistons and toe studs
- Programmable piston sequencer
- 15 reversibles including:
    Manual I/II reverse
    Full Organ
- Five balanced expression shoes with selector knobs
  on nameboard to assign functions
- Expression function selector system with six
  combination pistons
- Four Crescendo programs with bar graph indicator
- Record/Playback Sequencer
- Adjustable bench and music rack
- Six blowers (39.7 HP)
- MIDI Interface
- Blower room controlled for temperature and
  humidity

CONSOLE
- Bone and ebony covered manual keys with
  articulated touch
- Polished ebony and rosewood drawknobs with
  ivory resin faces and brass shanks
- Console platform
- Non-traditional controls located in drawers under
  the key desk
- Console Power switch for silent practice with
  combination action
- Technician call button (prepared)
- Pedal light
- "Coupler" light (behind music rack)
- Clock/Timer system
- Air fan
- Connector for TV monitor

PITCH=A440 @ 72° F.

MIXTURE COMPOSITIONS

Great Full Mixture IV–V (*ff*)

C1	C#14	A22	B36	A#47
15	12	8	8	5
19	15	12	12	8
22	19	15	15	12
26	22	19	19	15
26	22			

Great Mixture IV (*f*)

C1	D15	G#45	C#50
15	12	12	12
19	15	15	15
22	19	19	
26	22		

Great Sharp Mixture III (*mf*)

C1	C37	C49	F54
19	15	12	12
22	19	15	15
26	22	19	

Swell Cornet III (*mf*)

C1	E53
12	8
15	12
17	15

Swell Plein Jeu V (*f*)

C1	A#23	D#28	G#33	B48
15	12	8	8	5
19	15	12	12	8
22	19	15	15	12
26	22	19	19	15
29	26	22		

Solo Quint Mixture V

C1	B24	A#35	F#43	D#52
12	8	8	1	1
15	12	12	8	5
19	15	15	12	8
22	19	19	15	12
26	22			15

Grand Solo Tierce Mixture IV–VI

C1	D#16	G#21	A46	D51
15	12	8	5	5
17	15	12	8	8
19	17	15	12	12
22	19	17	15	15
	22	19	17	
		22	19	

Pedal Rauschquinte (II)
    12–15 throughout

Pedal Mixture (III)
    19–22–26 throughout

RECYCLED PIPES

ORCHESTRAL
Tibia Clausa: 1–12 Kimball,
    Remainder Wurlitzer
Phonon Diapason: Wurlitzer
Tuba horn: Wurlitzer
Orchestral Oboe: Wurlitzer
Vox Humana: Wurlitzer

PEDAL
Diaphone: Kimball, Opus 6644
Sub Bass: from 16' E–Kimball;
    (1–16 new by Fetzers' Inc.)
Open Wood: 1–12 Aeolian;
    13–30 Kimball;
    31–34 Schoenstein;
    (remainder new)

CHAPTER 8

The Console

The console is the command center of the organ. Some have likened it to the cockpit of an airplane. It is from here that the organist operates the instrument's various controls and plays the keys, which finally enables the organ to make music.

Organs are large, complex machines. Organists do not carry their instruments around with them. They cannot hold one in their hands, tuck it under their chins to bow it, or put the pipes to their mouths to blow them. It is as though they are playing their instrument by remote control. The organist is often some distance removed from the sound-producing pipes of the organ. The intimacy that other musicians have with their instruments usually is not part of the organist's experience. The placement of the console is sometimes such that he is unable to judge the balance between the various sections of the instrument. It is rather like asking the conductor of an orchestra to work from a podium out in the wings of the stage.

Given the challenges inherent in playing the instrument, the last thing an organist needs is a console that impedes his ability to easily control the organ's various functions. Anyone who has tried to operate a device whose controls are flimsy, unreliable, and poorly placed can appreciate the frustration of an organist trying to perform artistically from such a console. The console must be ergonomically designed with frequently used controls comfortably within reach. Controls should be clearly labeled, and move smoothly, quietly and reliably. The keys must feel crisp and solid, be carefully regulated for consistency of resistance and depth of travel, operate quietly, and have a surface that is neither slippery nor sticky to the touch. Therefore, the organ builder should lavish the same care and concern for quality and detail on the console as he does on the pipework.

Perfecting the Layout

Work on the Conference Center console began shortly following the signing of the contract. From the outset, we organists had three objectives in mind:

1. The layout should correspond insofar as possible to that of the Tabernacle organ to facilitate our moving from one console to the other.

2. The layout should be logical, with everything clearly labeled.

3. Controls should be designed and located to avoid "booby traps" (important functions easily overlooked) in performance, especially important under the pressure of live broadcasting.

A few departures from the normal arrangement of drawknobs are worth noting. In his cover letter of February 4, 1999 that accompanied the first drawing of the layout, Chuck Primich, Schoenstein's Design Director, explained:

> The Pedal division drawknobs are arranged such that those stops which are enclosed are in a parallel grouping to the unexpressive stops. This is certainly not the usual practice, however due to the comprehensive nature of the instrument we thought this concept worth your consideration.

Chuck's suggestion made perfect sense in view of the huge array of stops in the Pedal division, and we had followed a similar plan with the Pedal reeds of the Tabernacle organ during its renovation. Also, from the beginning Jack Bethards had conceived of the Choir division as a collection of ensembles, and the drawknobs were arranged accordingly, rather than strictly by pitch level.

The original drawing placed the Orchestral division stops on the left stop jamb, and the Solo stops on the right jamb. On the Tabernacle organ console, we were accustomed to having the gentler and more expressive Solo division knobs on the right jamb and the fiery reed and large principal chorus of the Bombarde on the left jamb. Hence, we proposed that the Orchestral and Solo division knobs exchange locations. We further suggested that the Solo and Grand Solo stop knobs be visually distinguished from each other in some way. This was accomplished by using wood of a contrasting color for the Grand Solo drawknobs.

One intriguing and useful feature of the Schoenstein specification, not available on the Tabernacle organ, was the ability to assign varying functions to the expression and crescendo pedals (sometimes referred to as "shoes"). Early in the design process, it was decided that this capability would be controlled by a separate combination action system with six adjustable pistons (labeled A through F). However, in Chuck's second generation console drawings, sent to us in mid-July 1999, this was still a "blind" system. A display on the nameboard would indicate which piston had been pressed, but there was no indication of what the resulting pedal assignment actually was. We viewed this as a potential booby trap. In a mid-August reply to Chuck's second generation drawing we wrote, "There is a feeling that we should be able to confirm at a glance exactly what the shoe assignments are. This implies some kind of visible display, but where and how need to be addressed." The ingenious solution came back a few days later. Chuck wrote:

> Jack and I both like the idea of miniature drawknobs set just above the LED display bezel. These would be connected to a regular drawknob mechanism and function in the same manner as any other drawknob. This really provides the best of all possible worlds as there would be no ambiguity about the expression arrangement, setting combinations would be simple, manually selecting the shoes would be easy, and there would be no need for a display indicating the piston in use.

Figure 8.1
See
Appendix 5

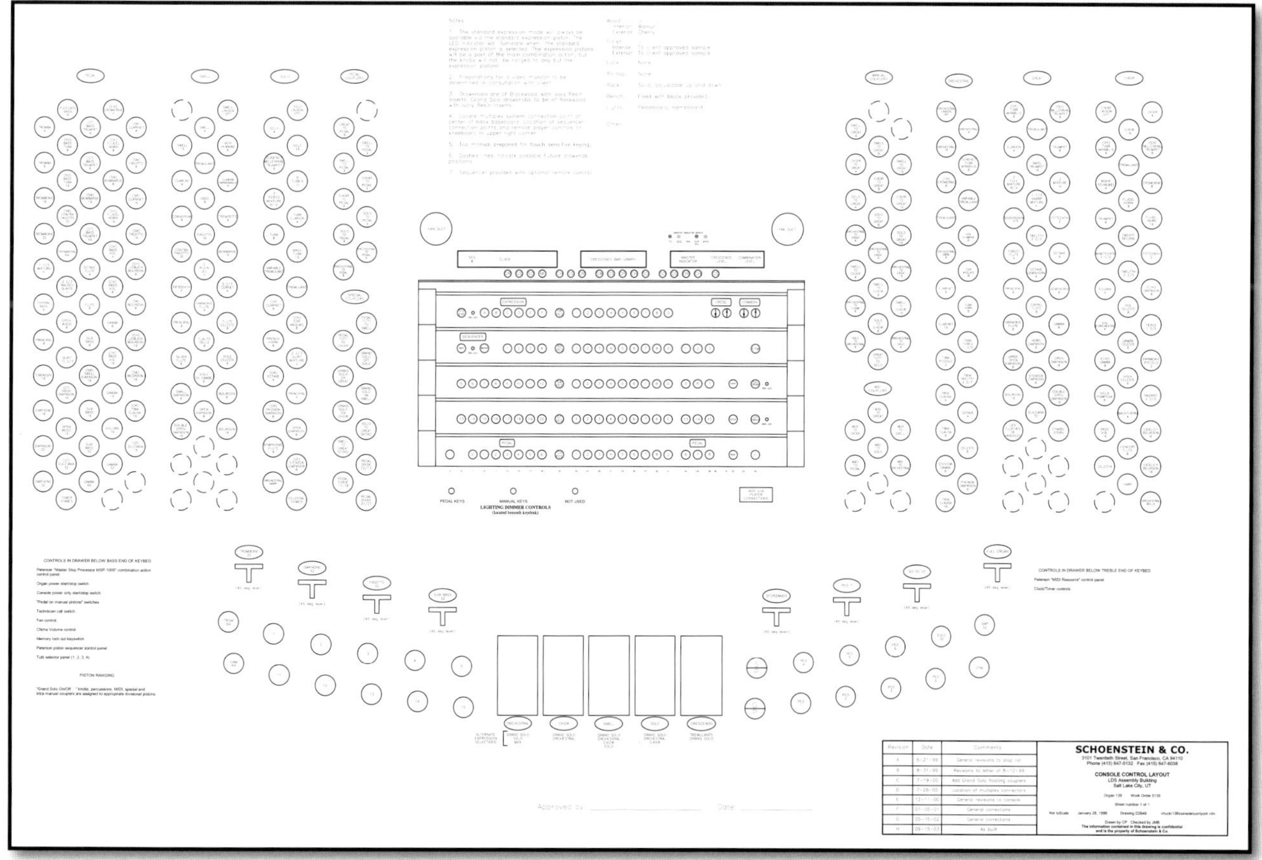

In mid-September, the third iteration of the console layout arrived, incorporating all the changes and decisions that had been made to that point. Even then, we suggested a few relatively minor changes in the location of some displays and controls. The final drawing of the console layout is shown as figure 8.1, also in Appendix 5. Note that the drawknobs controlling the swell pedal assignments were placed below the display bezel, rather than above it as Chuck had originally suggested.

In late September 1999, Chuck proposed that we consider another possibility:

> While working on the design and shop drawings, it occurred to me that you might like to have the jambs, and thus the overall console, a bit narrower and taller than we have planned right now. This would mean rearranging the drawknob layout in the Pedal, Swell, and Great divisions. If the alternate scheme should be your preference, I think that the work involved would be well worth the effort.

We gave serious consideration to Chuck's proposal, but after weighing its advantages and disadvantages decided not to pursue that option. We remembered that the Tabernacle organ console, following its installation, was cut down a few inches to lower its profile in order to improve the organist's sight line to the conductor. We felt it best to keep the top of the Conference Center console as low as practical for the same reason.

The Drawers

In the completed console, some controls are housed in drawers underneath the key desk on either side of the keyboards. The left-hand drawer contains the "Console Power" and "Organ Power" switches. The former turns on the console lights, controls, displays, and the combination action, allowing for silent practice. The latter turns on the organ's six blowers sequentially, ten seconds apart, to minimize a sudden power drain. In addition, the left drawer contains the controls for the MSP-1000 combination action and stop sequencer systems supplied by Peterson Electro-Musical Products, Inc. of Alsip, Illinois. A technician call switch (not used at present), the console fan on/off switch and a volume control knob affecting the Cymbelstern and Tower Chimes are also housed in the left drawer. The console fan is a simple device included for the comfort of the organist. Air from a fan housed in the console is directed through two adjustable tubes located just under the music rack on either

side of the nameboard. Schoenstein had included a similar fan in the Tabernacle organ console during its renovation that had proved very useful when performing under the hot lights required for television broadcasting.

The right-hand drawer contains a Yamaha MDF3 MIDI data filer that uses 3½" diskettes for organ recording and playback, a numeric keypad that allows instant access to the organ's 198 levels of combinations without scrolling, controls for the clock and timer, the Peterson MIDI Controller, and space for storage of pencils, erasers, and such. The numeric keypad was added by Peterson after the console was put into service, in response to our request to be able to change memory levels more quickly.

The Console Shell

Having determined the location of stops and controls, it was time to consider the appearance of the console shell. Chuck wrote on January 25, 2000:

> Here are the basic views of the console case. This design is similar to that which you have seen before, but has been adjusted to accommodate the stop jambs and to obtain correct proportions. I have developed the working drawings to the point of being sure that this design can be produced as shown. Once you have given approval of the design, I can send it to the wood shop in just a couple of days.

I felt it wise to show the drawings (figures 8.2 and 8.3) to Lee Gray rather than approve them unilaterally. Lee's creative mind immediately slipped into gear and

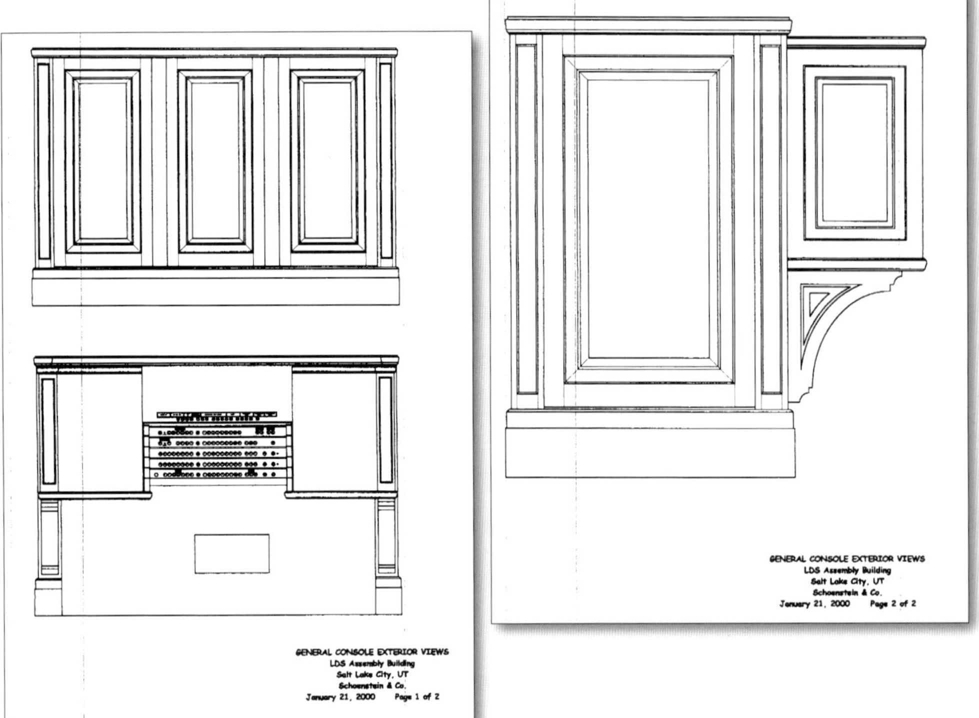

Figures 8.2 and 8.3

he quickly drew sketches of quite a different design (figure 8.4). After seeing Lee's drawings I responded to him in a memorandum dated January 28:

> I've shown your sketches of the organ console to the organists and others of the Choir staff. All are favorably impressed with the direction you have taken it. There is nothing "off the shelf" about any aspect of this instrument, and there is no reason to plunk down a [traditional] console in a room that is without precedent in so many ways.
>
> The only reaction I have received [to your sketch] that is the least bit negative is that the side view (which is, after all, the view that faces straight out into the room) is rather plain when compared to the front and back views. Also the gold inlay in the front could appear somewhat theatrical or even gaudy a la the Wurlitzer consoles from the early years of the 20th century.

We sent Lee's concept (figure 8.4) to Chuck. By mid-February, Chuck had responded with drawings of his own, based on what he called Lee's "very interesting and creative console design." Chuck modified Lee's drawings somewhat, both for practical and aesthetic reasons. His side view drawing is shown as figure 8.5. With just minor adjustments, the console shell was ready to go into production.

Paul Fetzer felt that his firm could not undertake building the console case woodwork, given the other work to which they were already committed. Schoenstein's woodworking shop was similarly encumbered, so Jack Bethards outsourced the job

Figure 8.4

to Richard Menacho, an independent artisan in the area. The woods used in the console include cherry (including the same cherry veneer used in the organ case and other areas of the rostrum), Karelian birch burl veneer and ebony.

The console was built 7' 5" wide, 4' 10⅝" high (the adjustable music rack extending above the cabinet top another 2⅞" in its highest position), and 3' 9" deep, with the pedalboard extending the total depth to 5' 6½".

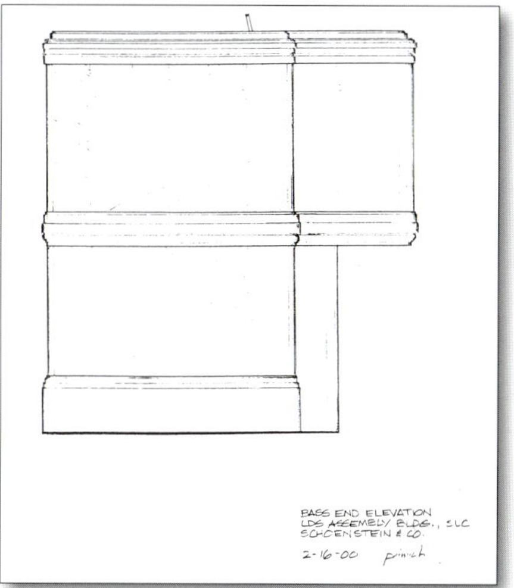

Figure 8.5

Assembly and Shipping

The keyboards and the mechanical and electrical systems were installed in the shell at Schoenstein's assembly shop. The keyboards, built by P & S Organ Supply Company Ltd. of Brandon, Suffolk, England, feature articulated ("tracker") touch and, with the exception of the bone coverings on the naturals, are identical to those on the Tabernacle organ console. The majority of the drawknobs are made of polished ebony (the Grand Solo knobs are rosewood) with ivory resin faces and brass shanks on actions provided by Harris Precision Products, Whittier, California. The expression shoes are cast brass, manufactured to Schoenstein's specifications. These keyboards, stop actions and expression shoes are standard on all Schoenstein consoles, an indication of the care taken with each instrument.

A view over the top of the console.

The console was shipped to Salt Lake City in August 2000 to be temporarily hooked up to as much of the organ as was playable for use at October conference. When it left San Francisco, several items had not been completed. The drawers had not been installed, nor had the toe studs, expression adjust system and various accessories. A temporary on/off switch had been wired. Following conference, the console was shipped back to San Francisco, completed, and returned to Salt Lake City in February 2001. The Tabernacle Choir's Christmas concerts were held in the Conference Center in December 2000. With the console gone, music was chosen for those concerts that could be accompanied by the orchestra, without organ.

The Bench

Strange as it may seem, the design of the organ bench was heavily influenced by the frequency with which the organ is seen on television. The necessity of clearing scores off the music rack quickly during a live broadcast while keeping the console uncluttered requires placing music on a shelf in the bench. We also needed the bench to be visually as open as possible to facilitate television cameras being able to show the organist's footwork. Finally, we wanted it to have a built-in height-adjustment mechanism, a feature we did not have at the Tabernacle where bench blocks were used. When we mentioned the difficulty of finding a bench that satisfied all three criteria to Lee Gray, he designed a bench for us. His design housed the height-adjusting mechanism in

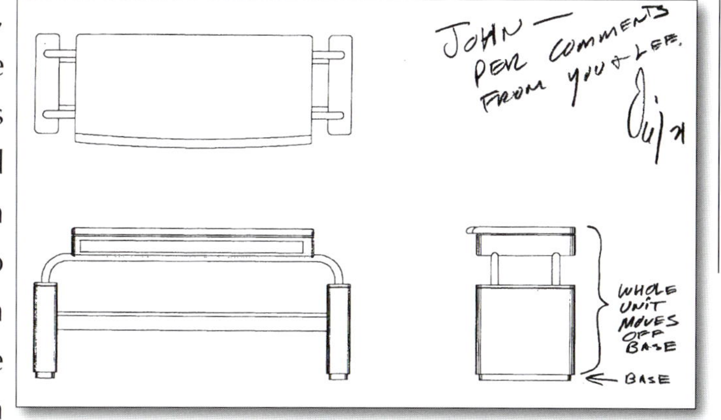

the sides of the bench, rather than under the seat. A thin connecting rod running unseen through the heel rest connected the two sides allowing them to operate simultaneously. A hand crank on the right side of the bench adjusted the seat to eight different heights over a range of nearly two inches.

Following our acceptance of Lee's original concept, one of his associates was assigned to have the mechanism fabricated. He, in turn, contracted with a local machine shop, and the resulting product was shipped to Chuck Primich at Schoenstein. After Chuck created a basic design for the bench's appearance that would incorporate the mechanism (figure 8.6), Fetzers' agreed to complete the bench. Paul Fetzer further refined the design of both the wooden portions and the mechanism. Conference Center Staging and Production Manager, Steven R. Wall, provided critical assistance in this process. Staging and Production machinist Blake Anderson implemented the resulting mechanical modifications, and Fetzers' clad the mechanism in wood to match the console shell. While waiting nearly three years to take delivery of the new bench in the fall of 2003, we used a bench belonging to Schoenstein that had been built by Æolian-Skinner.

Console shown with bench.

The Platform

The need to move the console both horizontally and vertically (from the choir level to the orchestra level) required building a platform on which the console was mounted. The platform, designed and built in-house, was made to be either rolled on casters or "flown" by hooking it to winches permanently installed on the grid overhead. A complete description of the platform's construction and function is given in Appendix 2.

Departures from the Contract

The contract specification, given in Chapter 7, listed nineteen items under the heading "Console." Our initial intention was to include everything in the contract that we could foresee might be useful. The majority of those items were provided as specified. Those not provided require some explanation:

1. *Five-manual and pedal open American-style case with adjustable bench and adjustable music rack all of oak and walnut or other hardwood to suit the auditorium décor.* The changes relative to the appearance of the console have been discussed above.

4. *Console platform with rollers and position lock.* The console platform has likewise been discussed.

9. *Multiplex system with multiple plug points on platform and in rehearsal/ storage area.* An offstage room was originally provided to house the console when it was not wanted on the stage. It was thought that this room could also be used for silent rehearsal. The finished room, however, was too small to be usable. The space was converted into badly needed restrooms for the choir and others working backstage. Due to the removability of the rostrum and choir staging modules, rather than multiple plug points on the platform, a single plug was provided with a long cord allowing console placement virtually anywhere on the rostrum.

11. *Music light in music rack base.* This was initially provided; however, the intensity of the light proved inadequate and the thickness of the base reduced visibility of the nameboard displays. The music light was replaced with a thin brass shelf.

13. *Radio broadcast "Stand By" and "On Air" lights.* As a carryover from the early days of radio broadcasting, these were found to be useful in the Tabernacle, but the Audiovisual Department determined not to use them in the Conference Center.

14. *Clock/timer system similar to that at the Tabernacle.* ("Broadcast Timer"). A clock with "stopwatch" function was initially installed; however, the "Broadcast Timer" was not. Again, this was a decision by the Audiovisual Department. The clock was recently interfaced with the house production clock, thus assuring precise time and eliminating the need to reset the console clock. Access to precise time would not be critical on most organ consoles, but for purposes of live broadcasting it is essential at the Conference Center. Experience in broadcasting from the new facility revealed the wisdom of finally including the Broadcast Timer function on the console. Now referred to as the "Plus/Minus Clock," installation was completed during 2008. During broadcasting, a display on the nameboard to the left of the clock shows a plus or minus figure in increments of five seconds. The display is controlled by production personnel who constantly compare the actual progress of a broadcast with projected running times. Both the conductor and organist have access to a Plus/Minus Clock, and can adjust tempos and add or delete musical material (a verse of a hymn, for example) to bring the broadcast to a timely conclusion.

16. *Temperature monitoring recording system for all divisions, blower and console.* This was felt to be unnecessary and was never installed. The blower room has sophisticated temperature and humidity control, and the organ chamber is likewise a stable temperature-controlled space. "Thermonunciators," Jack Bethards's trademark name for simple liquid thermometers, are installed throughout the organ.

17. *Prepared for intercom stations for auditorium/choir system and organ tuning system.* The Audiovisual Department felt that this need could be solved another way. Presently the technicians use two-way radios when tuning and have cell phones for other communication needs. In addition, landline phones are available both near the console and in the organ chamber.

18. *Prepared for Auditorium system public address speaker in console.* The Audiovisual Department felt that a public address speaker in the console could be problematic for them and it was not installed. When a monitor is needed for production purposes, a temporary external speaker is placed near the organ console.

19. *Prepared for TV monitor.* A decision on how best to accomplish this was not made in time to include it initially. A connector was later installed behind the music rack. This facilitates placing a six-inch LCD monitor on top of the console so it can easily be seen just above the top of the music rack. The TV monitor allows the organist to see the conductor when sight lines do not permit a direct view. The monitor attaches to a base that allows it to be angled to the organist's preference.

Two items listed in the contract specification under the heading "Mechanicals" need explanation:

5. *Prepared for touch-sensitive top manual.* We felt it would be wise to have at least one touch-sensitive keyboard for the sake of eventual use with the MIDI interface. However the keyboard manufacturer (P & S Organ Supply Co., Ltd.) was not prepared to supply a touch-sensitive keyboard. Rather than use keyboards from two different manufacturers, we decided to forego that requirement.

6. *Record/Playback Sequencer prepared for remote control operation.* Given the size of the Conference Center's main auditorium, we felt it would save considerable time walking back and forth between the console and the middle of the room if the playback sequencer could be operated remotely; however this technology was not available at the time.

A peek inside the back of the console.

An additional control that was not part of the contract was added to the Conference Center console by our organ technicians

and the Audiovisual staff. The daily organ recitals at Temple Square are strictly a one-person operation. The organist is responsible for the operation of the public address system, the lighting, the announcements to the audience and, of course, playing the recital. In the Tabernacle in recent years, the organist has been able to access several pre-set lighting effects from the organ console to enhance his performance. We desired that a similar system be made available in the Conference Center. While being depressed, a small button underneath the left key cheek disables Solo divisional pistons 1–8 and allows them to function as preset commands to the computer-controlled lighting system. Piston 1 turns the system on, brings up the house lights and illuminates the stage area. Pistons 2–7 turn down the house lights, spotlight the console and give the organist six different background colors around the organ case, ranging from a soft blue to vibrant magenta. Piston 8, pressed at the recital's conclusion, brings up the house lights and again brightly illuminates the stage area to facilitate picture taking by those in attendance. After about five minutes the lights fade, the system turns itself off, and the regular building illumination is restored.

The finished console is a remarkable piece of craftsmanship that meets all the criteria we set out to achieve. It is handsome to look at and pure pleasure to play.

Installation and Tonal Finishing

In an interview just a few months before the Conference Center opened for the April 2000 general conference, Alan S. Layton, a senior partner of Legacy Constructors[1] and President of Layton Construction Company, Inc., spoke as follows:

> This job has never been about how much money we could make. It's been about using our talents and our means and capability for the building up of the [Church].
>
> . . . We have had plenty of adversity and problems. But in spite of the difficulty, many little things have transpired . . . helping to get the work completed. We started building well before the design had been completed. There were phases of the work that we could not proceed with because we had to wait for information and there were some things that we had to redo because the information was changing.
>
> We need to give a great deal of credit to our subcontractors. They have been heroic. I don't think any of them realized what they were getting into, but they have stuck with the immensity of their commitment and worked as was necessary. . . .
>
> Workmen like a little overtime. . . .In the case of the [Conference Center], the number of hours these men have worked has been almost unbelievable and the sacrifice the families have made has been huge. . . . Yes, the additional money has been appreciated, but the family sacrifices have been far greater. These faithful workers, from the most skilled to the least, have recognized that this job was different; that this building was more about sacrifice of talent and time than it was about a paycheck.[2]

One of the setbacks experienced by the contractors was the result of a tornado that tore through downtown Salt Lake City on August 11, 1999, uprooting trees, damaging buildings, leveling an outdoor exhibition at the nearby convention center and traveling directly across the Conference Center construction site. A construction trailer was lifted off the ground and shifted a couple of feet; toolboxes weighing hundreds of pounds were moved substantial distances. The boom blew off one of the construction cranes and landed atop the roof of the building. Miraculously, only four of the nearly 1,000 workers on site were injured, and damage to the structure was minimal, considering the intensity of the storm.

Although Schoenstein's workmen were not affected by the tornado, they faced their own unique challenges and difficulties. The sentiments expressed by Alan Layton might just as well have been expressed by Jack Bethards, as his firm's experiences mirrored those of the general contractor almost to the letter.

The building's construction schedule was daunting. At the groundbreaking ceremony President Hinckley had voiced his desire that the building be completed in time for the April 2000 conference. He never wavered from that goal. Lee Gray recalls:

> One time Ted [Simmons] went to him and said, "President, could we maybe recognize the fact that the millennium starts in 2001, not 2000?" And the President smiled and said, "Think 2000." Well Ted pressed him a little more and said, "President, could we maybe think October?" Do you know the President's response to that? The President said, "At my age, I don't buy green bananas."[3]

In Schoenstein's December 1997 proposal to build the organ, Jack Bethards laid out an installation schedule as follows:

> The project will be starting 3 to 4 months later than originally anticipated so every element of scheduling is tight. Here is what we believe is realistic:

	Start	Finish
Major Component and Display Installation	1/1/00	4/1/00
This will take 5-6 weeks any time within this period that is convenient for you. (We will try to do all or part of this before the end of 1999, but cannot assure it.)		
Installation—Heavy Work	4/10/00	6/30/00
Requires layout space on stage, etc.		
Installation—Detail Work	7/1/00	8/31/00
Done in organ area.		
Preliminary Finishing	9/1/00	10/1/00
Requires silence during working hours.		
Use for [October] Conference		
Final Finishing	10/10/00	4/1/01
Dedication[4]		

The twelve-month delay between Schoenstein's being selected as the organ's builder and the eventual signing of the contract in January 1999, further exacerbated the scheduling problem. Yet Jack remained optimistic. In a letter to Tom Hanson dated May 6, 1999, Jack reviewed the history of the organ schedule:

> At the conclusion of my initial consulting assignment I suggested that production of the organ would have to start in September of 1997. On December 11, 1997 I set a schedule as part of my proposal to build the organ and at that time mentioned that we were already about three months late in getting started. Schoenstein & Co. was selected as your builder on January 14, 1998 at which time I immediately confirmed the potential order with our various suppliers and reserved time in our schedule. We then began the process of designing the case. We could not begin engineering of the internal components of the organ until the case was decided. This process was not completed until our contract was signed on January 26, 1999. At that point we were 14 months behind my original starting date. I kept the original December 11, 1997 schedule in the contract because I felt that we could still make the schedule inasmuch as we and all of our major suppliers had reserved time to get the work done.
>
> Tom, I still believe we can make the original schedule. However I doubt that there has ever been an organ produced on a tighter timetable. This means that everything must go exactly according to plan or else there will be delays. . . .
>
> . . . I want to assure you, also, that I see no problem in the installation of the case and display pipes from our point of view. Fortunately, our supplier, A.R. Schopp's has such faith in us that they went ahead and ordered all of the metal necessary for this huge pipe front even before the contract was signed.

The initial shipment of front pipes arrived for finishing at New Image Body and Paint on December 13, 1999, with the remainder scheduled to leave Schopp's factory in Ohio during the weeks of January 3, January 17, and February 7, 2000.

Schoenstein's vice-president, Robert (Bob) Rhoads, who, until his retirement, served as the firm's project manager at the Conference Center, arrived in Salt Lake City earlier, on December 12, to check conditions in the auditorium and make final arrangements for the arrival of the installation crew. Heavy construction work was underway throughout the space. Installation of the structural support for the case was continuing. While Bob found some things in order, he did express concern over unevenness of the concrete chamber floor, some potential sound traps in platform modules into which the bottom of the organ chamber area faces, and two doors high on the rear of the organ chamber that had not been shown on any drawings given to Schoenstein. The organ structure, as planned, would have made those doors inaccessible. Bob also questioned whether the ceiling over the chamber had been installed according to acoustical specifications.

Robert Rhoads, Conference Center organ project manager during the façade installation.

2000

With the promise of these issues being resolved, Schoenstein's installation crew arrived on site January 10, 2000, to find a virtual beehive of activity swirling around them. Some eighty subcontractors were employed during the course of the building project, with more than 1,000 workers at the site during peak construction periods. With the April general conference deadline looming, the auditorium was the focus of tremendous activity.

Organ builders are accustomed to installing instruments in finished rooms. The auditorium was far from finished, and conditions could most charitably be described as difficult. The Schoenstein crew arrived to find a pile of dirt and debris near the front of the auditorium and occasional puddles on the bare concrete floor. The only available lighting was from temporary work lights. Heat had not yet been turned on, so the building was cold and damp. There was a smoky haze in the air from welding and other construction activity in progress. The major backstage passageway leading from one side of the building to the other, located directly underneath the organ platform, was constantly clogged with workers and motorized vehicles of various kinds moving through. Frequently, multiple trades were trying to work in the same space. The Schoenstein crew often worked late at night, after other workers had left, in order to have the unhampered access they required. Initially, the choir risers were not in place, so the crew began working from floor level.

Installation and Tonal Finishing

Chests, toeboards and pipe racks were first to be installed. The men encountered occasional problems with structural steel members as they attempted to fit the organ components to the frame. In one case, a toeboard had to be remade. The façade pipes were still being painted at New Image while the installation was underway. Bob Rhoads informed Metro Foti of the order in which the pipes would be installed, so that Metro could paint them in that order and keep a steady supply coming to the Conference Center. During lulls, as they awaited the arrival of finished pipes, the crew began installing the organ's six blowers.

Fetzers' craftsmen attached finished wood panels to the case structure ahead of the large pipes being hoisted into place. In doing so, they started at the top of the case and worked down, rather than working from the bottom up as one might intuitively expect, in order to avoid a dropped tool from damaging finished casework below. Schoenstein's crew likewise worked with extreme care maneuvering the huge pipes into place to avoid collisions with the finished casework. Bob Rhoads obtained assistance from ironworkers still employed at the site, whose expertise in rigging and hoisting was of tremendous value.

Conditions in the auditorium steadily improved as conference weekend fast approached, and the room began to take on a finished appearance. The façade installation was finally completed in time. A Fetzers' employee inscribed on the inside of the organ case: "Last panels of organ installed 3/28/2000, 5:30 pm, EMH, Let's go home." Conference would convene four days later.

As the façade installation neared completion, Jack Bethards, normally upbeat and optimistic, wrote to Tom Hanson:

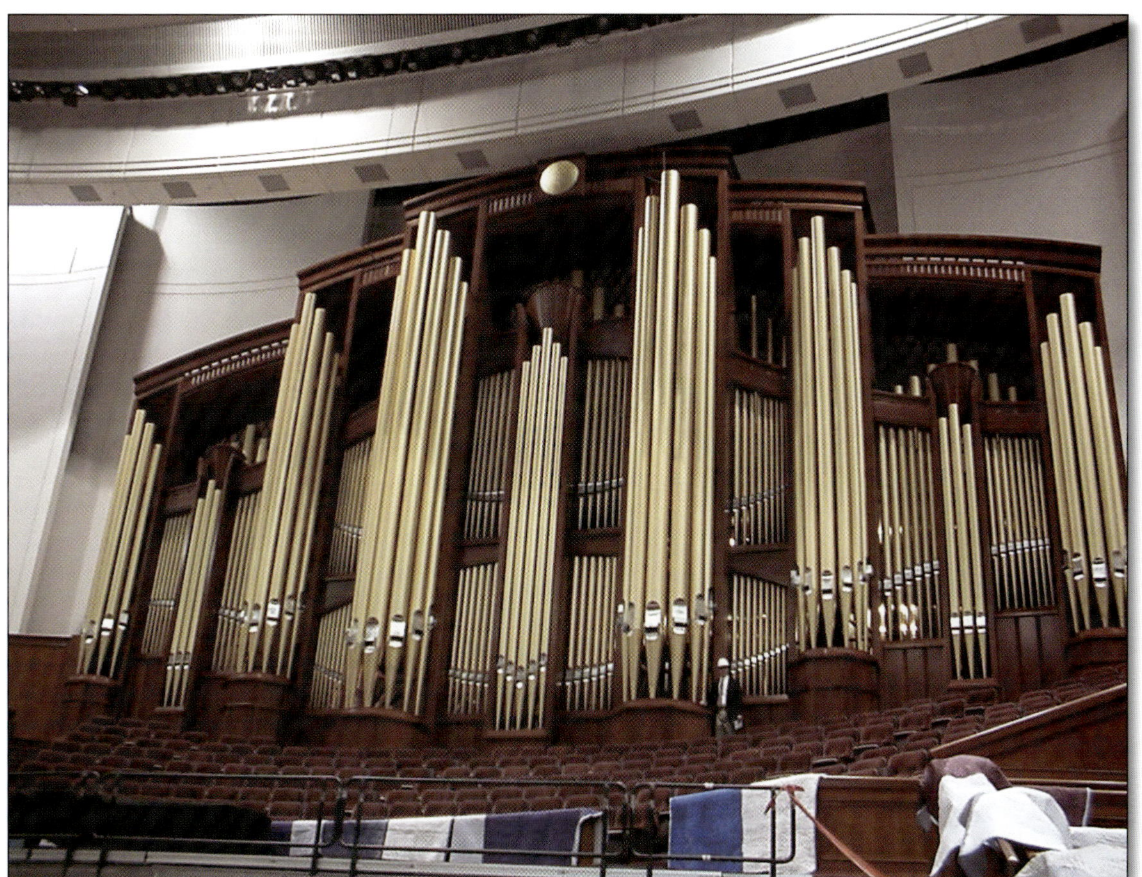

The façade installation was vastly more difficult than we had expected due to the amount of other work going on in the building. We expected some of these problems, but the reality was far worse than even our most bleak estimates. I lost both a lot of employee goodwill and money in the process. This is not to minimize the wonderful cooperation we've received from many people there. . .it's just one of those things, I guess, on a major, tight-deadline construction project. To put it simply, we can't afford to go through the same experience with the remaining divisions.[5]

The contractors managed to bring the project to a state of completion such that they were able to obtain a permit to occupy enough of the building to hold conference April 1–2. An organ was needed to provide music for the services. We considered two options. The first was to use the Tabernacle organ. As we envisioned it, the organ sound would be transmitted from the Tabernacle to the Conference Center sound system where it would be mixed with the live sound of the choir. The organist in the Tabernacle would follow the conductor by means of a closed circuit television monitor and would hear by wearing headphones. While to us that seemed like the simplest solution, the Audiovisual Department technicians, already concerned about a very complex and relatively untested sound system, preferred not to add this to their list of worries.

Preparing for April 2000 general conference with the Rodgers organ (hard hats required). Pictured (left to right) are David Bagley, Mark Anderson, Larry Hawkins and John Longhurst. Clay Christiansen is seated at the console.

Our second option was to bring in an electronic organ, just for that weekend. At our request, Heritage Church Organ Company, the local Rodgers Organ dealer, installed a three-manual Model 960D organ. Heritage's technicians had supplied instruments for the Tabernacle Choir on tour and had a good concept of what would be needed. David Bagley, one of the installers, later recalled:

> When we walked into the room I was talking with the factory about what we might need for audio, and I remember saying to Sandy McFerran, "whatever I just told you double it." She was shocked as I tried to convey to her the magnitude of the room. . . .
>
> I also remember that when the organ played, there was so much air moving from the subwoofers that several members of the choir thought the large pipes in front were playing.[6]

David explained that the installation required seventy-two speaker cabinets positioned on the catwalks of the organ case, powered by eight Rodgers 800-watt amplifiers plus an additional Walker amplifier for the Festival Trumpet.

The conference opened on Saturday, April 1. In his opening address to the congregation President Hinckley remarked:

> My dearly beloved brethren and sisters, what a magnificent sight you are, this vast congregation of Latter-day Saints gathered together in this new and wonderful hall.
>
> The organ is not completed, and there are various construction details yet to be attended to. But fortunately the work is far enough along that we are able to use it for this conference. A year or so ago in speaking concerning it, I expressed the opinion that we may not be able to fill it initially. It seats three and a half times the capacity of the

MAGNUM OPUS

Tabernacle. But already we are in trouble. People are filling all of the seats.

During the four general sessions and the priesthood session, we will be able to accommodate about 100,000. We had requests for 370,000 tickets. The Tabernacle and Assembly Hall will serve as overflow. But with all of this, many, very many, will be disappointed. We apologize. We ask for your forgiveness. We are powerless to do anything about it. So many wanted to attend this first conference in the new hall.[7]

The Rodgers organ performed competently, and the newly completed pipe façade added visual luster to its sound.

Once the façade was complete, Jack Bethards could see that some revision of the schedule was inevitable. In his March 15, 2000 letter to Tom Hanson he listed the rearranged shipping dates:

	Delivered
Blower room and Façade	Delivered
Swell (ready now—completed 11/99) and Solo	4/20/00
Choir and Orchestral	6/19/00
Great, Pedal and Console	8/22/00

The original goal had been to have the entire organ installed for October 2000 general conference in order to evaluate it with the room full before the final tonal finishing was begun. Jack explained:

It is likely that we will not meet our original objective of having the entire organ in good enough shape to play for the October conference. We should have enough ready to carry out the acoustical tests which are the main purpose for using the organ in October. The big question in all of this is how efficiently installation can proceed at the job site. We will know far more a couple of weeks after delivery of the Swell and Solo.[8]

As soon as the April general conference was finished, Jack wrote to Tom Hanson detailing a couple dozen items that needed attention prior to and during the next phase of the installation process. These included installing appropriate pick points in the chamber ceiling to facilitate hoisting and a ledger that would allow access to the doors that were not shown on plans provided to Schoenstein.

[The ledger would provide a place] on which to set the organ components and pipe platforms that span the last three feet to the back wall. The ledger must run the entire length of the back wall at levels to be specified in a drawing to be forwarded early next week. This will also improve the requested clear passageway to the transformer room by eliminating the posts we would require to the floor."[9]

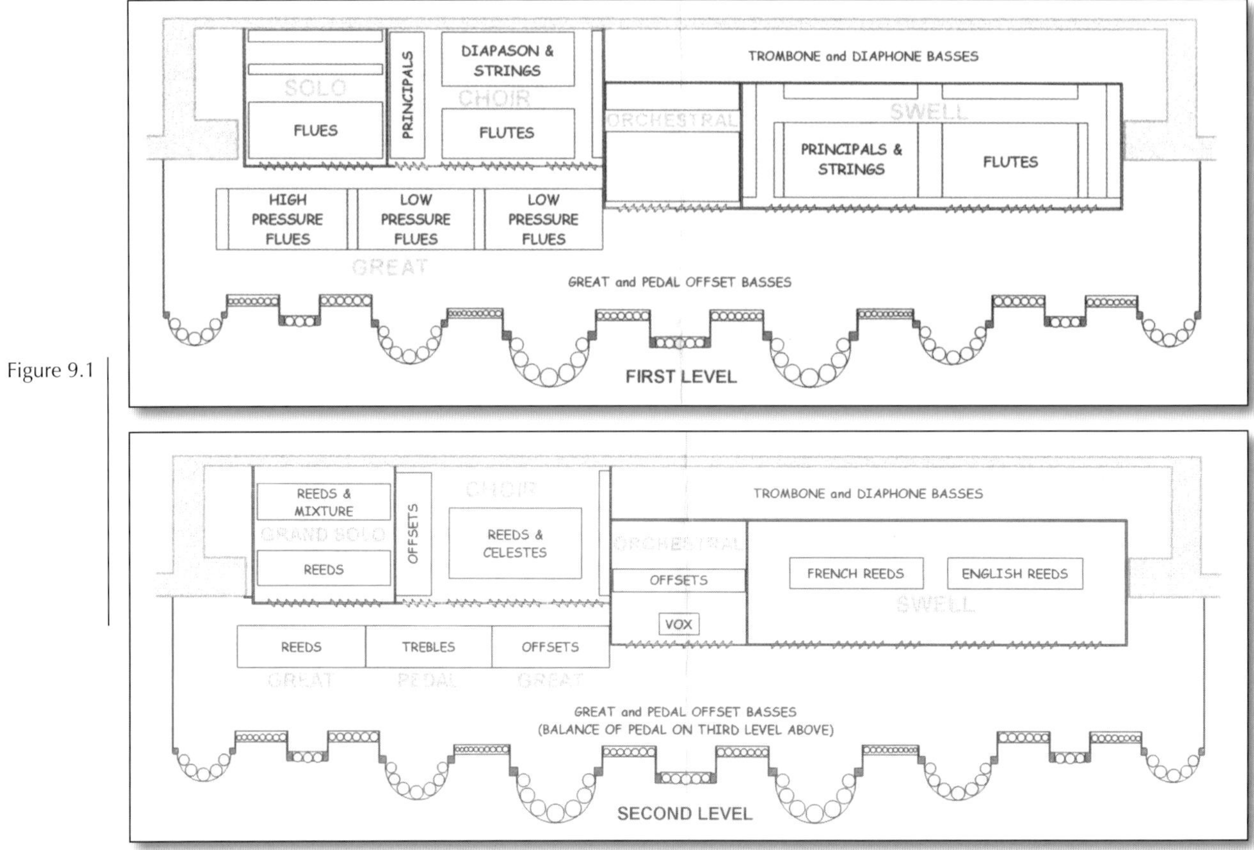

Figure 9.1

The Schoenstein crew returned in May to begin installing the Swell and Solo. With the façade already in place, their chief access for moving items into the organ space was through double doors that had been provided at the side of the chamber, stage right.[10] Outside the doors, a steel deck was built, onto which a forklift could place components prior to their being moved into the chamber proper. Access to the chamber determined, in large part, the order in which the organ was installed. The Swell, located at the far end of the space, stage left, was installed first, since it would not obstruct access to the rest of the space (see figure 9.1). The Solo was installed next. Located upstage of the double doors, it also would not block future access. The Great had to be installed last, as it stood immediately in front of the access doors.

Working conditions were markedly better than they had been during installation of the façade, yet there was still considerable activity to compete with, as other workers tried to complete various jobs in the yet unfinished building.   By this time, Bob Rhoads had retired from full time work with Schoenstein, though he continued to main-

Pipes and regulators awaiting installation.

tain a keen interest in the Conference Center job and returned occasionally at Jack Bethards's invitation.   Louis Patterson was asked to take over as project manager, and he saw the project through to completion.[11]   Throughout the project, Schoenstein's crews worked long hours, interfaced cooperatively with others, and took great care with every detail of their work.   Near the end of that May visit, I wrote to Jack Bethards,

> Jack, I must comment on the competence and professionalism of your crew. They are doing a beautiful job and have earned the respect and admiration of everyone involved. Several people have commented to me that they had no idea what was involved in the installation of the organ. We're all fascinated with the various phases of the work and just hope that our eagerness to observe the progress in no way impedes your men. If we get in the way, please tell us.[12]

Conference Center organ project manager Louis Patterson, seated at the console of the Schoenstein organ at First-Plymouth Congregational Church, Lincoln, Nebraska.

Following that first conference, the Church began scheduling other events in the Conference Center, somewhat cautiously at first, then with increasing frequency. These events were given priority over the need to finish the organ. Any event in that space requires an unexpected amount of time for stage setup, audio and lighting preparation, floral decoration, rehearsals, cleaning, the event itself, and finally the takedown afterward. As the organ installation progressed, it became increasingly challenging to find periods of time when Schoenstein's crews could work productively without interference. Tours were begun in order to satisfy intense public interest in seeing the new building. While the tours were not problematic during installation, during tonal finishing guides were asked to modify their normal route in an attempt to keep the auditorium quiet. Occasionally, guides were not informed of the change and unknowingly interrupted the painstaking tonal finishing process.

The first event following April general conference was a program presented June 23 to celebrate President Hinckley's ninetieth birthday. With the Orchestra at Temple Square participating, the organ's role in this performance was less exposed than it had been for general conference. Since the Rodgers organ was removed immediately following April general conference, the audio technicians agreed to pipe in the sound of the Tabernacle organ. I happened to be at the console and was most comfortable performing in my shirtsleeves, the only person in the dimly lit Tabernacle. The technology worked flawlessly.

In a July 17, 2000 letter to Tom Hanson, Jack Bethards summarized the current state of affairs:

> Installation of the blower room and façade are essentially complete. The Swell and Solo are complete with the exception of planting the smaller pipes. Choir and Orchestral are nearly finished in our erecting room and will be ready for shipping by July 28th or possibly the 26th. We will begin installation of these on the 31st. This is about 5 weeks later than the plan sent to you on March 15th. There are myriad reasons for this, but the main point, as stated before, is that the total time available for building the organ was reduced considerably because we couldn't get started until the façade design was settled. With such a tight schedule, every glitch has added delay. Our normal delivery time allows for such things. Here, we have no cushion at all.
>
> Some of the Pedal has been installed and more will be done in connection with the enclosed divisions; however, it will not be possible to complete the rest of the Pedal and the Great in time for the October conference. Nearly everything for these divisions is made; however, we need to erect them in our shop before we can ship.
>
> Our main concern for the October conference is having the console ready so that the divisions that are installed can be played. As you may know, Fetzers' had planned to build the console case for us so that it would match the other platform furnishings perfectly. Unfortunately, they were not able to follow through so we have been scrambling to get the job done locally. The console components are ready, but the case must be built and finished before we can install them in it. We have

been working out all sorts of changes to our normal console assembly routine and think we will make the deadline, but it's going to be close!

I have the Salt Lake crew and our crew here at the factory on maximum overtime. Our people have all agreed to give up their annual vacation so that the usual interruption in August will not occur. Every effort is being placed toward your job.

I have talked to John [Longhurst] about our expectations for the October conference. It is our hope that enough of the organ will be playing that we can accomplish our main objective of testing the acoustics with the building when full. There is no chance that the organ will be complete enough to give a full picture, but we hope to have enough going to set the bearings for the final finishing. John and I have talked about plans for the conference and he is getting prepared to be flexible on music selection depending on just how much of the organ is usable.

I want to emphasize that we have been receiving wonderful cooperation from all of your people. Everyone has gone the extra mile to be helpful to us. Our crew members have said many times how much they appreciate the support.

Tom, we are doing everything we can to make the October conference test of the organ successful. Once we are over that hurdle, things should progress smoothly to ultimate completion.

Richard Elliott inspects a Diaphone resonator. (Top)

Hoisting begins. Note windline stubs coming from blower room.

Jim Cullen monitors the hoisting process.

Note the arm of the crane and the chain fall used to facilitate the hoisting.

Richard Elliott admires the finished result.

The Diaphone vibrator boxes and lower portions of mitered resonators.

On their next visit, the crew undertook the installation of the eight largest diaphone pipes against the back wall of the chamber, before the growing organ structure further impeded access. These massive and extremely heavy pipes were built by the W. W. Kimball Company in 1924 for the organ in the Forum Theatre in Los Angeles, Kimball's Opus 6644.[13] Their resonators are made of two-inch-thick solid lumber. The opening at the top of the largest pipe (CCCC) is approximately twenty-four inches wide. Each pipe was constructed in three sections: the vibrator (which contains the action and valve portion that creates the sound), and two sections of resonator, which are bolted together after being hoisted into place.

High above the chamber floor, the platform on which the diaphone pipes stand was built in sections, a new section being constructed to accommodate each pipe before it was raised. On-site foreman, Chris Hansford, assisted by Joe Lambarena and Jim Cullen, constructed a hoist of 4 x 4 lumber in the manner of a jib crane, and this, combined with two chain falls, was used to lift the sections of each pipe into place. About a day's work was required to place and secure each of the eight huge pipes.

The diaphone chests were rebuilt by Ridges Pipe Organ Co. in Provo, Utah, and the pipes themselves were rebuilt by M. L. Bigelow & Co., of American Fork, Utah.[14]

At this same time, discussions were taking place about how best to protect the organ in case of fire. The architects assumed that installing sprinklers throughout the chamber would provide the best solution. Lead organ technician Robert Poll quickly stepped into that discussion with a memo to project architect Kerry Nielsen dated July 26, 2000.

> We would rather take the relatively low risk of a fire causing substantial damage in the organ than the much higher risk of almost complete destruction of the entire organ by water aimed at putting out a potentially small fire, or worse yet, sprinklers accidentally discharging without a fire which would cause substantial damage or quite possibly even destroy all or most of the organ's wood and leather components.

Consequently, a rather ingenious multi-pronged dry-alarm system was designed and installed through a collaborative effort. Heat and smoke detectors were located behind the case on the chamber's ceiling to sense a problem in the unenclosed areas of the instrument. In case of a fire, these sensors would activate an alarm and notify Church Security. Heat sensitive wire was run throughout the enclosed portions of the organ. The wire, rated at 155° Fahrenheit, was divided into four zones and was connected to a control panel at the entrance to the stairway leading to the organ chamber. Should excessive heat be detected, an alarm would be activated and Security notified. The control panel would identify the affected zone and display, in feet, where, along the length of the wire, heat was detected. Security would notify the fire department. Fire extinguishers were placed at the entrance as well as in the organ chamber to aid first responders, whether they be the organ technicians or Security officers, in putting down the fire. Only in the event a fire should remain unchecked or grow too fast to allow it to be effectively controlled, would sprinklers above the organ and choir area be charged and activated.

Left:
The boots and lower portions of the mitered resonators of the four 64-foot Trombone pipes.

Right:
Richard Elliott with sections of the 64-foot Trombone resonators.

In August 2000, following installation of the Choir and Orchestral framing, walls and chests, the four pipes comprising the 64-foot Trombone extension were placed adjacent to and stage right of the diaphones. Like the diaphones, these huge pipes were built in three parts: the boot (containing the brass reed and shallot that produce the sound), and the resonator, in two sections. A portion of the rear wall of the Orchestral division was removed to facilitate the installation. The boot and lower resonator sections were passed through the Orchestral enclosure to the back wall of the chamber. The upper, larger section of the resonator was hoisted up and over the top of the Orchestral enclosure with the same crane used for the diaphones.

More than a month in advance of October general conference, discussions were underway in an attempt to coordinate schedules leading up to the event, so that all involved could accomplish necessary work. The finished building was to be dedicated during the upcoming conference, and many were scrambling to complete their work in time. The last minute tuning of the organ posed a problem for the audio technicians who needed a quiet room in order to balance and refine the elaborate sound system. The seemingly interminable vacuuming of thousands of yards of carpet and upholstery along with technicians focusing hundreds of lighting instruments on the catwalks high above the auditorium made tuning challenging. With patience

The congregation joins the Mormon Tabernacle Choir in singing a hymn during general conference.

and cooperation from all parties, essential preparations were finally completed.

On October 8, 2000, during the Sunday morning session of the conference, ninety-year-old President Gordon B. Hinckley stood at the pulpit to address the capacity crowd in the Conference Center and millions more participating via the media. A few excerpts from his remarks and dedicatory prayer follow:

Before coming into the building this morning, we sealed the cover stone of the cornerstone of . . . this great new structure. That marks the completion of this building.

We preserve the symbolism of the cornerstone in remembrance of the Son of God, upon whose life and mission this Church is established. He and He alone, is the chief cornerstone. . . .

I am so grateful that this building is now complete. We occupied it for our April conference and on one other occasion last June. It was not entirely finished then. It is now declared complete with a permanent occupancy permit.

Today we shall dedicate it as a house in which to worship God the Eternal Father and His Only Begotten Son, the Lord Jesus Christ. . . .

We will also dedicate it as a house in which artistic performances of a dignified nature will be presented. . . .

This structure has been built of the finest materials by the ablest of craftsmen. We are indebted to all who have contributed to make of this a magnificent center for conferences of the Church and other purposes. . . .

I am so grateful that we have it. I am so grateful that it is completed. There is a little work of tuning up the organ, which will go on for some time. . . .

Now . . . if you will bow your heads and close your eyes, we will join in a prayer of dedication.

O God, our Eternal Father, with thankful hearts we approach Thee in prayer on this historic Sabbath when we dedicate this magnificent Conference Center. . . .

We thank Thee for the very many dedicated and highly skilled men and women who have worked long and hard to bring it to completion. May they have a sense of pride in their accomplishment. . . .

We dedicate it from the footings on which it rests to the top of its tower. We dedicate this magnificent hall, unique in its design and size, constructed to house the thousands who through the years will gather here to worship Thee and to be entertained in a wholesome and wonderful way. . . .

Though the earth tremble, may this magnificent edifice stand solid and safe under Thy watchful care. . . .

We dedicate the great organ, the beautiful halls and other rooms, the parking area, and all other features and facilities pertaining to this structure. . . .

May it give expression to the declaration of Thy people that "if there is anything virtuous, lovely, or of good report or praiseworthy, we seek after these things." . . .

Accept of our gratitude. . . .

Wilt Thou smile with favor upon us, we pray. . . .[15]

Jack Bethards, Bob Rhoads and Steuart Goodwin were all present during the conference, listening from all parts of the room, evaluating balances and timbres among the various stops of the organ and observing as it was used to accompany choral and congregational singing. The Swell and Solo divisions were installed and usable, along with a portion of the Choir. The borrowed stops from those divisions were available in the Pedal, plus a minimal number of independent Pedal stops. Virtually no tonal finishing had been done on the pipes. Steuart Goodwin was on site for two weeks prior to conference with his co-worker Wendell Ballantyne, to begin the regulation process. Except for that and for tuning, we were using pipes essentially as they came from Schoenstein's voicing room. It was quite surprising how well we got along with what at that time was perhaps half the organ. We used the three available divisions separately, and the Great as a coupling manual. What was even more amazing was the splendid effect the unregulated, unfinished organ had in the room. All were convinced that the organ was headed in the right direction and would ultimately be successful! A few days following the conference experience, Jack Bethards wrote to Tom Hanson:

Reflecting back after our return from Conference we can only conclude that the Conference Center in all regards is nothing short of a miracle! Something special was at work with the organ case as well. A case which is the product of so many different designers could have been a disaster. What came about, however, is a case which is very likely to be considered one of the greatest cases built since the turn of the 20th century. It looks wonderful in the hall and even better on television.[16]

Jack continued by suggesting that the case could be even more dramatic if the "boat bottoms" and details in the upper portion of the towers were highlighted with "some form of very gentle and subtle theatrical lighting." Our imaginative lighting technicians took that as a challenge and eventually created effective illumination by reflecting light from above off reflective surfaces installed within the organ case.

Temperature stability is a constant concern with regard to pipe organs, and in a building the size of the Conference Center it is hardly surprising that complete stability was not achieved immediately. As a follow-up to conditions at conference, Jack wrote to those involved with maintaining control over temperature and humidity:

> First, let me say how much all of us at Schoenstein appreciate the special care and attention you have given to the temperature and humidity requirements for the organ. With everything else you've had to worry about in the process of getting the building on-line, we are especially grateful of the intense effort placed against our relatively small part of the whole picture. . . .
>
> From our experience at conference, it seems that the organ pipe chambers maintain a pretty constant temperature equivalent to that in the auditorium. There was a big shift in temperature when the full HVAC system was put on-line just before the conference but otherwise things seem to be pretty steady. Our biggest tuning problem came from the wild changes in the blower room temperature. Obviously when very cold or very hot air is being pushed through the pipes it can change tuning drastically. The plan that I saw for monitoring and controlling temperature in the blower room looked good.[17]

Stability of ambient temperature and humidity, however, did not happen immediately.

Installation and tonal work continued during the ensuing months with short visits by Schoenstein's installers and two tonal finishing periods during October and December. While awaiting the August 2000 delivery and February 2001 re-delivery of the console, a single-manual keyboard was brought in to facilitate the testing of chests and initial tuning and regulation of pipes.

When the time arrived for a large number of Great and Choir pipes to be "planted" on their windchests, several volunteers were recruited to assist. The added manpower sped up the process, allowed Schoenstein's men to continue working on other facets of the job, and gave those involved satisfaction in having physically participated in the organ's installation. In addition to the Tabernacle organists and some of their children, the temporary workers included former and then current Tabernacle Choir conductors Jerold Ottley and Craig Jessop, along with Tabernacle Organist Emeritus Robert Cundick with some of his grandchildren and a few of their friends. As the work progressed over a two- or three-day period, all had an opportunity to work at the various tasks: uncrating, hoisting, carrying and planting. It was interesting to see how quickly even the younger workers learned the process, placing even the more complicated mixture pipes in the correct holes without error.

2001

The next issue to be resolved concerned the stability of the organ's structure during a potential seismic event. On July 17, 2001, Jack Bethards wrote to Tom Hanson as follows:

> Robert Poll and Harvey Wright [construction manager for Legacy Constructors] asked us to review the structural integrity of the organ installation. We have been doing so, paying particular attention to their concerns, but have waited until now to wrap up our analysis so that we could include all of the final adjustments to the set-up that we have been carrying out at the job site.
>
> It is our obligation to provide the Church with an organ structure built to our normal design standards which, in turn, are equal to or above the normal design standards of the organ industry. Our initial design fulfilled this requirement, but during the process of installation we made on-site changes which shifted some of the loads, particularly to the "roof" of the instrument. Therefore, we undertook the above mentioned design review completely independent of the original plans. In other words, a separate member of our design team reviewed the as-built structure of the organ. A preliminary summary of this study is attached. Please note that the façade and its steel structure are not included as they were furnished by others and that the internal structure (chest assemblies, bearers and legs) are not included because they met our standards and were not changed on-site.

All of us involved in the original design, as well as the installation, were pleased to see that the original structure, for the most part, is well above normal design tolerances. There are a few areas, however, which are adequate, but marginal. It is our practice to "over-engineer" and therefore we are going to provide additional bracing, etc. as indicated in the report.

This additional engineering work and the construction work, materials and labor necessary to add bracing to the instrument is included within the price of the organ.

We are submitting this for your review for two purposes. First, we welcome any suggestions which would further improve our approach prior to finalizing our plans. Second, if you wish to have additional bracing over and above that which is necessary to assure that the organ is up to our normal standards, it would be most efficient to incorporate such changes now. We will be glad to incorporate these into our work, but they will be at additional cost.

We are hoping that you could direct the appropriate persons to meet with Louis Patterson for at least a quick review while he is there this week. The objective is to complete, as much as possible, the manufacturing work on the additional bracing right away so that it can be installed on our next visit.

Tom Roberts, Schoenstein & Co. technician.

In the letter's final paragraph, Jack states that "the final details of the installation are nearly complete and that the tonal finishing is going extremely well." He closed by reminding Tom of the difficulty of finding quiet time in the building to do tonal work, a condition for which there was seemingly no remedy.

Tom Roberts, who at that time was a Schoenstein employee, carried out the structural analysis to which Jack referred. As a result of his very thorough study, Tom listed eight modifications to the existing structure which he identified as "required." He "recommended" an additional ten items be done. Schoenstein carried out all eighteen of those modifications. At the urging of Robert Poll, architect Kerry Nielsen asked Steven Judd from the Salt Lake City office of ABS Consulting to conduct an additional third-party review. "Mr. Judd recommended a few additional steps, including blocking between the organ chamber walls and the organ structure, and additional bracing and/or fastening plates along the front and rear of the organ structure. Steve

Judd also conducted the final inspection and accepted all the work."[18]

Work continued slowly through the remainder of 2001 with interruptions for October general conference, Christmas and other events sprinkled throughout the Conference Center's calendar. By the end of the year, the physical installation process was nearly finished. Steuart Goodwin made five trips to Salt Lake City during 2001 to do tonal work, mostly with Wendell Ballantyne, but also working with Jack Bethards and Frederick Lake, Schoenstein's head voicer.

2002

It was clear that 2002 would be just as difficult as 2001 had been. Salt Lake City was host for the 2002 Olympic Winter Games, and the Church scheduled cultural events for Olympics visitors in both the Tabernacle and Conference Center. General conferences in April and October plus smaller regional conferences scattered throughout the year, in addition to a Pioneer Day concert (a traditional July event commemorating the arrival of the Mormon settlers in the Salt Lake Valley) and the usual Christmas events, made scheduling for extended work on the organ extremely difficult. The building's management wondered whether Schoenstein's crew might even consider working through the night in order to have the quiet time they could not get otherwise. At the end of January 2002, ten months after Schoenstein's original completion date, Jack Bethards summarized the situation:

> We need to do three things to wrap the job up. First, there are some physical installation details which must be completed. Second, we must complete the structural strengthening work. Third, we have the tonal changes and finishing to do. We estimate two to three weeks of general installation work, two weeks of structural work, and three to four weeks of tone work. Everything but the tone work can be accomplished during normal Conference Center operational days, but we really need complete quiet for tonal work. We've been getting along ok with tonal work so far, but to do the final polishing, pulling everything together nicely, we need more ideal conditions.
>
> I've talked with our people and everybody here is willing to work two shifts starting very early in the morning and ending say at 10:30–11:00 at night, but the overnight shift is really impossible for us. I know that it wouldn't agree with my constitution and those of my crew members who have done it in the past say that they simply won't do it again.[19]

By this time, Schoenstein's crews were also heavily involved in the installation and finishing of other new instruments in Tennessee, Texas and Maryland, which made coordination with the Conference Center schedule even more difficult. Steuart and Jack came a few days before April general conference to "tidy up" the organ for that event, and Steuart and Wendell were able to work between April 24 and May 6. With cooperation from Conference Center management and other Church departments, particularly Audiovisual and Hosting (who were responsible for public tours), a schedule was worked out that allowed Schoenstein four additional periods of approximately a week to ten days each during May, August and September. The crews soon learned that if they sneaked in on Sunday, when the building was closed, they could work undisturbed by others.

In a mid-July letter, Jack posed two questions as he anticipated a complete tuning of the organ prior to the coming October conference. First was the matter of standard pitch for the organ. With the instrument being used frequently with the Orchestra at Temple Square, Jack wondered whether we might want it tuned at A=442, which many orchestras prefer, or the more traditional A=440. The second question involved the ongoing matter of temperature in the auditorium:

> We must know what temperature standard is to be established for the long-term at the Conference Center. You'll remember that we tuned the whole organ before the first conference at what we thought was going to be the correct temperature. Just a day or so before the conference, without any warning, the temperature was lowered so the organ has never been at the correct pitch. Re-pitching an organ of this size is a monumental task and should not be done unless absolutely necessary. It upsets regulation, especially in the reeds. I believe that it would be a good idea to get, in writing, a statement from the mechanical engineering department of the Church as to what temperature standards they plan to maintain. It's most likely that the present level is what we can expect in the future, but we certainly don't want any surprises in case there are some changes in the works. It's especially important to know if there are any cyclical changes in temperature planned. For example, if the hall is cooled down for major programs, we need to know when this happens as that will affect the choice of times to do touch-up tuning prior to events. Also, of course, we need to know what temperature to ask for during tuning sessions if temperature is to be different at performances.
>
> I'd like to have this information in early September. . . . I don't mean to make a federal case out of this, but it is terribly important. This organ has proven to be extremely stable in tuning and if we can establish

the pitch perfectly this time around, the organ should hold well for a long time without any more major tuning.[20]

After discussion with the conductors of the Choir and Orchestra, the decision was made to tune the organ at A=440. Technician Robert Poll immediately began to follow through on the temperature questions. I reported that information to Jack in an August 7 reply.

Following a ten-day period of tonal finishing in August, Jack wrote to Conference Center managers expressing appreciation for all that the crew had been able to accomplish, taking time to explain why silence was necessary for tonal work:

> Due to your great cooperation and that of all your people, we had a very productive session of tonal regulation. Thank you very much!
>
> When we were working, it occurred to me that people working in the Center must be wondering why we are so concerned about having absolute quiet when it looks as though we are not doing anything at all! Throughout the process there are long periods when we are doing no listening and, therefore, seem to have no need for a quiet background. These are times when we are working on the pipes. Sometimes we can fix a pipe in a few seconds. Sometimes one pipe may take ten or fifteen minutes to correct or even longer. There is no way to know in advance exactly how long each operation will take. Last week, for example, we had an unusually large amount of very difficult pipes and most of our time was spent working rather than listening.
>
> The reason that we need silence *throughout* [italics added] our work period each day is that we need to be able to listen to the pipe immediately after we attempt to correct it. On jobs where we haven't arranged for complete silence, it never seems to fail that the very moment we need to listen is the moment some other activity is going on. The kind of listening we are doing at this point in the job is critical.[21]

In two additional letters written that same day, Jack asked Robert Poll to help track down an unpleasant odor in the blower room that seemed to be worsening over time and asked Robert and me to assist in getting answers to continuing temperature fluctuations. During his last visit, he had noticed a consistent pattern of a two degree rise in temperature from early morning to evening, both in the chamber and at the console:

Obviously, this has many implications for the continuing care of the organ. For example, we must be wary of doing early morning touch-ups before conference or broadcast if the temperature is low. It is most critical, however, for our upcoming tonal finishing work where we are establishing the pitch of the reeds. Therefore, we need to get this figured out in the next week. We can work with whatever temperature picture we are given, but we need to know for sure whether this pattern is a continuing one and where we should peg the pitch.[22]

Toward the close of 2002, Jack asked the organists to prepare a "punch list" of items still needing attention. He had his own list, but wanted to be certain that nothing was overlooked. Our list, by this time, was relatively short:

1. Complete the regulation of unfinished voices (Symphonic Flute, English Horn, Tierce Mixture, others?)

2. Experiment with loudening Choir principals. We feel quite certain that we will want to proceed with this work.

3. Pedal 16s and 32s need more work to achieve optimal volume and evenness throughout their compass.

4. Evaluate French Horn, Orchestral Oboe, and Clarinet to see what voicing options might be available with existing pipes. The French Horn is quite full in the tenor octave, but becomes noticeably quieter and thinner as it ascends. Can the Orchestral Oboe and Clarinet take any loudening?

5. We may wish to soften the bottom octave of the Swell Contra Fagott. Also, we want to look carefully at the Choir flute stops to be sure that each is contributing optimally to the cornet.

6. There are a few isolated pipes in ranks already finished that need a bit more work to correct problems of speech or loudness.

7. Stabilize Swell wind.

8. Stabilize Tibia wind. This will make available several solo color possibilities in the *mp* to *f* dynamic range. If a normal tremulant could be available for use with the Tibias, it would make them even more useful for solo lines.

9. Minor adjustments of tremulants for speed and depth.

10. The expression shades are slow to respond. Can they be made to move more quickly?

In subsequent visits, the requested tonal work was done. The Tibia Tremulant was removed. The entire Orchestral division would now be affected by the regular Tremulant and Variable Tremulant. Items 7 and 10 turned out to be interrelated. The huge array of swell shades was rewired to reduce the time needed to fully open and close, and the wind to their motors was rerouted so that their operation would not upset the wind to the Swell chests.

We also called Jack's attention to some "bugs" in the combination action and in the MIDI recorder. Engineers from Peterson Electro-Musical Products, Inc. were quick to respond to those concerns. Peterson personnel made several modifications to the original systems over time, some at the factory in Alsip, Illinois, and some during trips to Salt Lake City.

2003

As 2003 dawned, the first order of business was to arrange time for Schoenstein crews to have access for additional mechanical and tonal work. A week for mechanical work was arranged for February 10–15, followed by tonal work from February 16 through March 2.

Tonal work included a careful evaluation of the Orchestral Wurlitzer reeds. After meticulous regulation, we still felt that the Clarinet needed to be louder. Several pipes from the Tabernacle organ's Corno di Bassetto were brought to the Conference Center for comparison with the Wurlitzer pipes. Based on that experiment it was decided to replace the Wurlitzer rank with a new Clarinet, to be built by Schopp's. Jack ordered several samples to try in the room, including one with a flared bell, which was felt to be rather brash. The new rank chosen was one closely related to a Clarinet built by E. M. Skinner.

The Salt Lake City chapter of the American Guild of Organists was to host the 2003 convention of Regions VIII and IX of that organization in June. One of the convention events was to be a gala inaugural concert on June 19 to which the public would be invited, to mark the completion of the organ and formally introduce it to the community. Also, during the course of the convention, four of Temple Square's daily organ recitals would be performed at the Conference Center by staff organists, and Jack Bethards was scheduled to present a lecture/demonstration featuring the new instrument. With more than 600 attendees representing churches and educational institutions from the entire western United States and some coming from other areas of the country, Canada, and England as well, Jack Bethards's goal was to have the organ completely finished for the convention.

By April, Louis Patterson had prepared a final work list of small items that needed attention. The list included such things as: checking tremulant adjustments; tracking down rattles; making a few adjustments to pipe racking; making the Choir Cromorne play in the Orchestral (in place of the removed Tibia Tremulant drawknob); installing new drawknobs for the Stentor Diapason (newly-extended from the Pedal Open Wood); fixing wind leaks; rewiring the Grand Solo expression shades; and re-winding the Tibia. The final item on the list was to pack and ship Schoenstein's tools and supplies back to San Francisco.

Panorama of the blower room.

One item on Louis's list was to check blower "cycling" on the high-pressure winding. As Robert Poll explains, "The original installation took some of the wind from blower #5 and ran it through blower #4 to step it up from 15" to 25". This created some turbulence and pulsing which, among other things, made the door on blower #5 intake flap and bang in rhythm."[23] After considering the options, the decision was made to replace blower #4 with a larger two-stage blower to provide the 25" wind. The new blower did not arrive until mid-August, and Louis returned to Salt Lake City to install it.

Louis devised a way to solve another perplexing problem. Jack explained it this way:

> When everything was said and done, we found we had no 16' C pipe for the 32' [Pedal] Diapason stop. After everything was installed and ready for final tuning and regulating, we found that the pipes from 16' C up were cut one pipe too short, and most of them were in the display and could not be changed. This was a pretty serious problem, because how do you fit a great big 16' Diapason into an organ [that is] all completed

and put together? Louis Patterson came up with an ingenious solution that had eluded all of us. Why not use one of the non-speaking (or dummy) display pipes? He found one that was just the right size, had an action made and installed, voiced it, and so now the stop is complete.[24]

2004

Completion of the final details of installation stretched into 2004. The decision to replace the original Wurlitzer Clarinet had not been made until spring 2003, and the replacement rank was not ready by the June inaugural concert. By September 2003, Jack reported that the new clarinet was "in progress." The new year saw Schoenstein simultaneously beginning to install an eighty-rank organ at St. Martin's Episcopal Church in Houston and moving their headquarters from San Francisco to a larger facility in Benicia. In a February 18, 2004 letter, Jack explained, "the Clarinet pipes are almost finished and ready for voicing." In planning what work might be feasible to accomplish prior to April general conference Jack suggested, "I know there's no chance to do everything on our 'punch-list.' We could get some things done, and we might be able to get the Clarinet installed and do some other tone work."[25]

Improved control of the environment in the organ area was achieved following a reworking of the cooling and humidification systems affecting that area. Schoenstein's "thermonunciators" now show that temperatures throughout the instrument generally vary no more than ±1°. The odor that was previously noticeable in the blower room had been eliminated.[26]

From the start of the erection of the steel frame and wood casework in late 1999 to the completion of the last pipe in the December 2004 tonal finishing session, the installation and tonal work on the organ stretched over a period of five years.

Tonal Finishing

Schoenstein's normal procedure, before finalizing the tonal design and scaling of a new organ, is to test sample pipes in the finished room, in order to determine the "acoustic profile" of the space. Because of the tight construction schedule at the Conference Center, this was not possible. Tonal decisions had to be made solely on the basis of theoretical projections by the acousticians. The first opportunity for Jack Bethards to hear any organ sounds in the finished auditorium came just prior to and during October 2000 general conference:

This was that great moment when we all breathed a partial sigh of relief that it looked like things would work out well. We could see a lot of work ahead of us, but it appeared that the design had generally hit the mark. There were all the usual speech problems, particularly in the larger pipes, and also rough balances plus lots of tuning still to do, but the picture was positive. I prepared a list of stops with guidelines for Steuart and Wendell, who concentrated their next visits on straightening out speech problems and doing preliminary regulation in the Swell.

Tonal finishing began in earnest in April 2001, when the whole organ could be auditioned. I made detailed notes of every stop and an analysis of the various divisions and of the tonal families throughout the instrument. This formed the basis for the regulation. Steuart and I then worked extensively on the Great division, finishing many stops including mixtures, and scheduling a few for revision.[27]

The meticulously detailed tonal finishing was accomplished by eight men, working in eight different teams, as determined by their availability and the needs of the moment. As tonal director, Jack Bethards was not only heavily involved in the actual finishing of the pipes, but also coordinated the entire effort. A tonal finishing status book was maintained both at the job site and at the factory that noted progress as each stop was worked on. Jack created tonal "punch lists," prioritizing items needing attention and indicating which team was to be responsible. When he was not at the job site, he maintained close contact with each of the teams as they worked. He determined or authorized any changes to the specification or modifications in scaling. While Jack set the overall tonal parameters and was a major participant in the process, he entrusted much of the detail to the expertise and artistic judgment of other skilled tonal finishers.

Steuart Goodwin was also heavily involved throughout the finishing process. At the beginning of the project, Jack suggested that Steuart should join him in the tonal work, thus continuing the team approach that was so successful in the Tabernacle

Steuart Goodwin works on one of the façade pipes.

Frederick (Fred) Lake, Schoenstein voicer, passed away in 2002.

Tonal finisher Wendell Ballantyne.

organ renovation project. In addition to leading tonal finishing teams, Steuart played a major role in all tonal aspects of the project, helping with scaling decisions, particularly in the diapason choruses, and suggesting tonal changes. In summarizing his work on the Conference Center organ, Steuart recalls:

> My active involvement spanned four and one-half years. I made at least 19 trips to Salt Lake for work first on the case design, then the tonal work. I spent approximately 105 days in tonal finishing. About 16 days were with Jack Bethards, 11 with Fred Lake and 78 days with Wendell Ballantyne.[28]

In addition to those already named, Schoenstein personnel Louis Patterson, Mark Hotsenpiller and George Morten participated in the tonal finishing, along with Fred Oyster and David Schopp of A.R. Schopp's Sons.

Following preliminary finishing work in October and December 2000, more substantial work was undertaken in April, July, September and November 2001; April, May, August and September 2002; February and March 2003; and final work in December 2004. Steuart and Wendell made extra trips for tonal work in between those listed.

The tonal finishing process was extended not only by the scheduling issues noted earlier, but also by the occasional decision to make tonal changes in the instrument. Jack Bethards explains:

Not all changes are made just because either the builders or musicians
don't like the effect of a stop. Some are forced on us by the laws of
physics. An organ stop has a very limited range of loudness within which
its tone and speech are perfect. This is particularly true of members of
the diapason family. If a diapason is pushed too far, it will become
"stringy." If it is softened too much, it will become "flutey." The scales
at the Conference Center were remarkably close on the mark, but in
a few cases, had to be changed. Re-scaling or making entirely new
pipes adds a lot of time, but making these decisions is one of the most
important parts of the process. One has to be willing to make tough
choices occasionally that involve throwing away a good deal of labor
and material and starting fresh. That, of course, is what separates a truly
custom-made organ from an ordinary one.[29]

While challenging and often frustrating both for Schoenstein's workers and
Conference Center management, the end result more than justified the time spent.
Tonal finishing is a cumulative process. In large measure, the success of each stop
is dependent on the work previously done on the stops to which it must relate. The
time between tonal work sessions allowed us to use each stop, as it was completed,
in various musical contexts to confirm that it fit properly into the tonal fabric, before
moving on. Reflecting on the extended time spent on tonal finishing, Jack Bethards
notes:

Whenever tonal finishing is spread over a long period of time, the
finishers gain a great deal of perspective and, if the organ is in use, can
evaluate it in a wide variety of musical contexts. Working in partnership
with the organists and conductors at Temple Square, we enjoyed the
advantage of informed musical judgment to aid us in all the decisions
made. The other benefit . . . is that each time we returned to Salt Lake
City, we had a fresh approach. Sometimes, when a [large] job like this
goes on without a break, perspective narrows, and judgment becomes
clouded. Although we could have wished for a more ideal schedule, the
final result was not compromised in any way, and was actually enhanced
by the circumstances.[30]

Over the course of the installation/finishing process, more than seventy trips
to Salt Lake City were scheduled for various Schoenstein employees who worked on
site for well over 6,000 man-hours.[31]

Having an extended length of time to complete the organ was a luxury that allowed adjustments and changes to be made and unanticipated problems to be solved before the instrument was declared finished. But with an organ this large in a space of unprecedented proportions, it was also a necessity. Viewing the project from the broader perspective that only time can afford, the delays that seemed so irksome at the time now seem to have been providential, allowing the organ to be brought to a degree of perfection that otherwise might not have been possible.

NOTES

[1]Because of the enormity and tight schedule of the Conference Center project, none of the local construction companies felt it had the resources to successfully bid on and undertake the job alone. Three of the area's largest and most respected firms, Okland Construction, Jacobsen Construction and Layton Construction formed a consortium named Legacy Constructors, which was awarded the contract for the building.

[2]Quoted in W. Dee Halverson, *The Conference Center: The Story of Its Construction* (Salt Lake City: Legacy Constructors, 2000), 51–52. The interview took place on December 9, 1999.

[3]Ibid., 31.

[4]Letter from Jack Bethards to John Longhurst, December 11, 1997.

[5]Letter from Jack Bethards to Thomas E. Hanson, March 15, 2000.

[6]E-mail from David Bagley to John Longhurst, January 20, 2009

[7]*Discourses of President Gordon B. Hinckley* (Salt Lake City: The Church of Jesus Christ of Latter-day Saints, 2005), 2:3.

[8]Letter from Jack Bethards to Thomas Hanson, March 15, 2000.

[9]Letter from Jack Bethards to Thomas Hanson, April 14, 2000. The transformer room is accessed through double doors at the rear of the organ chamber. The passageway leading to it needed to be clear to allow for the removal and replacement of large electrical transformers, in case of failure. The proposed ledger would facilitate that need by allowing the removal of previously planned organ structural supports.

[10]The large double door access was something of an afterthought. Originally, an opening about five feet square was provided in the floor of the chamber, next to the stairway, through which, it was thought, organ components and transformers could be raised or lowered. The architects soon came to realize the inadequacy of that opening relative to the organ's large chests, regulators, blowers, etc., and so the large double doors were added to address this.

[11]Louis Patterson was working as an organist and technician in Lincoln, Nebraska when the Schoenstein organ was being installed at First-Plymouth Congregational Church. Having provided some assistance both to Bob Rhoads and Jack Bethards during the installation and finishing of that instrument, he joined the Schoenstein firm in October 1999, and was subsequently named vice president and plant superintendent for the firm.

[12]Fax from John Longhurst to Jack Bethards, May 31, 2000.

[13]http://cinematreasures.org/theater/492/, accessed March 27, 2009. The Forum Theatre organ contained thirty-seven ranks over four manuals, including an eight-rank Echo division housed at the back of the auditorium. The Echo was fitted with an extra set of swell shades at the rear of the chamber that opened above the entrance to the theatre, thus allowing its sound to be heard

outside. In 1931, the organ was moved to the Wiltern Theatre, where it remained until 1979, at which time the Wiltern closed and the organ was dismantled. The diaphone pipes were found in storage at a warehouse in Kansas City. Jack Bethards chose to include a diaphone for the prodigious bass it produces, which he felt would be necessary in the vastness of the Conference Center.

[14]Shayne Ward, Bigelow's craftsman who spearheaded the diaphone rebuild, later recalled: "Each pipe was so heavy that, even though the larger resonators broke down into halves, a crew of several men was required just to move each half. Some pipes were in poor shape due to water damage. . . . We repaired the damaged pipes and painted them a dark green. . . .

We erected the shorter pipes that would fit under our 22-foot ceiling, but the longer pipes were left on the floor since there was not enough ceiling clearance to stand them up. Three blowers had to be connected in tandem in order to obtain the 25 inches of wind pressure necessary to operate these 'babies.' The first note played made it all worthwhile. It made such a rumble that the shop windows rattled. I was concerned that they would break! The sound was so deafening that I thought a helicopter was landing on the roof! I've never heard such a sound from an organ pipe!" E-mail from Michael Bigelow to John Longhurst, April 2, 2009.

[15]*Discourses of President Gordon B. Hinckley,* 2:57–69.

[16]Letter from Jack Bethards to Thomas E. Hanson, October 16, 2000.

[17]Letter from Jack Bethards to Sterling N. Jensen, et al., October 17, 2000. Sterling Jensen worked in the Church's Facilities Management Department and facilitated the Church's taking control of the building from Legacy Constructors. Decisions regarding temperature control fell under his jurisdiction.

[18]E-mail from Louis Patterson to John Longhurst, January 23, 2009.

[19]Letter from Jack Bethards to John Longhurst, January 30, 2002.

[20]Letter from Jack Bethards to John Longhurst, July 15, 2002.

[21]Letter from Jack Bethards to Brent W. Roberts, Richard H. Sawatzki and Steve Wall, August 27, 2002.

[22]Letter from Jack Bethards to John Longhurst, August 27, 2002.

[23]E-mail from Robert Poll to John Longhurst, February 2, 2009.

[24]Remarks prepared by Jack Bethards for his lecture/demonstration presented during the 2003 convention of Regions VIII and IX of the American Guild of Organists. The remarks were sent by Louis Patterson to John Longhurst in an e-mail, March 3, 2009.

[25]Letter from Jack Bethards to John Longhurst, February 18, 2004.

[26]E-mail from Robert Poll to John Longhurst, February 13, 2009. He explains further that the organ's six blowers are contained in a sealed room with a cooling unit and a temperature sensor.

The space above the blower room functions as an "air plenum mixing room." It contains a humidification unit controlled by a humidistat. Relative humidity in the mixing room is maintained at a constant 40%. "Make-up" air for the mixing room is drawn from the organ area through a baffled opening.

When the organ blowers are *off*, the blower room is maintained at the same temperature as the organ area, as measured by a temperature probe in the organ area and the sensor in the blower room.

When the organ blowers are *on*, the blower room temperature is controlled so that the temperature of the wind discharged from the blowers is the same as that in the organ space. To accomplish this, the blower room sensor is overridden, and the temperature measured by a probe in one of the wind lines is compared with that measured by the probe in the organ area. Filtered air from the air mixing room supplies the make-up air for the blower room.

[27]E-mail attachment from Jack Bethards to John Longhurst, April 13, 2009.

[28]E-mail from Steuart Goodwin to John Longhurst, January 27, 2009.

[29]E-mail from Jack Bethards to John Longhurst, April 13, 2009.

[30]Ibid.

[31]E-mail from Louis Patterson to John Longhurst, February 2, 2009.

The Finished Organ

The Symphonic Ideal

"Symphonic" is the term used by Jack Bethards to describe the character of the finished Conference Center organ and other recent Schoenstein instruments. It is an approach based on the assertion that the development of the organ through the centuries has been the result of a quest on the part of organ builders for ever-increasing musical expressiveness. Jack feels that the intense interest in historical, repertoire-specific instruments since the close of World War II represents a detour from the main path of organ building. "The time is past due," he claims, "to pick up the traces where the great innovators of organ building left off and continue the development of the organ's expressive qualities."[1]

For Jack, "symphonic" is different from "orchestral." An organ is not, has never been, nor ever will be a substitute for an orchestra, although at times it may have served as one. The two share a number of characteristics however, and those commonalities give an organ the potential for exhibiting symphonic qualities. Wide range, both of frequency and dynamics, variety of tonal color, and the ability to render long, sustained passages immediately come to mind. Beyond these are complete control of the entire range of timbres and dynamics, plus the ability to communicate articulation, accent and phrase. The Schoenstein symphonic approach to organ building seeks to narrow the gap between the ability of the orchestra and the ability of the organ to render these musically expressive elements. As Orpha Ochse observes:

> Bethards likes to explore any and all avenues that might contribute to the organ's expressive powers. Unhampered by precedent, his designs are sometimes radical departures from standard patterns. He is quick to admit that his style is not for everyone; on the other hand, it has much to offer organists who are particularly interested in using colorful registrations and kaleidoscopic tonal effects, and those whose performances include solos and accompaniments of an orchestral character. Focusing particularly on these concerns, Schoenstein & Co. has carved out a unique niche in the organ building market.[2]

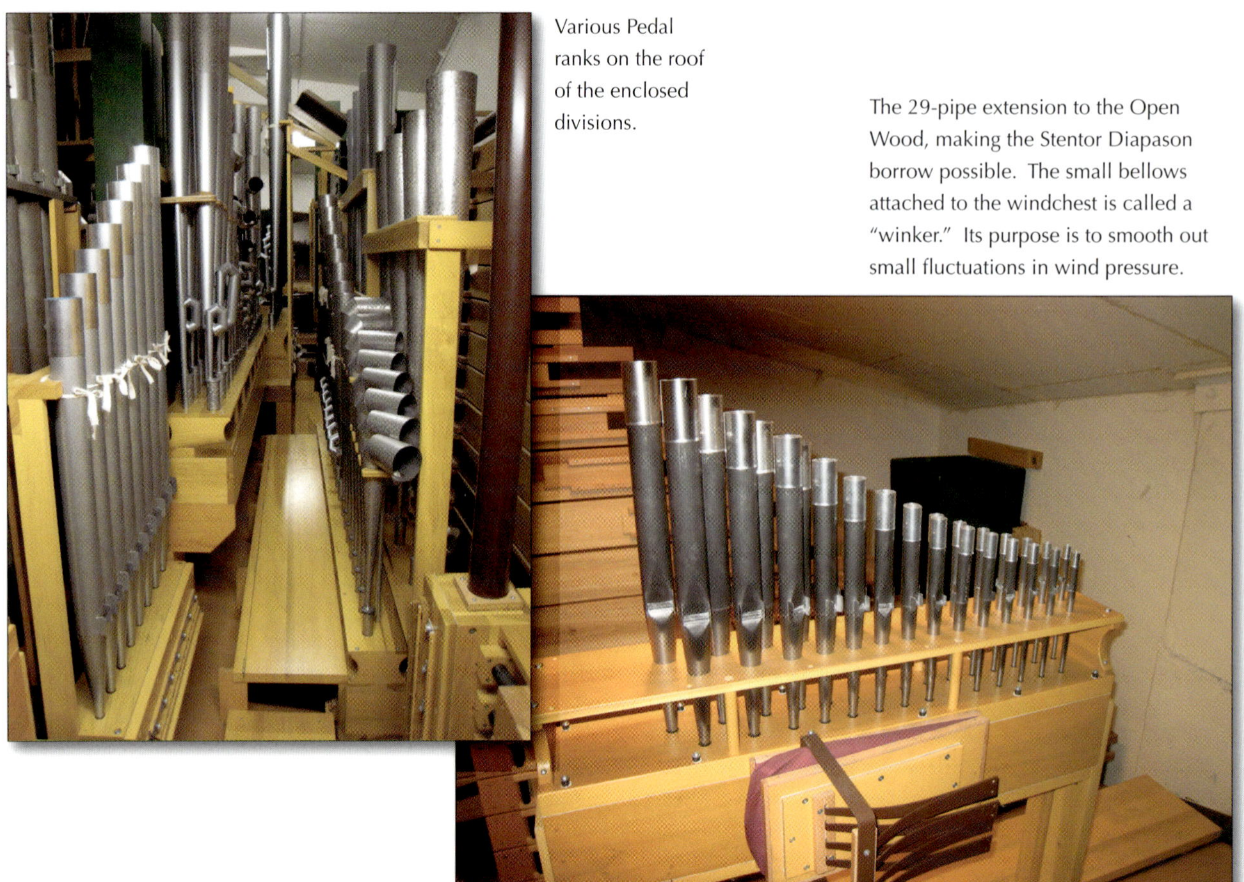

Various Pedal ranks on the roof of the enclosed divisions.

The 29-pipe extension to the Open Wood, making the Stentor Diapason borrow possible. The small bellows attached to the windchest is called a "winker." Its purpose is to smooth out small fluctuations in wind pressure.

Pipes of the Pedal Bourdon mounted horizontally atop the Solo enclosure's roof. Note how air to each pipe is tubed from the windchest.

Wood Pedal Violone pipes installed horizontally on the roof of the organ's expression boxes.

SIZE

Building a successful symphonic instrument requires that a number of criteria be met. First, any organ, symphonic or otherwise, need not be any larger than necessary to accomplish its musical purpose. Though the Conference Center organ's 130 ranks certainly comprise a large instrument—in fact, Schoenstein's *magnum opus* —when one considers that it is approximately two-thirds the size of the Tabernacle organ but must speak in a room with four times the seating capacity and nearly six times the cubic volume, its size is seen to be comparatively modest.

TONAL VARIETY

"In planning a symphonic organ," says Jack Bethards, "no tone color that might be useful is excluded from consideration, and if something new seems appropriate we will develop it."[3] This philosophy is evident throughout the Conference Center organ in such things as:

1. The inclusion of non-traditional theatre organ stops in a church/ concert organ.

2. Two Swell reed choruses, with both English- and French-style reeds side by side.

3. Vivid, highly differentiated colors representing all families of organ tone.

4. Use of proprietary stops, such as Symphonic Flute, Silver Flute, Tuben III and Pizzicato Bass, all Schoenstein originals.

An additional Bethards axiom relative to organ tone states, "Beauty of tone trumps all else in organ design. . . . The secret is committed voicing." He continues, "Great voicing imparts something extra to energize a tone and make it appealing. . . . An organ may look symphonic on paper, but if the character of tone is not beautiful, it cannot qualify. . . . [I]f beauty of tone can be combined with all of the flexibility promised in the symphonic ideal, the result can be sublime."[4] The meticulous care lavished on the tonal finishing of the Conference Center organ over an extended length of time by the finest artisans available paid off handsomely in this regard. The voicing produces a prompt, clean attack and a steady, clear, energized tone. Chiff and white noise in pipe speech are not part of Bethards's symphonic ideal.

Inside the Grand Solo enclosure. The Tierce Mixture is seen in the center; the tuba chorus reeds are to the left and right.

Inside the Solo enclosure

The upper Choir, showing the Lieblich Bourdon behind celestes and reeds.

Inside the lower Choir enclosure. The chest on the right contains string and diapason ranks; the chest on the left, flutes. The chest in the rear holds the principal ranks.

English reeds in the upper Swell enclosure.

148

Wurlitzer-style high-pressure regulators suspended from the ceiling of the upper Swell expression box. The regulators serve the Tuba Mirabilis and Pedal stops located on the roof above. Note the box on the left that houses the Voix humaine, expression louvers behind the regulators and French reed Schwimmer-style regulator with its Schoenstein identification tag and dowel-plugged pressure-testing hole.

To facilitate service and simplify the windchest layout, the bass pipes of the Orchestral Tibia were mounted from the ceiling upside-down. Note their leathered upper lips, and the tubing from the windchest to each pipe. Schoenstein uses green paint to identify wood pipes not of their construction (in this case used pipes).

Inside the Orchestral enclosure. The red wire, seen through the ladder rungs, is the heat-sensitive wire of the fire protection system.

Orchestral Vox Humana.

The Wurlitzer Orchestral Oboe with added tie-down hooks. The hooks keep the pipes securely in place on the high-pressure windchest, and when adjusting the tuning wire upward. The capped reed pipe at lower right is part of the Cor Anglais, with two of its top treble flue pipes to the left.

BALANCE

Balance, both horizontal and vertical, is a vital component of the tonal characteristics of the symphonic organ. By horizontal balance, Jack means the relationship between the various manual divisions of the instrument. He designs the Great and Swell to be approximately equal, though the latter is enclosed. The Choir division is subordinate. In the case of the Conference Center organ, the Solo flues are approximately equal to the Great flues, and the Grand Solo reeds can either match the Great reeds in power or crown the entire instrument, depending on the position of the expression louvers. The Pedal, containing both "straight," unenclosed stops and a large number borrowed from both the expressive and unenclosed manual divisions, is capable of providing a suitable balance to any manual registration.

Vertical balance involves the relationship between stops at various pitches in any given division. "To achieve balance there must be a center of gravity and in the symphonic organ it is at 8' [pitch] in the manuals. Each division should lay its foundation at the 8' level. This, after all, is where the music is written. In our symphonic concept, upperwork is considered a coloring agent, a way of adding a distinctive character to the 8' line."[5] As pitch levels become higher, pipe scales become smaller. If there is more than one mixture in a division, as is the case with the Conference Center organ, they tend to vary in color and dynamic as well as pitch level. Some may include a tierce, as in the Swell and Grand Solo. Over-emphasis of non-unison pitches is avoided. In the Choir, ranks at pitches that would normally comprise a mixture are available separately, allowing the organist to customize the composition of his "mixture." While flues and reeds are generally balanced, in a dry acoustic like the Conference Center, Jack finds it best for the organ's power to come from reeds, rather than brilliant flue upperwork.

WINDING

Winding of the instrument is another important factor in the symphonic scheme. Jack Bethards explains,

> We believe in providing absolutely steady wind using a multiplicity of regulators, not only to make available different wind pressures, but to assure consistent response from all pipes under all playing conditions. Most chests are fed by at least two steps of regulation, each with spring control, so that the final regulator in the system does not have too much differential for which to compensate. A moving bass line should not upset the treble; intervals and chords should not de-tune when wind

Regulators for the Orchestral division. Red springs are higher tension than green springs.

Windlines exiting the blower room.

One of several Schoenstein ten-stage expression motors.

demand is high. It's also important for the wind system to have more than adequate capacity to handle any demand and to have quick refill response so that staccato tutti chords will sound firm and full as they do in the orchestra.[6]

Schoenstein does not hesitate to use high wind pressures. Jack finds that some stops benefit from it for precision, beauty or smoothness of tone. While sheer loudness can be achieved by other means, carrying power, in a space like the Conference Center, is best achieved through use of higher wind pressure. The

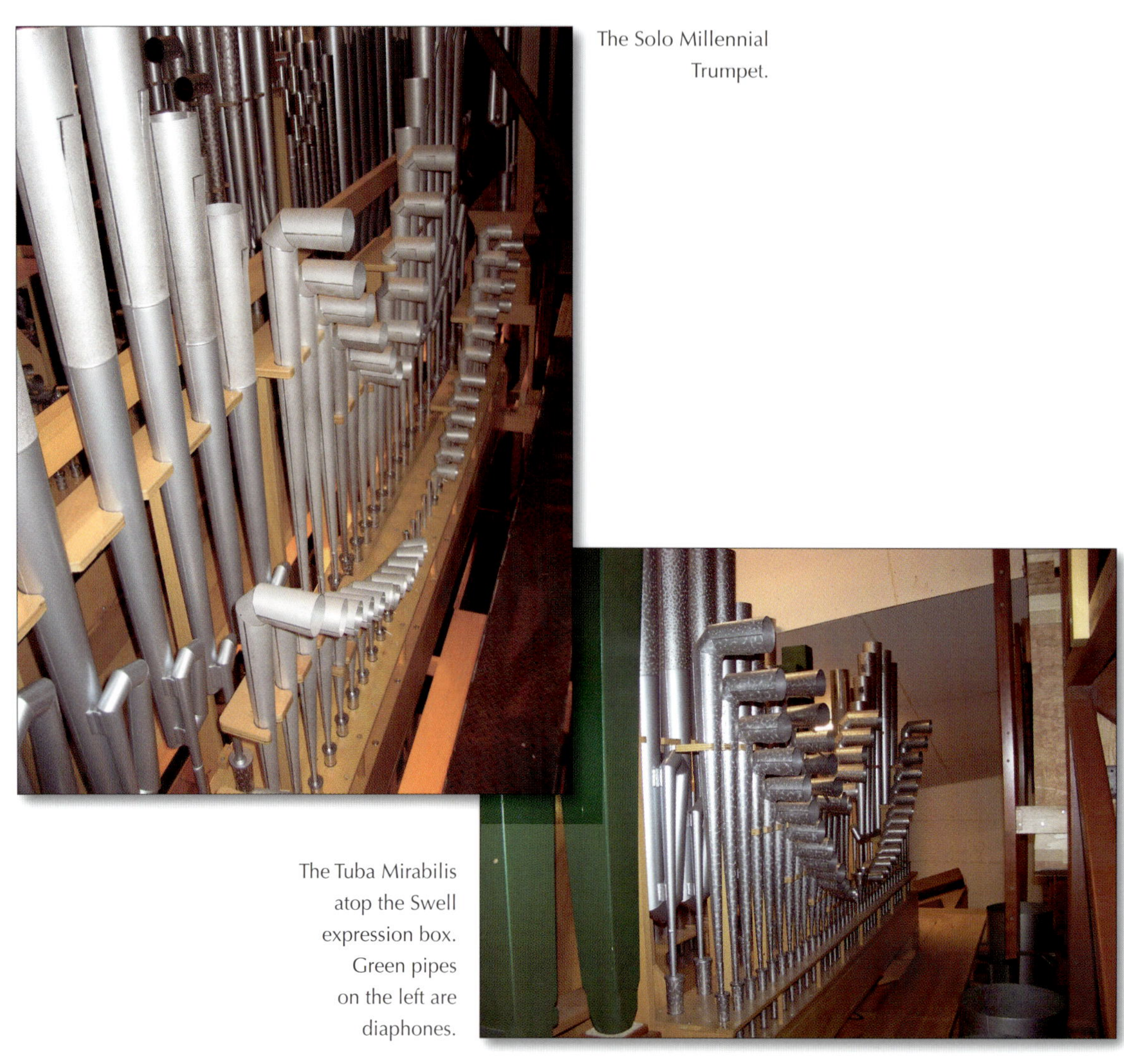

The Solo Millennial Trumpet.

The Tuba Mirabilis atop the Swell expression box. Green pipes on the left are diaphones.

Conference Center's winding system is complex. Six blowers, operated by motors totaling 39.7 HP provide wind to the various sections of the organ with different pressures through a veritable labyrinth of wind lines and regulators.

TREMULANTS

Related to winding is the matter of the organ's tremulants. In addition to normal tremulants available for all manual divisions, the Orchestral and Solo divisions include a Variable Tremulant, which allows the organist to adjust the speed of the beat from the console. Drawing either of the Variable Tremulants overrides the crescendo pedal function, and its position then determines the tremulant speed. Additionally, the two Vox Humana stops have separate tremulants, adjusted to maximize their effectiveness, as does the Orchestral Tuba Horn.

DYNAMIC CONTROL

To be successful, the symphonic organ must be able to offer three distinct types of dynamic control. Bethards labels them as continuous, discrete-terraced, and sudden. Continuous dynamic control is achieved by means of expression boxes and shades (louvers). The box must be sturdy and well built to be reasonably soundproof and to avoid soaking up lower frequencies. The shades must be responsive and silent, providing an effective seal when closed, and then open a full ninety degrees for maximum egress of sound. Counting the Solo and Grand Solo separately, the Conference Center organ has five expression boxes to aid in producing continuous dynamic control.

The discrete-terraced dynamic is dependent upon having several stops in the various tonal families at different dynamic levels. The addition or removal of stops, either by hand, by means of pistons, or through use of the crescendo pedal, then increases or decreases the dynamic level in a number of relatively small increments. The tonal resources of the Conference Center organ offer excellent control of discrete-terraced dynamics. The changes to the both the Great and Swell divisions during installation were made to further smooth out this type of dynamic build-up. A remarkably smooth, terraced crescendo from *pp* to *ff* using only the stops of the unenclosed Great division provides a remarkable demonstration of this concept.

Sudden dynamic changes are usually accomplished by moving to a different manual or by using a piston or the crescendo pedal. In addition, Schoenstein has introduced a device that they call the Sforzando coupler. At the Conference Center, either the Swell or Solo (or both) may be momentarily coupled to the Great by means of a toe lever. The preset combination on either of these divisions is added only while the Sforzando coupler is depressed. As soon as it is released, the coupler is disconnected. This device is most useful in effecting a momentary dynamic accent or adding a "stinger" at the end of a piece, where appropriate.

ACTION

In the broad sense, action refers to the entire chain of events that must occur between the pressing of a key and the resultant sound from the pipes. "Key action must be lightning fast both on attack and release and respond uniformly from all keys regardless of the number of stops or couplers employed. Stop action must be fast and clean, i.e. without any hesitation or gulping on draw or release."[7] On all its instruments, Schoenstein uses keyboards with articulated touch that give the player a positive feel for the point of electrical contact. The Conference Center organ uses

Flue pipes of the Great division.

Looking down at the hooded reeds of the Great division. In front are pipes of the high-pressure Millennial Trumpet.

Bird's-eye view of three 32-foot Trombone pipes. Closed louvers of the Swell enclosure are seen at bottom of photo.

Pedal Trombone and Diaphone pipes. Note the "Thermonunciator" mounted on the support to the right.

electro-pneumatic action with Pitman-style windchests. The final link in the chain is the speech of the pipes, which have been carefully regulated for promptness and steadiness.

In the successful symphonic organ, all of the above elements work together toward two main goals: clarity and beauty of sound, and flexible control by the organist of the resources and mechanics of what otherwise could be a very large and cumbersome machine. When an instrument meets both goals, the organist has the resources and freedom to realize and communicate to his audience the entire range of musical expression, from dramatic and forceful to the most subtle and intricate.

The Tabernacle and Conference Center Organs Compared

As organists at Temple Square, we are frequently asked two questions. What is the difference between the Tabernacle and Conference Center organs, and which do you prefer?

To answer the first question fully, requires some detailed explanation. Some of the comparisons are easy. The Tabernacle organ contains 11,623 pipes in 206 ranks over eight divisions. The Conference Center organ's 130 ranks include 7,708 pipes in seven divisions (counting the Solo and Grand Solo separately). Both instruments are played from five-manual consoles. The fifth manual at the Tabernacle plays an Antiphonal division, housed at the opposite end of the room from the main organ. The Conference Center organ's fifth manual controls the Orchestral division, a section of the organ made up largely of solo voices located with the rest of the instrument. Of the Tabernacle organ's eight divisions, four are unenclosed, while only two of seven are unenclosed at the Conference Center.

Beyond such statistics, the comparison becomes more complex. The key to their further differences lies in their respective tonal designs. The Tabernacle organ, finished in 1949 and built by Æolian-Skinner, is termed "American Classic." Without doubt, it is one of the finest examples of that style, designed by the movement's chief proponent, G. Donald Harrison. The Conference Center organ, completed in 2004 and classified as "American Romantic," was designed by Jack Bethards and built by Schoenstein & Co. It remains for history to define Mr. Bethards's ultimate place relative to organs in this style, but presently he is the leading exponent and chief innovator. As new organs are featured in trade magazines, we see other builders beginning to incorporate some of Jack's ideas into their instruments.

Consider the information in the following tables:

Table 1

Comparative Pitch Analysis of Manual Voices

Pitch	Tabernacle	Conference Center	CC in comparison
16′ and below	10%	13%	+3%
8′	42%	50%	+8%
5⅓′ and 4′	19%	16%	-3%
3$\frac{1}{5}$′	10%	6%	-4%
2′	8%	9%	+1%
Above 2′	11%	6%	-5%
Total	100%	100%	
Mixtures & Mutations	21%	15%	-6%

From Table 1 it can be seen that the Conference Center organ stresses 8-foot pitch to a considerable degree, with some additional emphasis on pitches lower than 8-foot. Remember that here only manual voices are being considered. Conversely, upperwork, including mutations and mixtures, is noticeably less prominent, conforming to the symphonic concept of vertical balance, discussed earlier.

Table 2

Comparison of Tonal Families Represented in Manual Voices

Tonal Family	Tabernacle	Conference Center	CC in comparison
Diapasons	14%	17%	+3%
Echo Diapasons	4%	7%	+3%
Diapason Mutations and Mixtures	17%	13%	-4%
Open Flutes	6%	8%	+2%
Stopped Flutes	10%	7%	-3%
Hybrids	3%	2%	-1%
Strings	14%	14%	–
Chorus Reeds	11%	17%	+6%
Color Reeds	6%	12%	+6%
Color Reeds (Baroque type)	4%	1%	-3%
Total	100%	100%	

Again consistent with the tonal philosophy discussed above, Table 2 points to an increased use of Diapason tone in the Schoenstein organ, as well as open vs. stopped flutes. The reliance on reeds over flue upperwork for power and brilliance is also clearly seen. The increased proportion of color reeds results from including a second solo division in the specification.

Table 3

Wind Pressure Comparison	Tabernacle	Conference Center
Lowest Pressure	$2\frac{3}{4}$"	$5\frac{1}{2}$"
Number of Voices on 10" pressure and above	9	23
Highest Pressure	15"	25"

Perhaps the most dramatic difference between the two instruments is seen in a comparison of wind pressures as shown in Table 3. The Conference Center organ's consistently higher pressures substantiate Schoenstein's objective to achieve greater carrying power in the larger building through increased wind pressure.

A few additional points are relevant. Tonally, the American Classic organ tends to emphasize blend among its stops, hence the contrast between stops is a bit more subtle. On the other hand, the Romantic organ tends to favor variety and contrast. Dynamically, American Classic voicing is often uniform throughout a stop's compass; Romantic voicing tends to become stronger as the pitch level ascends. A Romantic instrument will normally exhibit a wider dynamic range among its individual stops than does its Classic counterpart. For power, the Classic organ depends on a somewhat larger ensemble of moderately voiced stops, whereas the Romantic instrument uses a relatively smaller ensemble of more powerful individual voices. Relative to dynamic control, the Classic organ relies more on terracing while its Romantic counterpart favors having more of the organ contained in expression boxes.

The Romantic organ carries noticeably more weight in the pedal bass line. Direct comparisons between pedal division stoplists are made somewhat more difficult because of extensions and borrows, yet the figures in the table below are instructive. Table 4 compares the number of Pedal stops of the Tabernacle and Conference Center organs, at various pitch levels, as a percentage of the total number of ranks in each instrument.

Table 4

Comparison of Pedal Division Content

Pitch Level	Tabernacle	Conference Center	CC in Comparison
64′	0.0%	† 1.5%	+1.5%
32′	2.4%	5.4%	+3.0%
16′	6.3%	15.4%	+9.1%
8′	5.8%	11.5%	+5.7%
4′	2.9%	4.6%	+1.7%
2′	1.4%	0.0%	-1.4%
Mutations and Mixtures	7.3%	4.6%	-2.7%
Total	26.1%	43.0%	+16.9%
Total number of ranks	206	130	

† The Conference Center organ's two 64-stops extend down to GGGGG#.

The symphonic concept of vertical balance, with less emphasis on upperwork and non-unison pitches, is certainly evident in the Pedal when viewing the Conference Center percentages. Just as the manuals of the symphonic organ are tonally centered at 8-foot pitch, the Pedal is firmly grounded at 16-foot pitch. The increased number of available pedal stops on the Schoenstein organ adds versatility to the Pedal, as well as potential strength. For example, if one considers the Dulciana 16-foot to be a soft diapason, the Conference Center Pedal has four at 16-foot pitch, three unenclosed at varying dynamic levels, plus one under expression.

The availability of seven 32-foot stops in the Conference Center organ, six of which are full length, is remarkable. To yield a comparable ratio of 32-foot stops to its total number of ranks, the Tabernacle organ would need eleven 32-foot stops; the 346-rank organ at First Congregational Church in Los Angeles would have eighteen; and Philadelphia's 466-rank Wanamaker organ would contain twenty-five.[8]

Relative to the two instruments under discussion, it should be noted that the Tabernacle organ, as it was installed in 1949, already exhibited some Romantic and symphonic characteristics. It included several stops characteristic of the organs of E. M. Skinner, an important and influential builder of Romantic-style instruments in the early decades of the twentieth century. Also, the additions to the Tabernacle organ in the 1980s, carried out by Schoenstein, all tended to tilt it a bit further in the symphonic direction. As a result, the contrast between the two instruments is not quite as vivid as it might otherwise have been.

To summarize, one might think of the Tabernacle organ as genteel—beautifully refined, elegant and polite. Its tonal design tends to favor the Classic repertoire. The Conference Center organ comes across as being more assertive, more dramatic, and more heroic, placing greater emphasis on playing Romantic organ literature. Yet either is capable of exhibiting many of the characteristics of the other when called upon to do so. For example, Jack Bethards was very careful to ensure that his instrument could render "As the Dew from Heaven Distilling" (the organ's closing theme on *Music and the Spoken Word* broadcasts) "authentically," sounding like the Tabernacle organ. Both instruments are masterpieces of the organ builders' art.

Asking which organ we prefer is like asking a parent to name a favorite child. Each is different, yet wonderful. If one organ were favored over the other, it would likely be because of the rooms in which they are situated, rather than a preference for either instrument. The warm resonance and extended reverberation time in the Tabernacle are ideal for music in general and organ music in particular. The Tabernacle's size is better suited to the size of many recital and concert audiences. On the other hand, when audiences exceed the capacity of the Tabernacle—and there are many instances when that is the case—we are always happy for another opportunity to play the Schoenstein organ.

NOTES

[1]Jack M. Bethards, "A Brief for the Symphonic Organ," *The Diapason* 96, no. 9 (2005): 22.

[2]Orpha Ochse, *Schoenstein & Co.* (Richmond, Virginia: OHS Press, 2008), 20.

[3]Bethards, 23.

[4]Ibid., 24.

[5]Ibid., 24.

[6]Ibid., 25.

[7]Ibid., 25.

[8]The First Congregational Church organ contains six Pedal 32-foot stops in the Chancel organ, and two more in the Pedal of the Gallery organ. See http://fccla.org/music/organs.html (accessed March 5, 2009). The Wanamaker organ has seven 32-foot stops in the Pedal, and one in the Great. See www.wanamakerorgan.com/stoplist.php (accessed March 5, 2009).

Epilogue

An Inaugural Celebration

There have not been many organ concerts, in recent years, attended by 15,000 people! Nor are there many venues, with a pipe organ, that could accommodate such a crowd.

In June 2003, Regions VIII and IX of the American Guild of Organists joined to hold their biennial convention in Salt Lake City. Some 600 Guild members from throughout the western United States, and some from beyond, gathered to participate in the convention activities. One of the highlights of the convention program was the inaugural concert of the Conference Center organ. While an audience of 600 would fill many good-sized churches, in the cavernous Conference Center 600 people could seem like a poor turnout. The public was invited to attend, and they came by the thousands.

The program featured organist Todd Wilson, the Mormon Tabernacle Choir, and the Orchestra at Temple Square. Todd Wilson opened the program playing Joseph Jongen's *Symphonie Concertante* with the Orchestra at Temple Square, conducted by Craig Jessop. The Tabernacle Choir took to the stage for the second half of the program, performing Leonard Bernstein's *Chichester Psalms* and other selections from their upcoming tour to the northeastern United States. The organ was used prominently for the choir accompaniments with staff organists at the console. A small touring ensemble from the Orchestra augmented the accompaniments.

The Choir's tour was being billed as a seventy-fifth anniversary tour in recognition of their upcoming broadcasting milestone. Governor Michael Leavitt had proclaimed the day of the concert, June 19, as Mormon Tabernacle Choir Day. Prior to the concert, the Choir had hosted a banquet honoring the many skilled artisans who had contributed to the building of the organ. Most of the firms that had been involved sent representatives. Key Church employees who had lent their expertise and support were also invited to participate in the celebration. In his monthly message to the membership, Fred Swann, national president of The American Guild of Organists wrote:

> This summer, two events gave me the greatest inspiration I've had in years: performances of Bach's *St. John Passion* and the *Mass in B Minor* in St. Thomas Church in Leipzig, Germany, and, at an AGO regional convention, a stunning and moving performance by the Mormon Tabernacle Choir, orchestra, and organists on the new Schoenstein organ in the vast 21,000-seat Conference Center adjacent to Temple Square in Salt Lake City.[1]

This is not faint praise coming from a man who, during a long and distinguished career, has concertized worldwide and served as organist at three prominent American churches: New York City's Riverside Church; the Crystal Cathedral in Garden Grove, California; and First Congregational Church in Los Angeles.

Closing the Books

Between January 1999, when the organ contract was signed, and its completion in 2004, a number of changes were made that altered Schoenstein's costs. Some items specified in the contract, such as the console platform and bench, were ultimately supplied by the Church, rather than by Schoenstein. Conversely, changes to the stoplist, prior to and during installation resulted in increased costs to the builder. When longer periods of quiet for tonal finishing were not available, as required by the contract, additional shorter trips became necessary, thus increasing travel expenses. Inflation during the additional two years needed to finish the organ also increased the builder's costs. After the project was finally completed, these factors were carefully considered, and an equitable financial adjustment was made.

Closure of the Tabernacle

Soon after completion of the Conference Center, internal discussions began about closing the Tabernacle for an extended period for a thorough renovation, including seismic retrofitting and updates to critical systems. Extensive architectural and engineering studies were carried out, and finally the announcement came that the Tabernacle would close at the end of 2004. The exhaustive renovation took more than two years. The building finally reopened for the April 2007 general conference. During the twenty-seven-month closure, the daily thirty-minute organ recitals, a long-standing tradition on Temple Square, were presented in the Conference Center. This constant exposure to the organ over an extended period provided an opportunity for organists to explore the instrument in depth and to become even more intimately acquainted with its resources. Recital audiences were small, in comparison to the size of the room, and were seated in the heart of the auditorium.

Stephen Cleobury, Director of Music at King's College, Cambridge, performed on the Schoenstein in January 2005. The following November, Tabernacle Organist Richard Elliott played a program not only of traditional organ repertoire by Bach, Vierne and Cundick, but also a brilliant rendition of Mussorgsky's *Pictures at an Exhibition* during which he aptly demonstrated the organ's symphonic capabilities. The cherry atop the musical sundae came by way of a rousing Sousa march, played as an encore. In May 2006, Clay Christiansen, Richard Elliott and I recorded a CD, *Now Let Us Rejoice*, consisting of music based on hymn tunes. That recording was made at the same time the Tabernacle Choir was recording their *Showtime* album. In order to minimize the length of recording sessions for engineer Bruce Leek, we encoded the entire album on floppy discs in advance, using the organ's record/playback system. During the actual recording sessions, we simply inserted the discs and let the organ play itself.

During this time, the weekly broadcasts of the Tabernacle Choir also originated from the Conference Center, giving us organists an opportunity to work with the instrument in an accompanying role with music in a wide range of styles. All quickly came to appreciate its flexibility, its variety of tonal colors, its dramatic dynamic range, the usefulness of each of its special features and the richness of its overall musical sound. Tabernacle Choir conductor Mack Wilberg, who has written many wonderful compositions and arrangements for the Choir, soon began writing accompaniments that exploited the organ's symphonic capabilities. Accustomed to writing for orchestra, Mack quickly saw the potential of the new organ for comparable expressiveness. Along with orchestral reductions, he wrote several original accompaniments for two players at the console, thus allowing him the freedom to write simultaneous solo lines and thicker harmonic textures. A few of his scores effectively included the charming "pluck" of the Pizzicato Bass.

As part of the celebration marking the reopening of the Tabernacle, the Choir sponsored the Third American Classic Organ Symposium. Although the primary focus of the Symposium was on the newly renovated Tabernacle and its organ, the

Conference Center organ was also featured both in a lecture demonstration by Jack Bethards and in a recital by Ken Cowan. Mr. Cowan played a dazzling program, including Reubke's *Sonata on the 94th Psalm*, Mendelssohn's *Sonata No. 1 in F Minor*, *Harmonies du soir* and *Valse mignonne* by Karg-Elert, *Salamanca* by Bovet and transcriptions of movements by Weber and Wagner. Though the audience was of substantial size, no audio reinforcement was needed for the recital. Reporting on the event, Orpha Ochse wrote:

> We had heard a demonstration of the organ's colors and ensembles earlier in the symposium, but for many, this program was the first opportunity to hear it as a recital instrument. Cowan's program explored the organ's expressive range in a wide variety of styles, all associated with the romantic tradition. Here were kaleidoscopic color displays, sweeping dynamic changes, and even a nod toward theater organ style in Karg-Elert's *Valse mignonne*, a piece inspired by the composer's encounter with a cinema organ during his visit to the United States.[2]

Looking Back

President Gordon B. Hinckley passed away January 27, 2008, at the age of ninety-seven, but not before enjoying the fruits of his bold plan for a mammoth place of assembly for residents and visitors to Salt Lake City. His funeral on February 2 was the first one to be held in the building that bears the indelible stamp of his prophetic leadership. The large crowd that filled the Conference Center on that occasion was but a small measure of the worldwide respect and affection for this indefatigable man of God.

> Bring me men to match my mountains;
> Bring me men to match my plains,
> Men with empires in their purpose,
> And new eras in their brains.[3]

These words from "The Coming American," penned by Sam Walter Foss on July 4, 1894, describe not only the vision and determination of President Hinckley a century later, but also the many gifted individuals who came together for a brief moment in time to help make his vision a reality. All who were involved sensed the importance and singularity of the task.

The organ, though a relatively small part of the whole, is nevertheless an important part. Its dramatic casework looms above the rostrum and choir like the craggy peaks of the "everlasting hills" that surround the Salt Lake Valley. Its voice invites "everything that hath breath" to join in songs of praise. It speaks with authority, to match the sermons spoken from the pulpit. It speaks with beauty, to complement the anthems of the choir and the singing of the congregation. Its influence is already being felt in many ways, in many places.

The completion of the organ in 2004 marked the end of a more than seven-year odyssey that began with the April 1996 public announcement of the plan to build the monumental Conference Center. The journey was at once challenging, exhilarating, frustrating and rewarding. We could easily have followed the path of least resistance and saved ourselves a lot of work and the Church a lot of money. But the consequences of complacency far outweighed the risks of boldness.

As the Conference Center neared completion, President Hinckley expressed deep appreciation to all who played a part in its construction, including the men and women of Schoenstein & Co. and all the firms that participated in the organ project:

> To everyone who has worked on [this project], I wish to say that through all the years yet to come, you will be able to say with pride and satisfaction, "I worked on that building. I helped make it what it is. My sweat went into the construction of that sacred and beautiful house of the Lord." For I so regard it. I hope that there will always be pride on the part of those who worked on it as having done something unusual and even spectacular.[4]

"Unusual" and "spectacular" are words that aptly describe the Conference Center organ as well as the building itself. From the beginning, a special "something" seemed to be guiding both projects. Perhaps it was the same fervor that enabled the pioneer Saints to sing and dance their way across the plains, as they willingly sacrificed all to find "home" in a barren desert. Perhaps it was the faith of Joseph Ridges when, in the face of seemingly insurmountable obstacles, he, too, determined to build

Gordon B. Hinckley (1910-2008). President of The Church of Jesus Christ of Latter-day Saints, 1995-2008.

an organ in a magnificent new edifice on Salt Lake City's Temple Square. Whatever it was, the result is a stunning achievement in organ building at the dawn of the twenty-first century that will bless and inspire an untold number of listeners for generations to come.

NOTES

[1]Fred Swann, "Inspiration," *The American Organist* 37, no. 9 (2003): 3.

[2]Orpha Ochse, "The Third American Classic Organ Symposium," *The American Organist* 41, no. 10 (2007): 52.

[3]Hazel Felleman, *The Best Loved Poems of the American People* (New York: Doubleday, 1936), 107.

[4]Interview, January 4, 2000, quoted in W. Dee Halverson, *The Conference Center: The Story of Its Construction* (Salt Lake City: Legacy Constructors, 2000), 178.

APPENDIX 1
PIPE SCALE CHART

Notes:

1. Only the primary materials used to construct the stop are shown. Percentages indicate the amount of tin in the tin/lead alloy of metal pipes. The designation "zinc and xx%" means that the bass pipes of the stop are made primarily of zinc and the balance primarily of tin/lead alloy.

2. When two or more pitches are indicated for one stop, that stop has been extended or borrowed.

3. Mouth width, expressed as a fraction of circumference, is shown for metal pipes. Basic shape of shallot (tapered or parallel) is indicated for reeds. When mouth width is shown for wood pipes, the designation is for the metal trebles only.

4. Scale is shown in millimeters for metal flues and in inches for woods and reeds. The progression of measurements throughout the compass of the stop is indicated most often by a ratio showing at what point in the compass the scale reduces to one-half of the starting scale. Two numbers are given to avoid confusion. 16/17 means that the stop halves at the 16th step or 17th pipe of the progression. For members of the diapason family—the stops most sensitive to variations in the building's acoustical pattern—scales are indicated for each octave. For chorus reed stops the actual or theoretical scale for 8' C is shown to facilitate comparing the components of reed choruses. Stops that have variable scales to produce special tonal color effects are labeled "special." The most important designation in these cases is the starting scale. Other scaling details such as slotting, tapering, harmonic length, etc. are also indicated.

5. On compound stops, scaling is sometimes different for various ranks within the stop. The designation "U" indicates Unisons, "Q" indicates Quints and "T" indicates Tierces. In some cases, where scaling is shared by unisons and quints, the pitch of the rank is indicated by its position in the harmonic train e.g. 19th, 22nd, etc.

Stop/Material	Pitch	No. of Pipes	Mouth/ Shallot	Scale	Ratio & Details
GREAT					
Dulciana Zinc and 43%	32'	61	2/9	261.5	1 to 12-16/17, 13 to 61-18/19
Double Open Diapason Zinc and 43%	16'	61	2/9	250.4	13-148.9, 25-88.5, 37-52.6, 49-32.6, 61-20.2
Bourdon Wood	16'	61	—	$5^7/_8$" x $7^1/_2$"	37 to 61 - Pierced Stoppers
Large Open Diapason Zinc and 43%	8'	61	1/4	162.7	13-105.3, 25-65.3, 37-40.5, 49-24.1, 61-14.3
Open Diapason Zinc and 43%	8'	61	1/4	162.7	13-96.5, 25-57.4, 37-34.1, 49-21.1, 61-13.1
Horn Diapason Zinc and 43%	8'	61	2/9	148.9	1 to 17-16/17, 18 to 61-17/18 Slotted
Gamba Zinc and 75%	8'	61	1/4	90.7	18/19 - Slotted
Gemshorn Zinc and 43%	8'	61	2/9	148.0	16/17 ½ Taper
Harmonic Flute Zinc and 43%	8'	61	1/4	136.5	Special 1 to 30 - Slotted, 30 to 61 - Harmonic
Doppelflöte Wood	8'	61	—	$3^{13}/_{16}$" x $4^5/_8$"	$13-1^3/_4$" x $2^3/_4$"
Principal Zinc and 43%	4'	61	1/4	96.5	13-62.6, 25-38.8, 37-23.1, 49-13.7, 61-8.5
Octave Zinc and 43%	4'	61	1/4	92.4	13-54.9, 25-32.6, 37-20.2, 49-12.6, 61-8.1
Octave Gemshorn 75%	4'	61	2/9	84.4	17/18 $^2/_3$ Taper
Forest Flute 43%	4'	61	2/9	68.0	Special
Twelfth 43%	$2^2/_3$'	61	2/9	59.9	13-37.2, 25-23.1, 37-14.3, 49-9.3, 61-5.7
Fifteenth 43%	2'	61	1/4	50.4	13-31.3, 25-19.3, 37-12.0, 49-7.8, 61-5.0

Stop/Material	Pitch	No. of Pipes	Mouth/ Shallot	Scale	Ratio & Details
Seventeenth 43%	$1^3/_5'$	61	1/5	38.8	13-24.1, 25-14.9, 37-9.3, 49-6.0, 54-4.8 - Repeats above
Full Mixture (IV-V) *ff* 43%	2'	266	U - 2/9 Q - 1/5	50.4	1'-31.3, $^1/_2$'-19.3, $^1/_4$'-12.6, $^1/_8$'-8.1, $^1/_{16}$'-5.2
Mixture (IV) *f* 43%	2'	215	1/4	50.4	1'-31.3, $^1/_2$'-18.6, $^1/_4$'-12.0, $^1/_8$'-7.8, $^1/_{16}$'-5.2
Sharp Mixture (III) *mf* 43%	$1^1/_3'$	175	1/4	35.6	1'-28.7, $^1/_2$'-17.8, $^1/_4$'-11.0, $^1/_8$'-6.8, $^1/_{16}$'-4.6
Bass Trumpet Zinc and 43%	16'	61	Tapered	6"	$3^3/_4$" at 8', 57 to 61 - Harmonic
Trumpet Zinc and 43%	8'	61	Tapered	4"	45 to 56 - Harmonic, 57 to 61 - Flues
Clarion 43%	4'	61	Tapered	$3^1/_4$"	$4^1/_4$" at 8', 33 to 44 - Harmonic, 45 to 61 - Flues
SWELL					
Double Open Diapason Zinc and 43%	16'	68	2/9	229.6	13-136.5, 25-81.1, 37-50.4, 49-31.3, 61-20.2
Bourdon Wood, 33 to 68 - 43%	16'/ 8'	80	1/4	$6^{11}/_{16}$" x $8^1/_2$"	33 to 80-62.5-19/20 Stopped, 57 to 68 - Open Metal
Open Diapason Zinc and 43%	8'	68	1/5	162.3	13-96.5, 25-57.4, 37-35.3, 49-21.1, 61-13.5
Small Open Diapason Zinc and 43%	8'	68	1/4	136.5	1 to 12-16/17, 13 to 68-17/18
Silver Flute Zinc and 43%	8'	68	1/5	120.9	Special, Slotted
Viole de gambe Zinc and 43%	8'	68	1/4	87.9	17/18
Viole céleste Zinc and 43%	8'	68	1/4	65.4	1 to 24-24/25, 25 to 68-17/18
Flauto Dolce Zinc and 43%	8'	68	1/6	87.0	Special, 2/3 Taper, Slotted
Flute Celeste (TC) 43%	8' TC	56	1/6	65.0	Special, 2/3 Taper, Slotted

Stop/Material	Pitch	No. of Pipes	Mouth/ Shallot	Scale	Ratio & Details
Principal Zinc and 43%	4'	68	2/9	92.4	13-54.9, 25-32.6, 37-19.3, 49-12.6, 61-8.1
Harmonic Flute 75%	4'	68	2/9	71.0	Special, 1 to 17 - Slotted, 18 to 61 - Harmonic
Fifteenth 43%	2'	61	2/9	50.4	13-31.3, 25-19.3, 37-12.0, 49-7.8, 61-5.0
Cornet (III) *mf* 43%	$2^2/_3$'	183	U - 2/9 Q - 2/9 T - 1/5	59.9 48.2 38.8	1'-28.7, $^1/_2$'-17.8, $^1/_4$'-11.0, $^1/_8$'-7.1, $^1/_{16}$'-5.0 Same as above 13-23.1, 25-13.7, 37-8.5, 49-5.5
Plein jeu (V) *f* 43%	2'	276	2/9	52.6	$1^1/_3$'-38.8, 1'-31.3, $^1/_2$'-19.3, $^1/_4$'-12.0, $^1/_8$'-8.1, $^1/_{16}$'-5.2
Contra Fagotto Zinc and 43%	32'/ 16'	80	Tapered	10"	$5^1/_2$" at 16', $3^1/_4$" at 8', 57 to 80 - Harmonic
Bombarde Zinc and 75%	16'	68	Parallel	$5^{11}/_{16}$"	$3^{15}/_{16}$" at 8', 61 to 68 - Harmonic
Trompette Zinc and 75%	8'	68	Parallel	$4^1/_4$"	49 to 56 - Harmonic, 57 to 68 - Flues
Cornopean Zinc and 43%	8'	68	Tapered	$3^1/_2$"	33 to 56 - Harmonic, 57 to 68 - Flues
Oboe Zinc and 43%	8'	68	Tapered	$3^3/_4$"	57 to 68 - Flues
Voix humaine 43%	8'	61	Parallel	$1^9/_{16}$"	50 to 61 - Flues
Clairon harmonique 75%	4'	68	Parallel	$3^3/_4$"	5" at 8', 37 to 44 - Harmonic, 45 to 68 - Flues
Clarion 43%	4'	68	Tapered	$2^7/_8$"	$3^3/_4$" at 8', 21 to 44 - Harmonic, 45 to 68 - Flues
CHOIR					
Bass Viol Zinc and 43%	16'	68	2/9	142.6	16/17
Viola Pomposa Zinc and 43%	8'	68	¼	119.9	16/17, Flare by two scales
Viola Celeste Zinc and 43%	8'	68	2/9	87.3	1 to 20-24/25, 20 to 68-16/17

Stop/Material	Pitch	No. of Pipes	Mouth/ Shallot	Scale	Ratio & Details
Echo Gamba Zinc and 43%	8'	68	1/5	77.7	1 to 24-16/17, 25 to 68-24/25
Gamba Celeste Zinc and 43%	8'	68	1/5	77.7	1 to 24-16/17, 25 to 68-24/25
Viole d'orchestre Zinc and 75%	8'	68	1/5	40.0	23/24
Viole céleste Zinc and 75%	8'	68	1/5	40.0	23/24
Lieblich Bourdon Zinc and 43%	16'/ 8'	80	¼	229.7	1 to 12-16/17, 13 to 80-19/20, 30 to 66 - Chimneyed, 67 to 80 - $^2/_3$ Taper
Concert Flute Wood and 43%	8'	68	1/5	$4^1/_8$" x $5^1/_{16}$"	Open Metal at 45, 26.25, Special
Nachthorn 43%	4'	68	1/5	80.0	Special, Slotted
Nazard 43%	$2^2/_3$'	61	2/9	56.0	Special, 1 to 12 - Stopped, 13 to 42 - Chimneyed, 43 to 49 - $^2/_3$ Taper, 50-61 - Open
Harmonic Piccolo 43%	2'	61	2/9	48.2	Special, 50 to 61 - Harmonic
Tierce 43%	$1^3/_5$'	61	2/9	64.2	Special, 1 to 50 - $^2/_3$ Taper
Echo Diapason Zinc and 75%	8'	68	2/9	143.3	17/18
Fugara 75%	4'	68	2/9	84.4	17/18
Twelfth 75%	$2^2/_3$'	61	1/5	60.9	17/18
Fifteenth 75%	2'	61	2/9	49.7	17/18
Nineteenth 75%	$1^1/_3$'	61	1/5	37.3	17/18, 55 to 61 - Repeats
Twenty-second 75%	1'	61	2/9	29.2	17/18, 50 to 61 - Repeats

Stop/Material	Pitch	No. of Pipes	Mouth/ Shallot	Scale	Ratio & Details
Flügel Horn Zinc and 43%	16'/ 8'	80	Tapered	4"	$2^7/_8$" at 8', Capped, 67 to 80 - Flues
Trumpet Zinc and 43%	8'	68	Tapered	4"	43 to 54 - Harmonic, 55 to 68 - Flues
Cromorne 75%	8'	68	Parallel	1 - $^9/_{16}$"	55 to 68 - Flues
Rohr Schalmei Brass and 43%	4'	68	Tapered	$1^1/_4$"	40 to 68 - Flues
SOLO					
Open Diapason Zinc and 43%	8'	61	2/11	170.0	13-101, 25-63, 37-39, 49-24, 61-14.5
Symphonic Flute Zinc and 43%	8'	61	1/5	84.0	Special, 35 to 51 - Harmonic, 52 to 61 - Double Harmonic, 43 to 61 - Double Mouth 1/6 each
Principal Zinc and 43%	4'	61	1/5	97.0	13-57, 75-36, 37-22, 49-14, 61-8.8
Quint Mixture (V) 43%	$2^2/_3$'	288	1/5 15th-2/9	68.0	2'-55, 1'-33, $^1/_2$'-20, $^1/_4$'-13, $^1/_8$'-8.8, $^1/_{16}$'-5.7
French Horn Zinc and 43% Flues -	8'	61	Tapered	6"	38 to 61 - Flues
Bass Tuba Zinc and 43%	16'	61	Tapered	7"	4" at 8', 37 to 61 - Harmonic
Tuba Zinc and 43%	8'	61	Tapered	5"	25 to 58 - Harmonic, 59 to 61 - Flues
Tuba Clarion 43%	4'	61	Tapered	$4^1/_8$"	$5^1/_2$" at 8', 13 to 46 - Harmonic, 47 to 61 - Flues
Tierce Mixture (IV-VI) 43%	2'	309	1/5	U - 59.9 Q – 57.4 T – 54.9	1'-35.6, $^1/_2$'-22.1, $^1/_4$'-13.7, $^1/_8$'-8.8, $^1/_{16}$'-6.0 1'-34.1, $^1/_2$'-21.1, $^1/_4$'-13.1, $^1/_8$'-8.8, $^1/_{16}$'-6.0 1'-32.6, $^1/_2$'-20.2, $^1/_4$'-12.6, $^1/_8$'-8.5, $^1/_{16}$'-5.7
Millennial Trumpet Zinc and 75%	8'	61	Parallel	4"	33 to 56 - Harmonic, 57 to 61 - Flues
ORCHESTRAL					
Tibia Clausa Wood and 40%	16'/8' 4'/2'	97	—	$7^7/_8$" x $10^1/_8$"	Kimball, $4^5/_8$" x $5^3/_8$" at 8' Wurlitzer, 62 to 68 - Stopped Metal, 69 to 97 - Open Metal

Stop/Material	Pitch	No. of Pipes	Mouth/ Shallot	Scale	Ratio & Details
Phonon Diapason Zinc and Hoyt Metal	8'/4'	73	2/7	153.0	Wurlitzer
Stentor Gamba Zinc and 43%	8'	61	1/5	73.5	Special, Flare 4 Scales, Slotted
Celeste Zinc and 43%	8'	61	1/5	73.5	Special, Flare 4 Scales, Slotted
Clarinet Zinc and 43%	16'/8'	73	Tapered	$3^1/_4$"	$2^1/_4$" at 8', 69 to 73 - Flues
Tuba Horn Zinc and Hoyt	8'	61	Tapered	$4^7/_8$"	Wurlitzer, 57 to 61 - Flues
Cor Anglais Zinc and 43%	8'	61	Tapered	3"	50 to 61 - Flues
Orchestral Oboe Zinc and Hoyt Metal	8'	61	Tapered	$1^1/_2$"	Wurlitzer
Vox Humana† Hoyt Metal	8'	61	Tapered	$1^5/_8$"	Wurlitzer
Tuba Mirabilis Zinc and 43%	8'	61	Tapered	$5^1/_2$"	25 to 58 - Harmonic, 59 to 61 - Flues
PEDAL					
Gamba (*GGGGG#*) Zinc and 43%	64'/32'/ 16'/8'	60	2/9	369.9	16/17, 311.0 at 32', 184.9 at 16'
Diaphone Wood and 40%	32'/ 16'	44	Valve	26" x 26"	Kimball, 31 to 44 - Flues
Diapason Zinc	32'/ 16'	44	¼	459	16/17, Slotted
Sub Bass Wood	32'/16'/ 8'	56	—	$20^{13}/_{16}$" x 24"	17 to 45 - Kimball
Open Wood 1 to 30 (and Solo Stentor Diapason Zinc and 40% 31 to 73)	16'/8'	73	1/4	$13^{13}/_{16}$" x $16^3/_{16}$"	1 to 12 - Æolian, 13-30 - Kimball (71 at 2' C)
Violone Wood, Zinc and 43%	16'	32	2/9	$6^3/_{16}$" x $7^7/_8$"	19 to 32 - Metal
Quint Zinc and 43%	$10^2/_3$'	32	2/9	201.6	16/17

Stop/Material	Pitch	No. of Pipes	Mouth/ Shallot	Scale	Ratio & Details
Principal Zinc and 43%	8'	32	2/9	169.5	16/17
Flute Zinc and 43%	8'	32	2/9	148.9	16/17, Slotted
Choral Bass Zinc and 43%	4'	32	2/9	92	17/18
Octave Flute 43%	4'	32	$\frac{1}{4}$	76	Special, 18 to 32 - Harmonic
Rauschquinte (II) 43%	$2\frac{2}{3}$'	64	2/9	65.3	2'-52.6, 1'-32.6, $\frac{1}{2}$'-19.3, $\frac{1}{4}$'-12.6, $\frac{1}{8}$'-8.1, $\frac{1}{16}$'-5.5
Mixture (III) 43%	$1\frac{1}{3}$'	96	2/9	19th & 22nd 26th	$1\frac{1}{3}$'-38.8, 1'-32.6, $\frac{1}{2}$'-19.3, $\frac{1}{4}$'-12.6, $\frac{1}{8}$'-8.1, $\frac{1}{16}$'-5.5, $\frac{2}{3}$'-23.1, $\frac{1}{2}$'-18.6, $\frac{1}{4}$'-12.0, $\frac{1}{8}$'-7.8, $\frac{1}{16}$'-5.2
Trombone (*GGGGG#*) Zinc and 43%	64'/32'/ 16'	48	Tapered	22"	18" at 32', $11\frac{1}{2}$" at 16', $6\frac{1}{2}$" at 8'
Tromba Zinc and 43%	8'/4'	44	Tapered	$5\frac{1}{2}$"	

APPENDIX 2

The Console Platform

Information supplied by lead organ technician Robert Poll

Dimensions: 6"H x 7' 9"W x 6' 8"D

Materials: The perimeter frame is made of welded 2" x 6" tubular steel. The corners are rounded. The decking is 1" thick plyform (laminated plywood with thick, smooth, laminate facing, made to be used for forming concrete pours).

Structural Reinforcement: Six 2" x 5" tubular steel members oriented front to back which are welded to the inside of the perimeter frame. The bottoms of these rest on the floor together with the perimeter frame. The plyform deck is fastened to these with torx-head steel deck screws so that the top of the deck is flush with the top of the perimeter frame.

Finish: The steel tubing is powder-coated in lightly textured black. The plyform deck is painted to match.

Method of securing console to platform: The console floor is bolted to the plywood deck with six 3/8" diameter bolts.

Casters: There are four removable caster assemblies. Each assembly includes a 4" dual, flat-tire, ball-bearing, swivel caster. The swivel is lockable in four different positions. It is attached to the bottom of a typical utility trailer tongue jack with a crank for raising and lowering. The jack is attached to a welded steel framework consisting of 1/4" steel and 2" x 2" steel tubing, also 1/4" thick. The tube "stinger" of each caster assembly slides into a receiver welded into the steel frame near the front and rear corners of each side, much like the removable stinger holding the ball of a vehicle trailer hitch. Each stinger is secured in place with one 1/2" steel rod inserted at a right angle from the front or rear of the platform frame. The rod penetrates the stinger and threads into the opposite side of the receiver. On the outer end of each rod is welded a wing-nut-type device providing the necessary grip and torque to "finger-tighten" the rod in place. Once the caster assemblies are inserted and secured, the deck can be raised with the jack cranks and rolled in any direction.

Number of winches required to fly console/platform: Four

Method of cable attachment and flying: A rigging shackle is used to connect a steel-cable bridle to each caster assembly at a convenient point provided in the 1/4" steel. There are two bridles, one on each side, connecting to both casters on that side. Each bridle is made offset to compensate for the offset load distribution of the console on the platform. The cables from four separate winches (two per side) are then shackled to the bridles at four points. By slowing the two winches of the front, rear, or either side in relation to the two opposite as the platform is raised or lowered, the platform can be moved forward, backward, or from side to side (within limits) while remaining relatively level.

Approximate weight (including platform, console, casters, securing rods and cable bridle): 2,500 lbs.

Platform design and fabrication: Former Church employee Steven R. Wall, then Staging and Production manager.

Caster design and fabrication: Steven R. Wall and Steven L. Wall, then Staging and Production welder.[1]

Bridle design: Lee Alger and Steven L. Wall

Bridle fabrication: Rocky Mountain Wire Rope & Rigging, Inc.

NOTE

[1]Steven L. Wall continues as welder, but also serves as the main Staging and Production lead as well. The two Steven Walls are unaware of any family relationship.

APPENDIX 3

Graffiti Found Inside the Organ Case

With few exceptions the names and sentiments that follow were written by skilled craftsmen, representing a variety of trades, in an effort to express their pride in having been part of such a monumental project and their desire to be remembered for their contribution.

Inside CCCC of Pedal Diapason 32-foot pipe (employees of A.R. Schopp's Sons, Inc., builders of most of the pipes in the Conference Center organ):

David Schopp 2/24/00	Mark Trainer
Ron Brimlow	Larry Hively II
Ron Miller	Brian Rudolph
Rob Beck	Cye Proctor

Also inside that pipe:

New Image Body Works [the firm that applied the finish to the pipes]

Metro Foti

Poncho

Inside the pipe written vertically through the open tuning slot:

Chris Blea 3/18/2000

THANH 3/18/00

Roy 14th

Esteban Hernandes

New Braunfels, Texas 3/22/00

On a separate piece of wood attached in plaque-like fashion on the top center plywood framework of their "boat bottom," behind the gold medallion: Some of the writing was smeared by the lacquer during the finishing process at Fetzer's.

LOUCHARD YACHT RESTORATION

PORT TOWNSEND, WA

1999

DAVE FISH

STAN DELO

GUY HUPY

ED LOUCHARD

STEVE CHAPIN

RUSSELL BROWN

Elsewhere on the case:

> Rick Barnett and crew built this organ
> for the future enjoyment of our families.
> Completed installment of all wood components
> 2/8/2000

> It was worth every sliver.
> Mel Whiting
> Fetzers

> Edgar Glz[?] & Chucky GB
> Build all frames & wood & the choir modules;
> we clean, clean & clean everywhere too!
> We're [smiley face] for have contributed
> in the building of this stage &
> concrete walls as well.
> Thanks everyone!
> "The Mamilas of LLC"

There are three different places with names that are difficult to read that appear to be part of the claim: "I shipped the organ!" or "I shipped this 2000"

There is a signature of "Patience" [elsewhere printed as "Patience Fetzer"]which appears to be connected with the printed statement "I did this for you."

> Last panels of organ installed 3/28/2000 5:30 pm
> EMH [probably Estaban Hernandez whose name appears several times along with Rick Barnett]
> Let's go home

> Joe F. Lambarena [Schoenstein employee]
> Helped install display
> 2/3/99 thru 3/13/00

Conference Center
The Church of Jesus Christ of Latter-day Saints
Salt Lake City, Utah

By Jack M. Bethards

Reprinted from the January 2004 issue of *The American Organist*

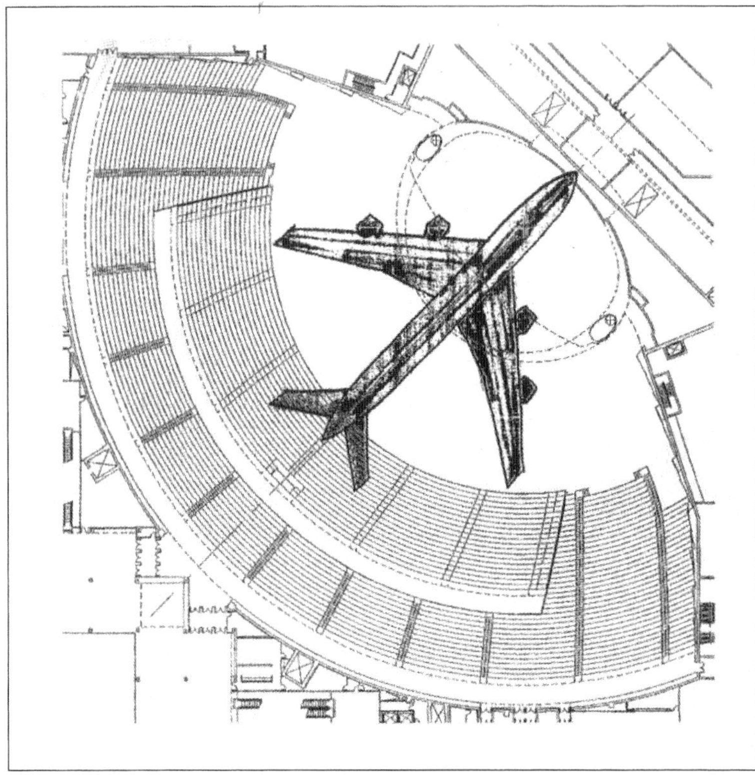

COVER FEATURE
CONFERENCE CENTER
THE CHURCH OF JESUS CHRIST
OF LATTER-DAY SAINTS
SALT LAKE CITY, UTAH
A SYMPHONIC ORGAN FOR THE WORLD'S LARGEST THEATER AUDITORIUM
SCHOENSTEIN & CO. ORGAN BUILDERS

The Builders' Perspective

It's downright confounding to think of a five-manual organ with 130 ranks, seven 32' stops—two of them extended into the 64' range—and wind pressures up to 25" as a *Multum in Parvo* job (that's what the British call a small organ that sounds big). Yet, when we realize that this substantial instrument is in a 21,333-seat auditorium—fully carpeted with upholstered seats, acoustically treated walls and ceiling—into which a Boeing 747 would comfortably fit, the reality of that description sinks in. This is the largest theater-style auditorium ever built. The next largest is the Auditorio Nacional in Mexico at about 11,000 seats. For comparison, remember that Radio City Music Hall has about 6,000 seats, and a typical symphony hall about 2,000. Organs have been built for majestic spaces with reverberant resonance, but never before has one been designed for an 8.5 million cubic foot space with an acoustic planned primarily for the spoken word. The prospect of doing this was daunting to say the least. Very few concert organs in theater acoustics have been successful, even in buildings a tenth the size. There were no examples of buildings—let alone organs—to study. We had to start installation before the building was completed, so there was no opportunity for tonal testing or even a hand clap in the finished space. We had a theory, but that was all!

Before outlining the nerve-racking, but exhilarating process of designing and building this organ, let me answer the questions we are most often asked.

Is an auditorium this large really necessary? The original plan was for one even larger, but this was the largest that could be built on the site with today's technology. The members of the Church of Jesus Christ of Latter-day Saints gather together twice each year for their General Conference. In the last few decades requests from members to attend have flooded in by the tens of thousands. The Tabernacle and all the other Temple Square overflow facilities could barely hold the church leadership, let alone all the members who wished to attend. Church president Gordon B. Hinckley decided that the problem must be solved and ordained the building of the Conference Center.

What is General Conference? Like most people, when I heard the term I thought of a convention business meeting. Nothing could be further from the truth. General Conference, held on the first weekend of April and October each year, is a series of five religious services with messages of instruction and inspiration from the General Authorities of the church and sacred music usually led by the Tabernacle Choir. The organ provides accompaniment for the choir and support for the robust singing of over 21,000 congregants, but there are no organ solos except for soft prelude and postlude selections.

Why is the building shaped and furnished like a theater? It was important to have a semicircular (pie-shaped) design to bring the people as close as possible to the speakers on the rostrum, because the spoken word is the central aspect of General Conference. Perfect sight lines and clear sound were equally important. This shape, combined with acoustically absorptive materials, is the opposite of what is traditionally desired for choral and organ music.

Does a modern auditorium of such vast proportions have the proper atmosphere for religious services? General Conference is a deeply meaningful religious experience and a kind of homecoming or family gathering for members of the church. The Tabernacle has been its home since the early days. Moving into a new site is a bit like asking the Vatican to abandon St. Peter's. Therefore, it was of primary importance to create an atmosphere in the new building reminiscent of the traditions of past conferences and, indeed, of the church's history. A warmly welcoming, familiar and comfortable place of religious purpose was the program set before the architects. All of us in the organ profession must be very gratified that the church authorities found the organ to be the most perfect means to make the members feel at home in the new building. The organ's physical design would be a gentle reminder of the Tabernacle's pioneer case; the sound of a real pipe organ, containing sonic elements of the Tabernacle instrument, would be an equally strong reminder of the building's purpose.

Does the Auditorium have other uses? We found out just how many when we attempted to schedule tonal-finishing work! As soon as the building opened, its usage multiplied. It plays host to regional conferences of the church, special musical events such as Pioneer Day in July and Christmas programs plus pageants, meetings, and special events such as the program the church put on for the 2002 Winter Olympics. The stage platform area is designed for flexibility. It can be converted from the choir and rostrum setup (shown on the front cover) to a setting for orchestra and choir only, or to a completely clear stage—from first row of orchestra seats to the organ case. Ultra-modern rigging, lighting, and audio equipment make varied uses possible. The building is completely climate-controlled 24 hours a day—a great advantage for the organ.

MAGNUM OPUS

Six sets of expression shades, variable tremulants, and crescendo functions are assigned to five balanced pedals by these miniature drawknobs, which in turn are controlled by six independent combination thumb pistons.

Given the size of the building, why isn't the organ larger? Our charge was to make an instrument large enough to get the job done but no larger. Because of the stage requirements, there were space limitations. The budget was to be reasonable and the organ had to be practical to maintain. Also, we were convinced that the number of ranks was not the answer to filling the room with sound. Overly large designs can be counterproductive, smothering themselves in cramped layouts.

I heard that the organ was to be amplified. Is that so? It was never intended to amplify the organ independently by placing microphones in or near the organ. However, we knew that the choir's sound would have to be reinforced and that the organ would be picked up along with it. We also thought that this system would be needed to help project the sound of the organ to the far reaches of the balconies. Much to our surprise and relief, the organ required no amplification at all to be heard clearly throughout the building. The acoustic surpassed even our highest expectations, thanks to the brilliant engineering of acoustical consultants Jaffe Holden Scarbrough of Norwalk, Connecticut.

MUSICAL OBJECTIVES

Our first objective was to create a tone of beauty and nobility without the coarse, shrill loudness that could so easily result from an effort to fill such a large space with sheer force. Certainly, room-filling power is important, but not nearly as important as balancing with the choir. The Tabernacle Choir is used to singing with the full resources of the Tabernacle organ and they were not enamored with the idea of full organ having to issue from closed expression boxes! Another point, the full significance of which was not obvious until the building was in operation, is that it is primarily a recording and broadcasting facility from the point of view of the worldwide church membership. Every significant event is broadcast and translated into 50 languages over the church satellite network. The Sunday radio and television program, *Music and the Spoken Word*, originates from the Conference Center on many occasions. The organ, therefore, had to have a character of tone that was appropriate for broadcasting and recording where subtlety and control are more important than loudness.

Our second objective was to provide all the tonal resources necessary for choir accompaniment. An organ of 130 ranks should be able to handle the bulk of the organ solo repertoire, but this was our last concern. The Tabernacle Choir has an unusually wide-ranging repertoire, as they say, "from Bach to Broadway." They are used to being accompanied by one of the largest and most elegant organs in the world. Our charge was to provide every sound at every dynamic that a choral conductor could ask for. The recently formed Orchestra at Temple Square, a first-rate symphony orchestra, performs often at the Conference Center, and the organ has to acquit itself well in the orchestral repertoire.

There are three features of the divisional layout that are designed specifically to enhance accompaniment capabilities. In working with the Tabernacle Choir over the years, the organists all wished that they could have more solo tone colors available for counter-melodies and melody reinforcement at contrasting dynamic levels. In other words, two

Solo divisions. The Conference Center has three—the Solo, Grand Solo, and Orchestral. The Symphonic Flute and French Horn of the Solo, the Tuba and Tuben of the Grand Solo, and all the stops of the Orchestral fill this need. The Orchestral division is especially interesting because it includes several voices borrowed directly from the theater organ. The Conference Center organ is truly an eclectic one designed to cover the greatest possible repertoire. Borrowing sounds from the theater organ is no different than borrowing sounds from the French Romantic or English Romantic traditions. Any tone that is attractive and useful and that does not detract from the overall ensemble can be included. We picked several distinctive Wurlitzer voices not found on the typical concert organ. It is very important to note, however, that we were not attempting to insert a small theater organ into the instrument, just as we would not graft onto it a neo-Baroque positive. It turned out that these theater-inspired voices have been extremely useful in all kinds of musical contexts that have nothing to do with theater music. They are simply beautiful sounds that work well.

The Choir division is also geared toward maximum accompanimental flexibility. It has a complete selection of strings of different scales from Viole d'orchestre to Viola Pomposa, flutes of different types at all pitches of the cornet, and a chorus of small diapasons with pitches individually controllable. This arrangement provides a nearly limitless array of combinations in both tone color and pitch to create new and interesting effects. The Swell division, which is always the workhorse in choir accompaniment, is especially well developed, with several variations in diapason and flute tone, as well as both French- and English-style reed choruses.

Our third objective was to include some of the more important musical effects of the Tabernacle organ, while at the same time providing overall contrast to it and the other organs on Temple Square. The Aeolian-Skinner is noted for its clarity, and that was a quality the Tabernacle Choir could not live without. The scintillating string ensemble of the Tabernacle organ and its exceptional wealth of *mezzo-forte* voices were effects we wanted to capture in the new instrument. A direct imitation would not only have been impossible but inappropriate in the Conference Center acoustic; the objective was to create equally pleasing sounds with a different accent. In the simplest terms, both organs are eclectic. The Aeolian-Skinner is an American Classic instrument, whereas the Schoenstein organ is an American Romantic one. Other organs on Temple Square lean toward the French and German, so we leaned slightly in the English direction.

Our fourth objective was to duplicate the Tabernacle console arrangements as far as reasonable to make transferring from one instrument to the other as easy as possible considering the pressure of constant performances and broadcasts with limited rehearsal schedules that face the organists.

Finally, we limited ourselves to the smallest stoplist that could achieve the four goals above. We avoided any specialty stops that would be seldom used. For example, there was no need in this instrument for whisper-soft stops that would be lost in this acoustic. There were practical benefits to the *Multum in Parvo* approach, too: tuning stability through logical layout, keeping primary flues and primary reeds each on one level; more economical maintenance.

The following table compares various halls showing the sonic work the Conference Center organ must do:

Hall	Seats	Cu. Vol.	Ranks	Seats/Rank	Cu. Ft./Rank
Conference Center	21,333	8,500,000	130	164	65,385
Atlantic City Convention Hall	40,000	14,700,000	449	89	32,739
London Royal Albert Hall	6,080	3,060,000	172	35	17,790
Mormon Tabernacle	6,500	1,495,000	206	32	7,257
Dallas Myerson Hall	2,179	845,000	84	26	10,059
Cleveland Severance Hall	1,890	554,000	94	20	5,894

Appendix 4

The Great reeds and Solo Millennial Trumpet viewed from above

If we apply to other halls with similar acoustics the Conference Center's ratio of seats to ranks (164 seats per rank), we can see just how small the Conference Center organ is in proportion to the hall:

Hall	Seats	Ranks
Conference Center	21,333	130
Royal Albert Hall	6,080	37
Myerson Hall	2,179	13
Severance Hall	1,890	12
Average large church	1,000	6
Average medium church	500	3

DESIGN THEORY

Every organ design should be based on a solid foundation of musical/acoustical theory, just as every composition should be based on a thorough understanding of harmony and form. For this organ we had a definite theory and a strong conviction that it would work—but no proof! Our system has worked well in moderate-sized buildings with dry acoustics, but would the same principles apply here? Since we had nothing else to go on, we decided to take a deep breath and bet our reputation that they would.

Our first principle in dealing with a dry acoustic is to "fight fire with fire." It seems logical to think that a thin, bright tone will pierce through a dry acoustic, but the exact opposite is true. A dry acoustic requires exceptionally warm, rich, and mellow tones with the center of gravity at 8' pitch. Acoustical resonance is what smooths out and adds beauty to tones that otherwise would be brittle. Without such resonance, the tone must fend for itself and be beautiful up close without the halo of reverberation. Fifty percent of the Conference Center manual voices are at 8' pitch. There are nine 8' diapasons as well as numerous flutes, smooth-toned reeds, and strings. These, along with the softer, smoother 16' and 4' voices, produce a broad tonal foundation.

The second principle is to dominate the stoplist with tones of a naturally projecting character, such as highly energized diapasons, keen strings, open and harmonic flutes, and English-style chorus reeds. These stops, which have a good balance of fundamental and overtones within themselves, can impart power without harsh loudness.

The third principle in dealing with a dry acoustic is that dramatic power must come from reed choruses rather than mixture choruses. The brilliance from the overtones in high-pressure chorus reeds is much more satisfying than the piercing shrillness that results from over-driven mixtures. Mixtures are vitally important in any large organ, but in our concept they provide tonal color—not power.

Perhaps the most thrilling characteristic of the pipe organ is its room-shaking bass. To produce the proper gravity in a room of over eight million cubic feet requires moving a lot of air. Therefore, we included 16' and 32' stops representing each family of tonal color and several dynamic levels. Given the size of the room, it seemed not inappropriate to extend two of the stops into the 64' range. The most interesting bass stop is the Diaphone. In this country diaphones have been associated almost exclusively with theater organs; in England, they were more widely used. The diaphone is a valvular reed developed by Robert Hope-Jones. It yields a magnificent, fast speaking, fundamental bass unequaled by any other class of stop. We were fortunate to acquire a fine example made by Kimball originally for the Forum Theatre in Los Angeles.

The proper and judicious application of high wind pressure is critical to the success of all these concepts. High wind pressure is not employed to produce loudness. The virtue of high wind pressure is twofold. First, it provides a kind of tonal quality that projects sound very efficiently. You have probably experienced the amazing projection achieved by great singers and instrumentalists. Their tone is not loud, but is infused with an intensity that projects. The Wurlitzer organ is another good example. Wurlitzer organs are capable of filling large, acoustically dead motion picture theaters with rich and full tone. The same Wurlitzer organ voiced in the same way can be placed in a small broadcasting studio with an equally fine result. You can stand next to a Wurlitzer organ with no sonic discomfort; its sound projects without extreme loudness. The second virtue of high pressure is the production of sonorous quality in solo stops. High pressure is particularly helpful in reeds, as it also promotes stability. In the Conference Center organ we applied high pressure liberally, but not throughout the instrument, because there is no doubt whatsoever that certain classes of tone fare much better on moderate pressure. This includes, of course, the traditional diapason choruses. In summary, there are certain tonal characteristics that are best achieved with different wind pressures, and to create an instrument of broad tonal scope that can work in a dry acoustic, both approaches should be employed.

Finally, although we consider unenclosed voices a luxury on small organs, there is no doubt of their value in large schemes. We designed a large Great, which is capable of a smooth crescendo buildup by itself. All of the tonal families are well represented and enhanced by the freshness of unenclosed placement directly behind the facade. This is where the application of moderate wind pressure is most valuable. The largest enclosed division, the Swell, has a very complete diapason chorus, as does the Solo. Therefore, we have the luxury of unenclosed Great and Pedal choruses in contrast to expressive choruses in both Swell and Solo. A choir can be backed by all manner of plenum effects at many dynamic levels.

TONAL FINISHING

In scaling and designing the pipes we used the acoustical projections of Jaffe Holden Scarbrough. A theory, which fortunately worked out in practice, is that in order to have good bass in such a huge building, we would have to use extra-large scales. Treble scales would also have to be large, because there were no nearby reflective surfaces to aid in treble projection. It was almost as though the organ were located outdoors!

Our approach to tonal finishing followed the same pattern as our tonal renovation of the Tabernacle Aeolian-Skinner organ, which was completed in 1989. As at the Tabernacle, hall scheduling made it impossible to conduct long periods of tonal regulation. We never had one longer than ten days. Even then, the complete silence that we are used to in churches didn't happen except on Sundays and holidays. But this turned out to be an artistic advantage in both projects. We would do some work, evaluate it, and make refinements before moving on. The breaks between tonal finishing sessions allowed us to think through the balancing and detailed polishing of the instrument while it was being used and tested in a variety of applications. Because of the hall's varied bookings, we were able to test the organ with the Tabernacle Choir and various visiting organizations, as well as orchestra. Tonal finishing was a 32-month process.

We started this job realizing that we might have to make some major changes after hearing the organ in its final acoustical setting. Building an organ based entirely on theoretical concepts and mathematical projections is a dangerous business. We were prepared for the worst. Much to our great surprise and relief, the projections turned out to be right on the money, and the instrument performed generally as we had hoped it would. The acoustic turned out to be much like a good symphony hall of the less resonant type. We faced a huge job of tonal regulation, but no more than what we expected in any instrument of this size. We did make some tonal

The console is made of cherry, kerulian birch burl veneer, and ebony with polished bone and ebony manual key coverings, polished ebony and cherry drawknobs on brass shanks, and cast brass expression shoes.

changes, but we were gratified that none of these contradicted our design theories. To the contrary, changes were necessary only where we were not quite bold enough in following our original concepts! These were: emphasis on 8' foundation tone, adequate wind pressure, and emphasis on open rather than stopped flutes.

Even with fairly large scales specified for the diapasons, we increased the scales slightly on the Great Large Open Diapason and the Great Principal. The instrument had commanding reeds and a powerful solo flute, but no diapason of similar character. Therefore, we extended the Pedal Open Wood into a Stentor Diapason on the Solo (scale 38 on 25" wind pressure). We raised the wind pressure of the Solo from 10" to 11½" and of the Grand Solo from 15" to 17½". We knew at the outset that normal stopped flutes were not terribly effective in large buildings so we included only a few. The results proved the point and caused us to eliminate two more and replace them with diapasons! The straight 8' Stopped Diapason in the Swell was replaced with the 8' Small Open Diapason. The 8' Chimney Flute in the Great gave way to an 8' tapered principal (Gemshorn). These aided greatly the dynamic buildup in these divisions.

We also discovered that our system of double expression, which is very effective in smaller buildings, did not mean much in a building of this immense size. With the long distances between the pipes and the listeners, a single swell box is quite adequate to reduce volume to *ppp*. We modified the double expressive box and shades of the Grand Solo to make it an entirely separate subdivision of the Solo. Being separately couplable, the Grand Solo Tuba chorus topped by a Tierce Mixture serves as the capstone of other divisions.

FACADE

That the facade turned out so well is another one of the miracles of this job. It could have been a real disaster, because it was truly a design by committee. Emphasis was placed on the facade because it is the main design feature of the entire auditorium. Our first instinct was to do something completely different than the Tabernacle. We tried Modern, Greek revival, and many other concepts.

Soon it was made clear that we must arrive at something that would be a reminder of the Tabernacle, but an imitation of that case would be doomed to failure on the grounds of both appropriateness and accuracy. Four groups were involved in the design: Bill Williams, project architect of ZGF, Seattle, Washington; the church architects and design experts under the direction of Leland Gray; Paul Fetzer of Fetzers' Inc., Salt Lake City, the architectural millwork firm engaged to build the facade along with the other woodwork of the building; and Steuart Goodwin from our firm. Steuart suggested that by employing two large towers, a group of smaller towers and flats, and gold-finished front pipes we would echo the feeling of the Tabernacle no matter how far afield we went with other elements. He developed the initial design. Scott Bleak of the church's Architecture and Engineering Division suggested the unique idea of bridging all of the towers with one sweeping connective element at the top. We wanted the facade to be as acoustically transparent as possible and to include reflective elements to help project sound forward. Paul Fetzer worked out all these details, as well as the decorative elements and structure of the woodwork. The design team worked tirelessly to achieve a result that was acceptable to each party and one that appears to have been happily embraced by the leadership and membership of the church.

COLLABORATION

The time schedule, which was shorter than we would expect, even for a modest-sized church organ, combined with the size of the instrument made it impossible for us to accomplish this project without a lot of extra help from our many trusted suppliers and colleagues. A.R. Schopp's Sons Inc. of Alliance, Ohio, made almost all of the pipes and, in addition, all of the windchests and most of the wind regulators. Peterson Electro-Musical Products of Alsip, Illinois, made the combination action and relay equipment. Walker Technical Company of Zionsville, Pennsylvania, furnished the digital percussion effects. Fetzers' Inc. of Salt Lake City manufactured and installed all of the facade woodwork. The gold finish of the front pipes was executed in Bountiful, Utah, by New Im-

age Body Works. M.L. Bigelow & Company Inc. of American Fork, Utah, was very helpful to us throughout the project, particularly in restorative work of the Diaphone pipes. We could not have done this project without the help of the skilled and diligent organ technicians of the Tabernacle, Robert Poll and his associate, Lamont Anderson.

Our longtime colleague Steuart Goodwin collaborated on this project as he did on the Tabernacle renovation, helping with design work, voicing, and supervising massive amounts of the tonal finishing. Our project manager for the first portion of the work was Robert Rhoads, who was succeeded after his retirement by Louis Patterson.

All of us at Schoenstein wish to thank the Conference Center team under the direction of Tom Hanson for their generous cooperation and support, and especially the Tabernacle Choir staff: Tabernacle organists John Longhurst, Clay Christiansen, and Richard Elliott; Temple Square organists Bonnie Goodliffe and Linda Margetts; music director Craig Jessop and associate director Mack Wilberg; choir president Mac Christensen and past president Wendell Smoot. Working on Temple Square, serving the Mormon Tabernacle Choir, is a once-in-a-lifetime experience that we have been blessed to enjoy twice.

Finally, we must recognize perhaps the most important collaborators of all, the great builders of the past who handed down knowledge and inspiration. Three of them even provided pipes—Wurlitzer, Kimball, and Aeolian—three giants of American organbuilding.

JACK M. BETHARDS
On behalf of all the organbuilders:

Wendell Ballantyne	Joe Lambarena
David Beck	Luis-Alonzo Lopez
Ann Bharoocha	Fernando Martinez
Filiberto Borbon	George Morten
Peter Botto	Mike Ohman
Jim Cullen	Louis Patterson
Mary Dunwell	Sharon Powers
Manuela Esteva	Chuck Primich
Steuart Goodwin	Bill Ramsay
Vicente Guerrero	Robert Rhoads
Chris Hansford	Tom Roberts
Nathan Hansford	Don Siler
Mark Hotsenpiller	Cindy Smith
Eldon Ives	Chet Spencer

CONSOLE CONTROL LAYOUT

Drawn by Chuck Primich

Schoenstein & Co.

9-15-2003

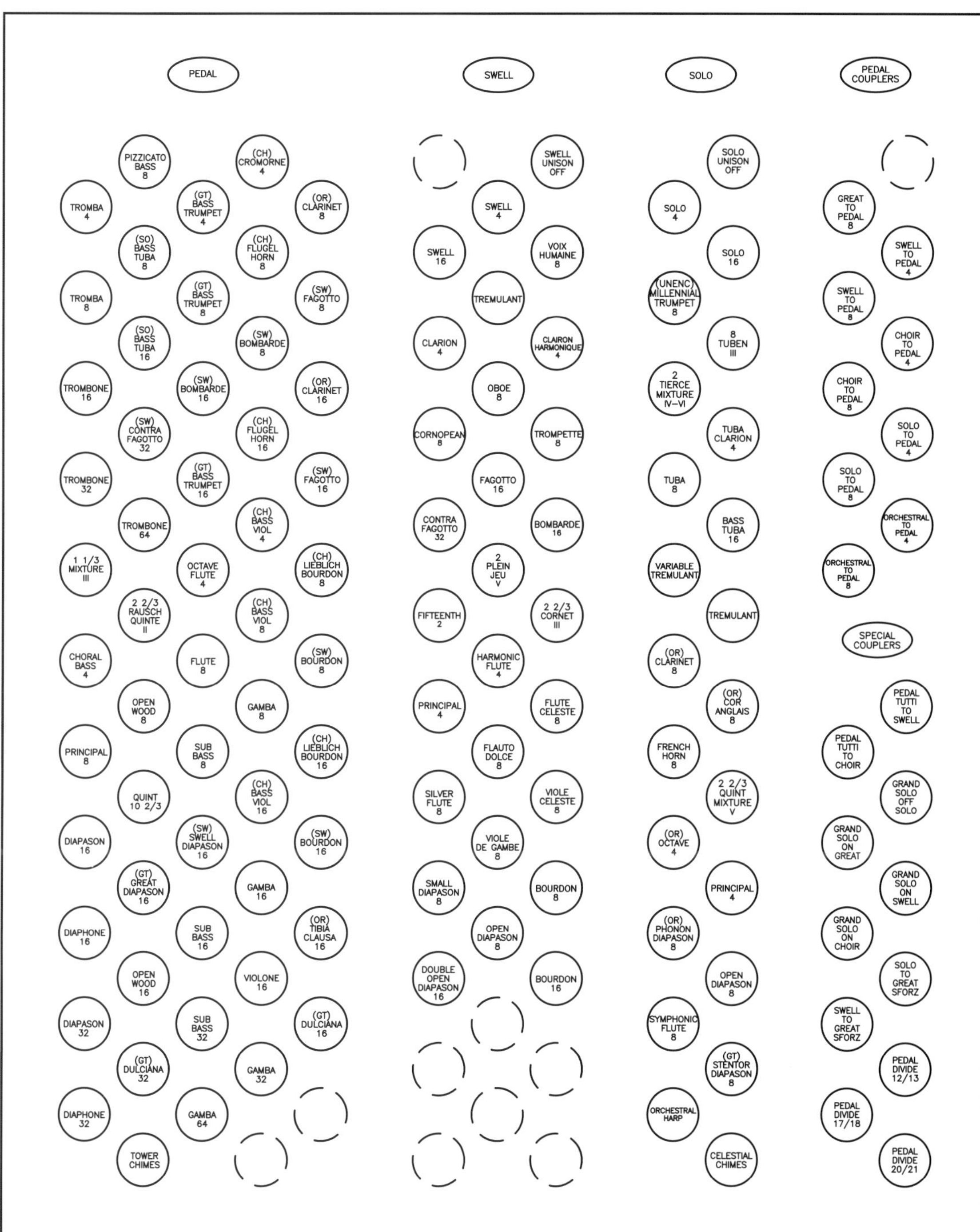
PEDAL
SWELL
SOLO
PEDAL COUPLERS

PIZZICATO BASS 8
(CH) CROMORNE 4
TROMBA 4
(GT) BASS TRUMPET 4
(OR) CLARINET 8
(SO) BASS TUBA 8
(CH) FLUGEL HORN 8
TROMBA 8
(GT) BASS TRUMPET 8
(SW) FAGOTTO 8
(SO) BASS TUBA 16
(SW) BOMBARDE 8
TROMBONE 16
(SW) BOMBARDE 16
(OR) CLARINET 16
(SW) CONTRA FAGOTTO 32
(CH) FLUGEL HORN 16
TROMBONE 32
(GT) BASS TRUMPET 16
(SW) FAGOTTO 16
TROMBONE 64
(CH) BASS VIOL 4
1 1/3 MIXTURE III
OCTAVE FLUTE 4
(CH) LIEBLICH BOURDON 8
2 2/3 RAUSCH QUINTE II
(CH) BASS VIOL 8
CHORAL BASS 4
FLUTE 8
(SW) BOURDON 8
OPEN WOOD 8
GAMBA 8
PRINCIPAL 8
SUB BASS 8
(CH) LIEBLICH BOURDON 16
QUINT 10 2/3
(CH) BASS VIOL 16
DIAPASON 16
(SW) SWELL DIAPASON 16
(SW) BOURDON 16
(GT) GREAT DIAPASON 16
GAMBA 16
DIAPHONE 16
SUB BASS 16
(OR) TIBIA CLAUSA 16
OPEN WOOD 16
VIOLONE 16
DIAPASON 32
SUB BASS 32
(GT) DULCIANA 16
(GT) DULCIANA 32
GAMBA 32
DIAPHONE 32
GAMBA 64
TOWER CHIMES

SWELL UNISON OFF
SWELL 4
SWELL 16
VOIX HUMAINE 8
TREMULANT
CLARION 4
CLAIRON HARMONIQUE 4
OBOE 8
CORNOPEAN 8
TROMPETTE 8
FAGOTTO 16
CONTRA FAGOTTO 32
BOMBARDE 16
2 PLEIN JEU V
FIFTEENTH 2
2 2/3 CORNET III
HARMONIC FLUTE 4
PRINCIPAL 4
FLUTE CELESTE III
FLAUTO DOLCE 8
SILVER FLUTE 8
VIOLE CELESTE 8
VIOLE DE GAMBE 8
SMALL DIAPASON 8
BOURDON 8
OPEN DIAPASON 8
DOUBLE OPEN DIAPASON 16
BOURDON 16

SOLO UNISON OFF
SOLO 4
SOLO 16
(UNENC) MILLENNIAL TRUMPET 8
8 TUBEN III
2 TIERCE MIXTURE IV–VI
TUBA CLARION 4
TUBA 8
BASS TUBA 16
VARIABLE TREMULANT
TREMULANT
(OR) CLARINET 8
(OR) COR ANGLAIS 8
FRENCH HORN 8
2 2/3 QUINT MIXTURE V
(OR) OCTAVE 4
PRINCIPAL 4
(OR) PHONON DIAPASON 8
OPEN DIAPASON 8
SYMPHONIC FLUTE 8
(GT) STENTOR DIAPASON 8
ORCHESTRAL HARP
CELESTIAL CHIMES

GREAT TO PEDAL 8
SWELL TO PEDAL 4
SWELL TO PEDAL 8
CHOIR TO PEDAL 4
CHOIR TO PEDAL 8
SOLO TO PEDAL 4
SOLO TO PEDAL 8
ORCHESTRAL TO PEDAL 4
ORCHESTRAL TO PEDAL 8

SPECIAL COUPLERS
PEDAL TUTTI TO SWELL
PEDAL TUTTI TO CHOIR
GRAND SOLO OFF SOLO
GRAND SOLO ON GREAT
GRAND SOLO ON SWELL
GRAND SOLO ON CHOIR
SOLO TO GREAT SFORZ
SWELL TO GREAT SFORZ
PEDAL DIVIDE 12/13
PEDAL DIVIDE 17/18
PEDAL DIVIDE 20/21

Center console.

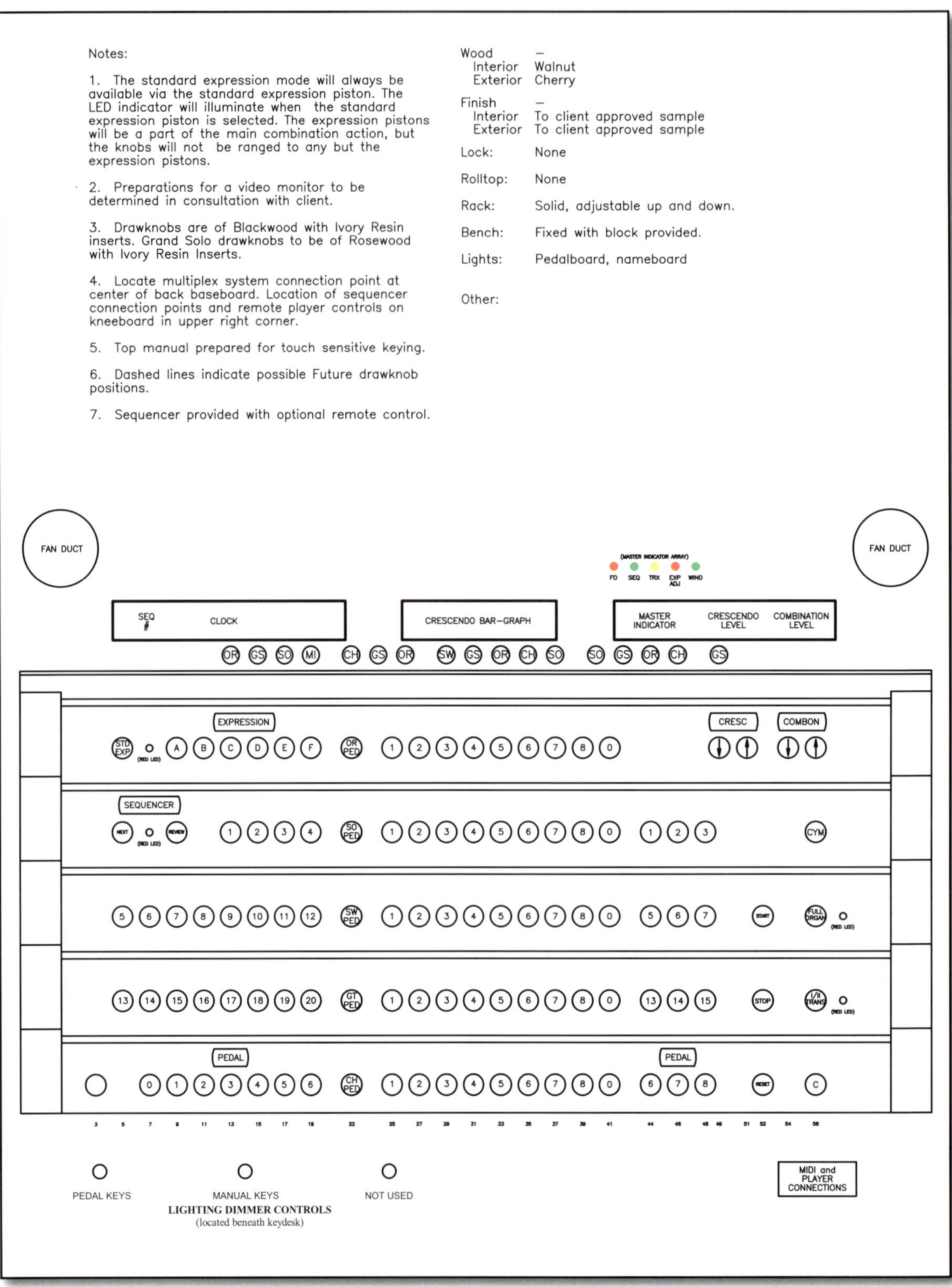
Notes:

1. The standard expression mode will always be available via the standard expression piston. The LED indicator will illuminate when the standard expression piston is selected. The expression pistons will be a part of the main combination action, but the knobs will not be ranged to any but the expression pistons.

2. Preparations for a video monitor to be determined in consultation with client.

3. Drawknobs are of Blackwood with Ivory Resin inserts. Grand Solo drawknobs to be of Rosewood with Ivory Resin Inserts.

4. Locate multiplex system connection point at center of back baseboard. Location of sequencer connection points and remote player controls on kneeboard in upper right corner.

5. Top manual prepared for touch sensitive keying.

6. Dashed lines indicate possible Future drawknob positions.

7. Sequencer provided with optional remote control.

Wood   —
  Interior   Walnut
  Exterior   Cherry
Finish   —
  Interior   To client approved sample
  Exterior   To client approved sample
Lock: None
Rolltop: None
Rack: Solid, adjustable up and down.
Bench: Fixed with block provided.
Lights: Pedalboard, nameboard
Other:

FAN DUCT
FAN DUCT

(MASTER INDICATOR ARRAY)
FO   SEQ   TRX   EXP   WIND
                       ADJ

SEQ #   CLOCK
CRESCENDO BAR–GRAPH
MASTER INDICATOR   CRESCENDO LEVEL   COMBINATION LEVEL

OR GS SO MI   CH GS OR   SW GS OR CH SO   SO GS OR CH   GS

EXPRESSION
STD EXP   (RED LED)   A B C D E F   OR PED   1 2 3 4 5 6 7 8 0   CRESC   COMBON

SEQUENCER
NEXT   (RED LED)   PREV   1 2 3 4   SO PED   1 2 3 4 5 6 7 8 0   1 2 3   CYM

5 6 7 8 9 10 11 12   SW PED   1 2 3 4 5 6 7 8 0   5 6 7   START   FULL ORGAN   (RED LED)

13 14 15 16 17 18 19 20   GT PED   1 2 3 4 5 6 7 8 0   13 14 15   STOP   T/A TRANS   (RED LED)

PEDAL   PEDAL
0 1 2 3 4 5 6   CH PED   1 2 3 4 5 6 7 8 0   6 7 8   RESET   C

3 5 7 9 11 13 15 17 19 22 25 27 29 31 33 35 37 39 41 44 46 48 49 51 52 54 56

PEDAL KEYS   MANUAL KEYS   NOT USED
LIGHTING DIMMER CONTROLS
(located beneath keydesk)

MIDI and PLAYER CONNECTIONS

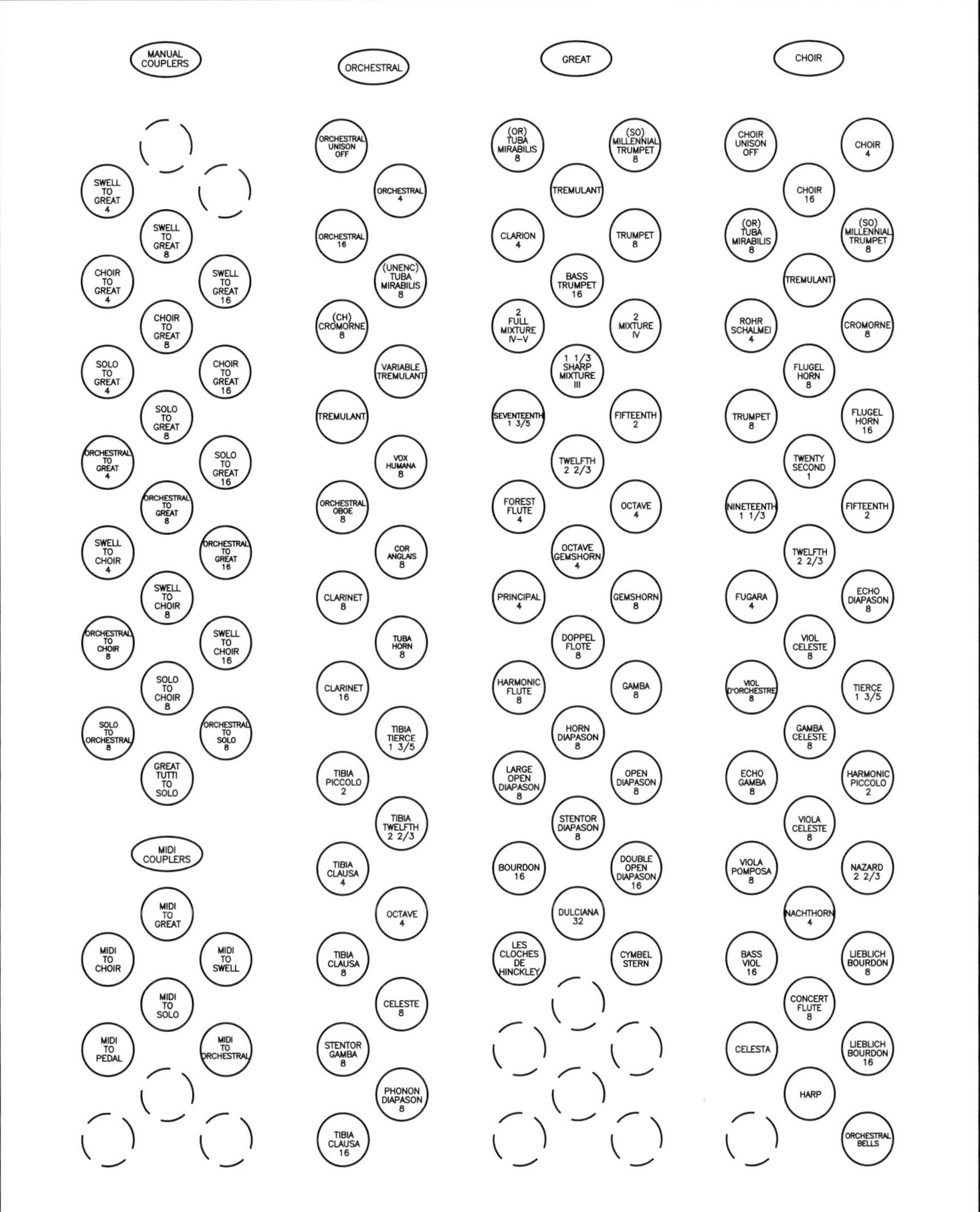
MANUAL COUPLERS
ORCHESTRAL
GREAT
CHOIR
SWELL TO GREAT 4
SWELL TO GREAT 8
SWELL TO GREAT 16
CHOIR TO GREAT 4
CHOIR TO GREAT 8
CHOIR TO GREAT 16
SOLO TO GREAT 4
SOLO TO GREAT 8
SOLO TO GREAT 16
ORCHESTRAL TO GREAT 4
ORCHESTRAL TO GREAT 8
ORCHESTRAL TO GREAT 16
SWELL TO CHOIR 4
SWELL TO CHOIR 8
SWELL TO CHOIR 16
ORCHESTRAL TO CHOIR 8
SOLO TO CHOIR 8
SOLO TO ORCHESTRAL 8
ORCHESTRAL TO SOLO 8
GREAT TUTTI TO SOLO
MIDI COUPLERS
MIDI TO GREAT
MIDI TO CHOIR
MIDI TO SWELL
MIDI TO SOLO
MIDI TO PEDAL
MIDI TO ORCHESTRAL
ORCHESTRAL UNISON OFF
ORCHESTRAL 4
ORCHESTRAL 16
(UNENC) TUBA MIRABILIS 8
(CH) CROMORNE 8
VARIABLE TREMULANT
TREMULANT
VOX HUMANA 8
ORCHESTRAL OBOE 8
COR ANGLAIS 8
CLARINET 8
TUBA HORN 8
CLARINET 16
TIBIA TIERCE 1 3/5
TIBIA PICCOLO 2
TIBIA TWELFTH 2 2/3
TIBIA CLAUSA 4
OCTAVE 4
TIBIA CLAUSA 8
CELESTE 8
STENTOR GAMBA 8
PHONON DIAPASON 8
TIBIA CLAUSA 16
(OR) TUBA MIRABILIS 8
(SO) MILLENNIAL TRUMPET 8
TREMULANT
CLARION 4
TRUMPET 8
BASS TRUMPET 16
2 FULL MIXTURE IV–V
2 MIXTURE IV
1 1/3 SHARP MIXTURE III
SEVENTEENTH 1 3/5
FIFTEENTH 2
TWELFTH 2 2/3
FOREST FLUTE 4
OCTAVE 4
OCTAVE GEMSHORN 4
PRINCIPAL 4
GEMSHORN 8
DOPPEL FLOTE 8
HARMONIC FLUTE 8
GAMBA 8
HORN DIAPASON 8
LARGE OPEN DIAPASON 8
OPEN DIAPASON 8
STENTOR DIAPASON 8
BOURDON 16
DOUBLE OPEN DIAPASON 16
DULCIANA 32
LES CLOCHES DE HINCKLEY
CYMBEL STERN
CHOIR UNISON OFF
CHOIR 4
CHOIR 16
(OR) TUBA MIRABILIS 8
(SO) MILLENNIAL TRUMPET 8
TREMULANT
ROHR SCHALMEI 4
CROMORNE 8
FLUGEL HORN 8
TRUMPET 8
FLUGEL HORN 16
TWENTY SECOND 1
NINETEENTH 1 1/3
FIFTEENTH 2
TWELFTH 2 2/3
FUGARA 4
ECHO DIAPASON 8
VIOL CELESTE 8
VIOL D'ORCHESTRE 8
TIERCE 1 3/5
GAMBA CELESTE 8
ECHO GAMBA 8
HARMONIC PICCOLO 2
VIOLA CELESTE 8
VIOLA POMPOSA 8
NAZARD 2 2/3
NACHTHORN 4
BASS VIOL 16
LIEBLICH BOURDON 8
CONCERT FLUTE 8
CELESTA
LIEBLICH BOURDON 16
HARP
ORCHESTRAL BELLS

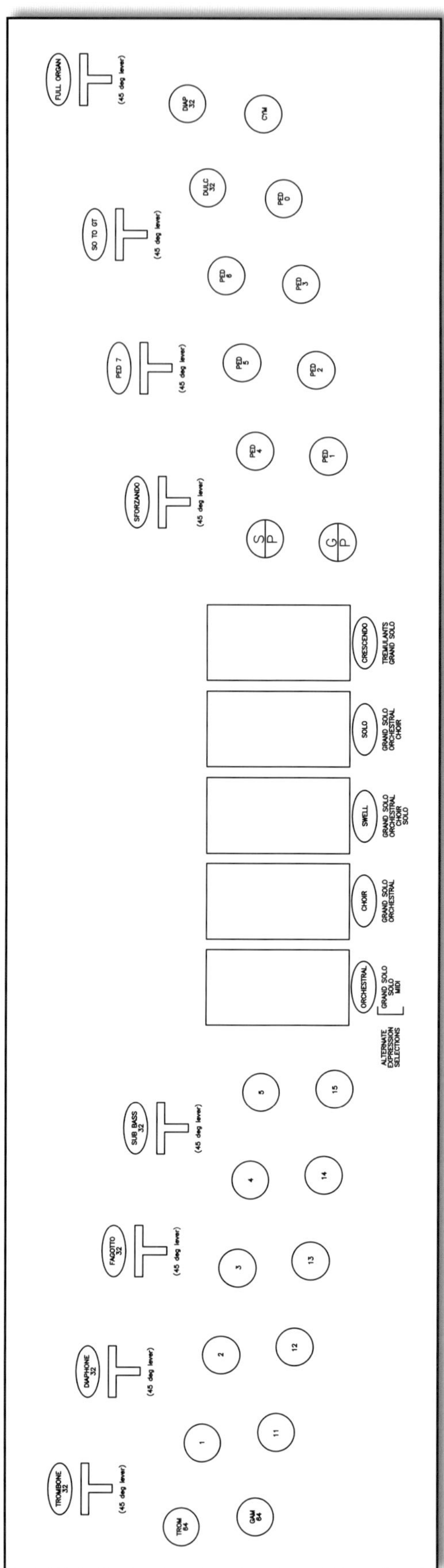

Swell shoes, toe studs and Levers.

APPENDIX 6

SCHOENSTEIN & CO.
PIPE ORGAN TONAL COLOR WHEEL

Schoenstein & Co.
Pipe Organ Tonal Color Wheel

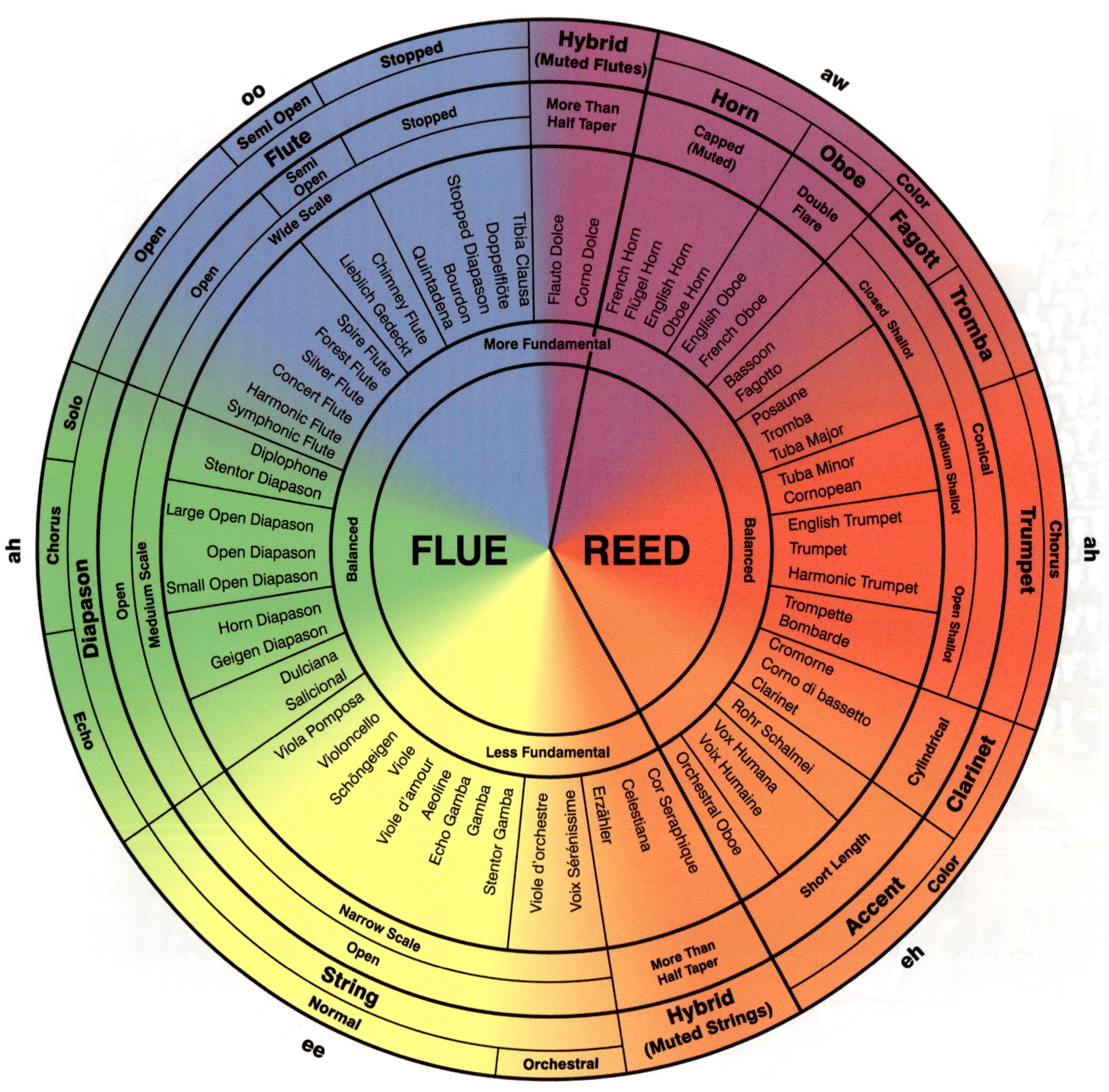

Color wheel layout by Brian White, whitesgraphics.com
Colorization by Blake Palmer, carrprinting.com
Copyright © Jack M. Bethards, 2007

<h1 style="text-align:center">READING THE COLOR WHEEL</h1>

The color wheel is divided into four main rings, as delineated by the five bold circles. The four rings are most cearly seen just to the right of the twelve o'clock position on the wheel. In other areas of the wheel, the outer two rings are often subdivided. The following text describes the content of the wheel, starting at its perimeter and working inward toward the core.

VOWEL SOUNDS

Describing organ tone in words is difficult and often misleading. Bright, dark, rich, warm, brilliant, wooly and sweet are just a few of the common attempts to picture organ tone. Saying that a stop sounds like an oboe, for example, doesn't help much either. Is it an oboe in a French band or in an English orchestra? Six of the most basic vowel tones are shown at the outer edge of the wheel to introduce a more accurate system of description. There are dozens, if not hundreds, of minute variations in vowel sound, any of which might be employed to illustrate the kind of organ tone one is either hearing or wishes to hear. Consonants may be used as well to describe the percussive onset of some tones.

FIRST (OUTER) RING

The outer ring of the wheel indicates twelve major categories of organ tone. The number of categories could be decreased to six by reducing the reed family to chorus reeds and color reeds and by combining the two hybrid groups into one. Conversely the number of categories could be increased to seventeen, thus revealing more detail, by dividing the flute family into open, semi-open and stopped flutes; the diapason family into chorus, solo and echo diapasons; the string family into normal and orchestral strings.

SECOND RING

The second ring describes the elements of pipe construction that contribute most to the distinctive character of each group. Among flues, the most important determinant is the scale—a pipe's diameter relative to speaking length. Next in importance are the treatment of the top end of the pipe (open, semi-open, stopped) and the shape of the pipe body (parallel or tapered). Among flutes, tone quality is so greatly affected by the opening at the top that they are divided into three distinct tonal groups based on this characteristic alone. The strongly tapered (muted) flue pipes are called hybrids because they have an unusual tone that is difficult to place squarely in the flute or string category. This elusive quality is part of their charm. (Mildly tapered construction also affects tone, but this and myriad other more subtle construction features cannot be shown with clarity on the color wheel.)

In the reed family, the shape and length of the resonator, as well as the shape and opening of the shallot (the organ's equivalent of a mouthpiece) are the most important among many variables. Scale, of course, also plays an important role; however, there are great variations in scale within each reed group—not a continuum as found in flues (string to diapason to flute.)

THIRD RING

The third ring gives specific examples of 8-foot stops of various dynamic levels in each tonal category, using nomenclature found in Schoenstein organs. Dozens, if not hundreds, of other names would serve just as well. One example is the term "principal," which is synonymous with "diapason." Some names are unique to Schoenstein organs, but in those cases, stops with more common names, which are in the same category, are also included for clarity—for example Viole d'orchestre, which is in the same class as Voix Sérénissime.

FOURTH RING

The essence of tone color is harmonic structure—the relative strength of a tone's harmonic components. The most elementary description of tone color derives from the balance between a tone's first harmonic or fundamental frequency, and all its upper harmonics or overtones, considered as a group. Tones with what we may consider a "normal" balance (between the fundamental and all upper harmonics) are capable of producing what is called "chorus tone" in the organ. These are the trumpets and diapasons at the right and left sides of the ring respectively. At the bottom of the ring are stops with less fundamental in relation to upper harmonics, with a tone often described as "bright." At the top are stops with more fundamental in comparison to upper harmonics, sometimes called "dark." Although it is not possible to include in this highly simplified presentation, a detailed analysis of each stop would reveal widely varying proportions between the fundamental and the various upper harmonics from one stop to the next around the wheel. Thus, some stops can be described and recognized by the prominence of certain harmonics. A keen ear can detect if a stop has, for example, a prominent third harmonic (an octave plus a perfect fifth above the fundamental). Two groups of stops—the clarinet and stopped flute families—emphasize all the odd-numbered harmonics. Note that these are roughly opposite one another on the color wheel. The two hybrid groups emphasize the fifth, sixth and seventh harmonics, giving them their mysterious quality.

FLUE AND REED

The inner core of the wheel divides all organ tone into two categories based on the method of tone production—flue or reed. Flue pipes generate tone by wind blowing across the lip of the pipe, which causes the column of air inside the pipe to vibrate. A flue pipe generates its tone very much like a simple whistle or the flute of the orchestra. Reed pipes generate tone with a thin, brass tongue (reed) vibrating against a small, open-faced, hollow tube (shallot). The resulting tone is then amplified and modified by a resonator (often conical in shape), which comprises the top portion of the pipe. A reed pipe generates its tone much like the clarinet of the orchestra.

LOUDNESS AND PITCH

Loudness and pitch affect our perception of tonal color. Extremes of either can obscure tonal color or create what appear to be variations. For example, a diapason voiced loudly can become stringy and the same pipe voiced softly can seem fluty. Many tone colors when voiced softly can take on a "grey" or nearly neutral tone, which can be very valuable, especially for accompaniment. Around the tonal color wheel, stops that are normally loudly voiced may appear next to ones that are usually soft. Relationships are based entirely on tone quality, irrespective of loudness.

Many stops lose their distinctive color as they approach the top of their pitch range; the same is true of some stops toward the bottom of the compass. The color wheel considers stops as they sound in the mid-range of the manual keyboard.

USING THE COLOR WHEEL

Diapason, flute, string, and reed are just about as useful in describing organ tone as are sweet, sour, bitter, and salty in describing food flavors. A simple system is better than no system, but as a tool for description or analysis of tonal design or registration, the standard "four families of tone" is limited and misleading. It certainly doesn't create much enthusiasm for the nearly limitless subtle variety of tone colors that can be produced by the pipe organ. Take the reeds for example. One may well wonder how it is possible to put a Trumpet, a Clarinet and a Vox Humana into the same category. What about open flutes and stopped flutes? What about different scales of strings: one that might have the bite of a reed and another almost diapason-like breadth? These questions prompted a search for a way to categorize the vast array of organ tones in a more systematic way.

Music has always been related to color, and musicians often describe not only timbre but also tonality in terms of color. Organ consoles sometimes have red color engraving on reed stop knobs; some French Romantic organs use different colors for each of the major tonal families. A color wheel, therefore, seems to be an appropriate way to present the families of organ stops, showing how they are related in a continuum, depending on their harmonic content and thus the vowel sound they produce. It is very interesting to see how the relationships among visual colors (primary, secondary, etc.) correspond to the relationships among tone colors.

PRIMARY COLORS

The primary colors (red, blue and yellow) cannot be made by combining other colors; they are unique. The primary tone colors of the organ are flute, string and trumpet. They, too, are unique. The most striking example of a secondary color that may be synthesized by combining primary colors is the diapason, which can be imitated, if not replaced, by combining a flute and a string. We see this often on small instruments where the Swell uses a flute and a string as the foundation of the division. How can the diapason be omitted from the list of primary colors when it is universally recognized as the most important stop of the organ? An analogy is that green may be the most important color in a forest painting, but that does not make it a primary color.

THE DIAPASON

Diapason tone is unique to the organ. It is the signature sound, well known to even the most casual listener. The terms "diapason" and "principal" are synonymous, but at Schoenstein we reserve "principal" for the 4-foot member of this tonal family, which is used to set pitch for tuning. Diapason is the tone color that sets the organ apart from other instruments and therefore is the most important of all flue stops. Diapason tone is poised at the mid-point between pure string and pure flute tone. This is the characteristic that also makes it one of the most difficult stops to design and voice perfectly. If the scale is a bit too wide, the stop will tend toward the flute character. If it is a bit too narrow, it will tend toward the string character. Given the influence of the acoustic into which the organ plays, achieving this perfect balance is one of the most challenging aspects of the organ builder's art. This explains why diapason tone has differed so much among various builders and national traditions over the centuries. The sound of the diapason and the emphasis placed on diapason tone is what most commonly defines a personal or national style of organ building—and what most often invites criticism.

THE ORGAN'S TWO PILLARS OF TONE

If the diapason is the monarch of the flues, certainly the trumpet is the emperor of the reeds. It is the dominant sound of the reed family and the only primary "inimitable" reed tone; it cannot be synthesized by combining two other reed stops. What makes the diapason and the trumpet the pillars upon which the structure of an organ is built is their unique ability to create a true chorus effect. The term "chorus" is often used loosely, by applying it to a group of stops of different pitches that are in the same tonal family. Sometimes a group of flutes at 16', 8', 4', 2^2/$_3$' and 2' is called a chorus. This is not correct. That same group of pitches in the diapason family, however, could be called a chorus, following this definition: a chorus is a group of stops of the same tone color, sounding at different pitches of the harmonic series, that has both strong fundamental and brilliant overtones and is commonly played together **in chordal texture**. A chorus is possible only when the various pitches can interlock with each other and fuse to make a single blended block of sound. This fusing requires production of the most natural singing vowel tone, the "ah." The tone must have a balance of fundamental and overtones such that the overtones of a lower pitch interlock with the fundamental and overtones of each successively higher pitch.

Certainly stops from other tonal families can be combined in this way, but such an ensemble is not normally used in chordal texture. For example, the grouping of flutes mentioned above is most effectively used in playing a single melodic line. An ensemble of strings or specialty color reeds can produce interesting special effects, but their lack of fundamental precludes sustained use as a chorus.

The two pillars of organ tone, capable of producing a chorus, are the tonal backbone of the organ. One or the other, or most often both together, are necessary to give the organ's full ensemble its sense of grandeur and magnificent power. Often in the Anglo-American tradition, one division of an instrument (commonly the Great) has a diapason chorus as its primary focus while another division (usually the Swell) has trumpets as its power center. The full Great will have a diapason color with some trumpet accent. The full Swell will consist of trumpet 16', 8' and 4' plus a mixture to add a diapason accent. In the full organ ensemble, with all divisions coupled together, the diapasons and trumpets may be of equal power, or one may slightly dominate the other depending on the acoustical and musical circumstances, but the diapason chorus and trumpet chorus are the essential elements of organ architecture on which the rest of the structure depends. The term "quasi-chorus" may be applied to several tonal groups. These include stops that can produce a chorus-like effect for limited use. For example, an ensemble of echo diapasons (dulcianas and salicionals) can produce a sound like a diapason chorus heard at a distance, a most useful timbre in choir accompaniment. Reeds of the tromba family can make a fine multi-pitch ensemble effect, but their emphasis on the fundamental doesn't permit the kind of balance and blend found in the trumpet chorus. Exactly the opposite imbalance–emphasis on overtones–limits the usefulness of ensembles built on fagott tone. A mixed group of color reeds such as a Clarinet at 16-foot pitch, Flügel Horn at 8-foot pitch and Rohr Schalmei at 4-foot pitch can yield a chorus-like effect on the Choir manual. Also, a stop of this type can be used as a substitute 16-foot voice to give a lighter effect to a trumpet chorus.

DESIGN AND REGISTRATION

The main purpose of the color wheel is to provide some practical help in both organ registration and tonal design. Here are just two points relative to registration that the wheel helps illustrate. The Diapason is a closer relative of the Harmonic Flute than is the Bourdon. Therefore in playing one of the beautiful Harmonic Flute solos in the French Romantic repertoire on an organ without one, it might be wiser to substitute a broad-scale diapason, rather than a stopped flute with its emphasis on off-unison overtones and consequent "hollow" tone color. On the other hand, a stopped flute serves as a nice substitute for a Clarinet, especially if augmented with flute-toned mutations reinforcing the off-unison overtones, since the Clarinet shares a similar harmonic make-up. Thus, looking at tones near one another or opposite one another on the color wheel provides insight as to how tones may be combined or substituted.

Thinking of tone colors in this format helps in deciding which stops to include in an organ design. For example, note the close relationship of the Flauto Dolce, Corno Dolce, French Horn and Flügel Horn. Each one of these stops exhibits a mysterious, muted quality. If that effect is desired, the color wheel shows choices that might be overlooked if these stops were not arranged together based on tonal quality. In a small symphonic organ we often include the Corno Dolce or Flügel Horn where the more specialized Flauto Dolce and French Horn are not practical. Thus an important effect is included by substituting these stops for a soft string and an Oboe. A Swell division should have flute, string and diapason tone at 8-foot pitch. Where there is space for only two 8-foot stops, the color wheel illustrates interesting possibilities to provide diapason quality: one combines two primary colors–a flute and a string; the other selects, in addition to a flute, a tone on the border between string and diapason tone–a Salicional or a Viola Pomposa–thus providing an alternate foundation not dependent on the flute, but light enough to be effective in string passages.

In a large instrument, where an important effect is a crescendo using only string stops to develop a build-up of tone, the difference between the hybrid muted flutes and the hybrid muted strings becomes important. Many people think of these as one tonal category, but their musical effect is quite different and must be taken into account. If a build-up is to be of pure string tone throughout, the starting point must be in the muted strings. On the other hand, if the desired effect is to start with a dark, mysterious tone color, gradually infusing it with the light of string tone as the build-up develops, then it is best to start with muted flutes.

If a very colorful tone with edge is required, it may be obtained with either an Orchestral Oboe or a Viole d'orchestre. The question becomes, which is more valuable in the tonal structure? Their close relationship, as shown on the wheel, presents the interesting option of substituting string tone for reed tone or vice versa.

The color wheel helps in making choices among flutes and color reeds for maximum variety and tonal interest. If an organ has only two flutes, one should be stopped or semi-open and the other open. If two color reeds are desired, one should be from the upper part of the wheel and one from the lower part for maximum tonal differentiation. An Oboe and Clarinet offer more variety than an Oboe and an English Horn.

In choosing the type of heroic reed to include on a larger instrument, a proper match with the room acoustic and musical needs is best made from a careful analysis of the various stop options, ranging from Bombarde to Harmonic Trumpet to Tuba Minor and Tuba Major. These stops graduate from light fundamental and strong overtones to heavier fundamental and weaker overtones.

One should not infer that the color wheel can be used as a pattern for the design of a particular organ. A well planned stop list does not have to include stops from every one of the tone wheel categories. There are no established proportions among tonal elements. The design of an organ depends on acoustical and musical requirements–not on a formula. The color wheel reveals possibilities for creative design through a systematic approach for placing tones in categories and illustrating their relationships.

NOMENCLATURE ODDITIES

Pipe organ nomenclature can certainly be confusing. This is especially true of names that we know from the symphony orchestra. For example, the French horn in the symphony orchestra offers a wide variety of tone colors, ranging from the brilliant hunting horn effect (*schmetternd*) to dark and covered melodic beauty (*gestopft*), depending on many factors, including the position of the hand in the bell and the angle of the bell. The French Horn of the organ imitates the dark and mellow moods of the orchestra's French horn, but the role played by the heroic character of the orchestral French horn is taken by the organ's Tuba Minor, which is a member of the trumpet family.

The tuba we most often hear in the symphony orchestra is the bass tuba. We forget that there is a whole family of tubas, and that the Tuba Major we hear in the organ, a member of the organ's tromba family, is like the tenor tuba or one of the treble Sax horns of the orchestra or band. The trombone leads to the opposite misunderstanding. In the organ, the name Trombone is usually reserved for a deep bass reed, whereas in the orchestra, the trombone we hear most often is the tenor trombone.

Oboe is another confusing organ name. The Orchestral Oboe sounds very little like the oboe of the symphony orchestra despite its name. The French Oboe or Hautbois is probably most like the orchestral instrument. The English Oboe and the capped Oboe Horn are only distant sonic relatives of the orchestral double reed instrument. Bassoon tone of the orchestra is seldom captured in the organ. The organ Bassoon is usually more closely related to brass tone than to woodwind tone. The English Horn is more successful, but the Saxophone is a stop that has been attempted many times without much success.

Everyone knows that the Vox Humana sounds nothing like a human voice. If the Vox Humana does have a vocal sound, it is the sound of a large choir of voices heard from a great distance. It is, of course, a choir with a somewhat unfashionable vibrato!

The stops that sound most like their orchestral counterparts are the open flutes. These have a quality similar to the traverse flute of the orchestra. Other successful parallels to orchestral sound are the Clarinet, the Trumpet and the narrow scale strings. On the other hand, there are stops developed over the centuries of organ evolution that we continue to call by names that we know are far off the mark, such as the Stopped Diapason, which is a flute.

Sometimes one name is used to describe two or more different tone qualities. For example, a Gemshorn can be slightly tapered and a member of the diapason family or strongly tapered and a member of the hybrid (muted string) category, sounding much like an Erzähler. For this reason the Gemshorn does not appear on the color wheel.

Remember, too, that the name of a stop may not indicate its proper tonal family relationship. Each builder has a system of nomenclature, and often names are assigned to stops at the request of a client or organist. The ear is the only reliable guide to assigning a stop to one of the color wheel categories.

The color wheel is an attempt to show the ever-changing and delightful kaleidoscope of musical beauty and drama that the thoughtfully designed organ is capable of producing. Perhaps it may open new avenues of thought about organ registration and design.

TIMELINE

YEAR	MONTH	EVENT
1996	April	Conference Center announced at general conference
	May	Jack Bethards recommended as consultant
	December	Trip to see organ at Ellis Auditorium, Memphis
1997	April	First meeting with President Hinckley and Ted Simmons
	May	First trip to California to inspect electronic organs
		Second trip to California to inspect electronic organ
		Memo written recommending pipe organ for CC
		Meeting with First Presidency to recommend pipe organ
	June	First Presidency approves pipe organ for CC
	July	Groundbreaking for CC
	August	Schoenstein responds to inquiry regarding their interest in being considered as a possible builder of CC organ
		Trip to California to examine pipe organs
	September	Visit with Mander and Harrison & Harrison in London
	October	Trip to Colorado Springs to see additional pipe organ
		Three preferred builders chosen
	November	Letters sent to prospective builders requesting proposals
		Trip east to visit shops of two prospective builders
	December	Visit to Schoenstein shop in San Francisco
		Proposals sent from prospective builders following shop visits
1998	January	Trip to examine organs by the three prospective builders
		Schoenstein selected to build CC organ
	February	Work begins on case design and stoplist
1999	January	Contract signed with Schoenstein
	February	First drawing of console layout sent
		Decision to revise Orchestral division to include theatre stops
	July	Second generation drawing of console layout sent
	September	Third generation drawing of console layout sent
	November	Blowers delivered to CC
	December	First shipment of façade pipes arrives for painting
2000	January	Schoenstein crew begins façade installation
	March	Last of display pipes delivered to CC
	April	CC opens for general conference
		First *Music and the Spoken Word* broadcast from CC
	May	Swell and Solo divisions delivered; installation begun
	June	Celebration for President Hinckley's 90th birthday
	July	Decision to float Grand Solo
		Choir and Orchestral divisions delivered; installation begun
		Blower room installation completed
	August	Incomplete organ console arrives at CC
	September	Tonal work and tuning on portions of Sw., Ch., & Solo
	October	General conference: CC dedicated; organ first played publicly
		Console returned to Schoenstein shop to be completed
	December	First Presidency Christmas Devotional in CC for first time
		First Tabernacle Choir Christmas concerts in CC

2001	All Year	Installation and tonal work continue
	January	Roof pedal chests and pipes installed
		(Violone, Open Wood, Bourdon, Trombone from 16-foot C)
	February	32-foot Trombone installed
		Completed console returned to CC
	March	Great delivered and installed
	May	Wiring completed
		Sw. 16' Bourdon removed; modified to serve as 16'–8' stop
		Millennial Trumpet heard for first time
		Winding completed
	July	Great reeds installed
		New Swell Small Open Diapason installed
	August	Tuba Horn installed (last rank to be placed in organ)
2002	All Year	Tonal work continues
	February	2002 Winter Olympics
	April-May	Stentor Diapason chest and pipes added to roof
		Structural bracing completed
		Completing installation; tools and supplies shipped back
		to California
2003	February, March	Tonal finishing sessions
	June	A.G.O. Regional Convention in Salt Lake City
		Inaugural organ concert featuring Todd Wilson
	Mid-August	Installation of Blower #4 replacement
2004	January	CC organ featured in *The American Organist* magazine
	May	Installation of replacement Clarinet stop
	December	Final tonal finishing
2005	January	Tabernacle closes for 27-month renovation
		Choir broadcasts and daily organ recitals now held in CC
		Stephen Cleobury organ recital in CC
	September	Delivery of custom bench from Fetzers'
	November	Richard Elliott organ recital in CC
2006	All Year	Choir broadcasts and daily organ recitals continue in CC
	May	*Now Let Us Rejoice* recorded on CC organ
2007	March	Tabernacle reopens for April general conference and is
		rededicated March 31
	April	Third American Classic Organ Symposium
		Ken Cowan organ recital in CC
	August	*Music and the Spoken Word* moves to CC through Labor
		Day; crowds too large for Tabernacle
2008	June – August	2 pm organ recitals held in CC Memorial Day through
		Labor Day. Noon recitals continue in Tabernacle
	February	Peterson doubles combination action memory levels to 198

A GLOSSARY OF ORGAN TERMS

Italicized words are defined in a separate entry. CC stands for Conference Center

8'. (read eight-foot pitch). A *stop* that sounds at the written pitch. In other words, middle C, played on an 8-foot stop, will sound the same pitch as middle C played on the piano.

4'. A *stop* that sounds one octave (the first overtone) above 8-foot pitch.

2⅔'. A *mutation* stop that sounds an octave plus a perfect fifth (the second overtone) above 8-foot pitch.

2'. A *stop* that sounds two octaves (the third overtone) above 8-foot pitch.

1⅗'. A *mutation* stop that sounds two octaves plus a major third (the fourth overtone) above 8-foot pitch.

1⅓'. A *mutation* stop that sounds two octaves plus a perfect fifth (the fifth overtone) above 8-foot pitch.

1'. A *stop* that sounds three octaves (the seventh overtone) above 8-foot pitch.

10⅔'. A *mutation* stop that sounds an octave plus a perfect fifth (the second overtone) above 32-foot pitch (which is a perfect fourth below 8-foot pitch).

16'. A *stop* that sounds one octave below 8-foot pitch.

32'. A *stop* that sounds two octaves below 8-foot pitch.

64'. A *stop* that sounds three octaves below 8-foot pitch.

American Classic. An eclectic tonal approach to organ building that was developed in America beginning in the 1930s and brought to its zenith by G. Donald Harrison, who designed the Salt Lake Tabernacle organ. Such organs are characterized by moderate *wind* pressures, articulate *voicing* and an abundance of *mixtures* and *mutations*, in an attempt to more successfully render European organ music of the 17th and 18th centuries.

American Romantic. A term used by Schoenstein & Co. to describe the characteristics of American organs built during the early decades of the 20th century and contemporary instruments, such as the one in the CC, built in a similar style. Such instruments tend to employ higher *wind* pressures and smooth *voicing*. These organs strive for greater dynamic range and a wide variety of tonal *color*—expressive characteristics of the symphony orchestra as applied to the organ.

Blind function. An action taken that alters the number of *stops* sounding without physically moving the *drawknobs*. The most common blind functions are the *crescendo pedal* and the *full organ* piston.

Blower. A large fan (turbine), powered by an electric motor, that produces compressed air (*wind*) to blow the pipes.

Borrowed stop. A *stop* made available on a *keyboard* other than its home keyboard is said to have been "borrowed" or "duplexed." On the CC organ, for example, the Cromorne has been made available on the Orchestral keyboard by "borrowing" it from the Choir *division*.   In the case of borrowed stops, the home division is shown in parentheses following the stop name.   Borrowing is common from the manual divisions into the Pedal to add flexibility and to conserve space and cost. Also see *extended stop.*

Case. The woodwork containing the display pipes of the organ. The front of the case is often rather elaborate, helping to create a dramatic visual effect.

Choir. The name of the lowest *manual* on the CC organ, and the home manual for the stops in that *division*. The Choir stops are *enclosed*, and are generally designed to be somewhat softer than those in other divisions of the organ.

Chorus. In organ *registration,* a chorus is an *ensemble* of *voices* (stops) at a variety of pitches. The more pitches present, the fuller the chorus is perceived to be. Often choruses are built using stops from a single *tonal family.* At other times, stops from different tonal families are blended, resulting in a hybrid chorus.

Color. In music, color is often used synonymously with "timbre," referring to the characteristic quality of sound produced by a particular instrument or, in the case of the organ, a particular *stop.*

Combination action. A system for storing a number of preselected *registrations* that can later be recalled by pressing a *piston* or *toe stud.*

Console. The control center for the organ, at which the organist sits to play the instrument.

Coupler. There are two general kinds of couplers: "intermanual," and "intramanual." <u>Intermanual</u> couplers enable *stops* to be played on *keyboards* other than their home keyboard. A Swell to Pedal coupler, for example, will cause any stops drawn in the Swell division to be played also on the Pedal keyboard (*pedalboard*). A Choir to Great coupler would cause any stops drawn in the Choir division to also play on the Great keyboard. With an 8-foot coupler drawn, all stops sound at their nominal pitch on the keyboard to which they are coupled. A 4-foot coupler (often called a super-coupler) causes them to sound an octave higher than their normal pitch, and a 16-foot coupler (often called a sub-coupler) causes stops to sound an octave lower than their normal pitch. <u>Intramanual</u> couplers affect the way stops sound on their home keyboard. If Choir to Choir 4' were drawn, for example, all stops drawn from the Choir division would sound not only at their nominal pitch, but also an octave higher when playing on the Choir keyboard. Similarly Choir to Choir 16' would cause any stops drawn to sound an octave lower than normal on the Choir keyboard. The Choir Unison Off coupler turns off all

Choir stops at their nominal pitch on the Choir keyboard, while still allowing the 4-foot and/ or 16-foot couplers to function, if drawn.

Crescendo pedal. A large pedal, sometimes called a "shoe," located in front of and above the *pedalboard.* The crescendo pedal, as it is depressed, adds stops in a predetermined order, thus gradually increasing the dynamic volume of the instrument. Since the *drawknobs* do not move as stops are added, this is referred to as a *blind function.* On the CC organ, a multi-segment LED bar graph on the nameboard indicates the position of the crescendo pedal. Of the five shoes on the CC organ, the crescendo pedal is the one farthest to the right (a position similar to that of the accelerator in an automobile).

Diapason. [dahy-uh-**pey**-zuhn, -suhn] See *Principal.*

Diaphone. A unique class of pipes whose tone generators use a valve to vibrate the air column, rather than a reed tongue. Developed around the turn of the 20th century by Robert Hope-Jones, diaphone pipes consist of a vibrator assembly (that generates the tone), and a resonator, like that of a *reed* pipe. More often found in theatre organs, diaphones are capable of producing solid, majestic bass power, perfectly suited to the immense size of the CC. The technology used in diaphone pipes is similar to that used in foghorns.

Division. Sometimes called "department," a division is a major section of the organ. Each keyboard generally controls a single division of the instrument; however, in the CC organ the fourth keyboard controls both the Solo and Grand Solo divisions. The divisions of the CC organ are Choir, Great, Swell, Solo, Grand Solo, Orchestral, and Pedal. The pipes from each division are usually housed together within the instrument, with the exception of the larger Pedal pipes. Because of their immense size, in the CC organ the largest Pedal pipes are located along the back and sidewalls of the organ space, mounted horizontally at the top of the instrument, and in and immediately behind the case.

Drawknob. Sometimes also called *stops*, the drawknobs, located on jambs to the right and left of the keyboards, control which *ranks* of pipes will sound when the keys are played. Pulling out a drawknob readies the pipes of that stop to play, and pushing it in "stops" those pipes from sounding. "Pulling out all the stops" is a commonly heard phrase derived from organ playing, meaning to use every resource at one's command.

Eight-foot pitch. The foundation pitch, or "center of gravity" for organ *manual divisions*. See *8'*.

Enclosure, Enclosed. Organ pipes are designed and *regulated* to speak at just one volume level. To create the impression that they can play louder or softer, they must be placed in a sealed enclosure, or *expression box*, fitted with *louvers* (sometimes called expression shades) on the front that can be opened and closed by means of an *expression pedal* to allow more or less sound to be emitted from the box into the auditorium. On the CC organ, five *divisions* are enclosed: Swell, Choir, Solo, Grand Solo and Orchestral.

Ensemble. In organ registration, an assortment of appropriate *stops* chosen by the organist to create a particular musical effect. Also, see *chorus*.

Expression box. Sometimes called "swell box," the expression box is an *enclosure* that allows for gradations in the perceived dynamic level of pipes contained within it.

Expression pedal(s). Large pedal(s) (sometimes called "shoes") located above and in front of the *pedalboard*. These pedals cause the *louvers* of an *enclosure* to open and close, thus giving the organist dynamic control over pipes within the enclosure. The CC organ has four such pedals, the functions of which can be variously assigned.

Expressive. A term associated with pipes that are *enclosed* in an *expression box*, thus giving the organist dynamic control of their sound. Also see *enclosure*.

Extended stop. By adding twelve pipes (one octave) to the upper end of an existing *rank*, a 16-foot *stop* can also be played as an 8-foot stop, or an 8-foot stop as a 4-foot stop, etc. The practice of "extension" is commonly encountered in the Pedal division to save space and control cost, and may occasionally also be found in the manuals. In the CC organ, for example, the Swell 8-foot Bourdon is an extension of the 16-foot Bourdon. The fact that only twelve pipes are shown in the stoplist for the 8-foot Bourdon indicates that it is an extension, and the extended stop has the same name (Bourdon) as its parent stop. In the CC organ, many of the ranks in the Swell and Choir divisions contain sixty-eight pipes in order to extend their range by seven notes when 4-foot *couplers* are used. Also see *borrowed stop*.

Façade. The face or front of the organ *case*. The façade is designed to make an attractive visual statement, utilizing both pipes and woodwork. The pipes in the façade are often real, working pipes.

Flue. An organ pipe whose tone is generated by *wind* blowing across the lip of the pipe, which causes the column of air inside the pipe to vibrate. In contrast to *reed* pipes, a flue pipe generates its tone very much like a simple whistle or the flute of the orchestra.

Flute. A *flue* pipe of wide *scale*, which tends to emphasize the fundamental tone over harmonic development, producing a tone rather flute-like in quality. There are many varieties of flute tone, depending on the particular way the pipe is constructed.

Full organ. A *reversible* device (*piston*, *toe stud or toe lever*) which, when pressed, turns on a very large, preset *ensemble* of *stops*. On many organs this function is called "Tutti" or "Sforzando."

Grand Solo. A *division* of the CC organ played from the fourth *keyboard* from the bottom. The Grand Solo is *enclosed* and contains a heroic tuba chorus, plus a brilliant mixture that can crown the entire organ.

Great. On the CC organ, the Great is the name of the second keyboard (counting from bottom to top). It is the home keyboard for the stops in that *division*. The Great is considered an organ's main division.

Hybrid. A *stop* constructed and *voiced* to exhibit characteristics of two *tonal families*.

Keyboard. A set of keys used to play a musical instrument. Organs usually contain multiple keyboards, the CC organ having six—five of which are played by the hands (*manuals*), and one played with the feet (pedalboard). Most organs, including the CC, have manuals that contain sixty-one keys and a *pedalboard* with thirty-two keys.

Louvers. Sturdy slats that are placed on the front of an *enclosure* in Venetian blind fashion. The louvers can be opened and closed from the *console* to adjust the amount of sound being emitted from the enclosure. In the CC organ, the louvers, each 7" wide and $1\frac{1}{2}$" thick, are installed vertically. Louvers are sometimes referred to as "shades" or "shutters."

Manual. A *keyboard* that is played with the hands. The five manuals on the CC organ are, from bottom to top, *Choir*, *Great*, *Swell*, *Solo* and *Orchestral*. Like many organs, the CC organ's manuals contain sixty-one keys, spanning five octaves from bass (or low) CC to c^4, three octaves above middle C.

MIDI. An acronym for Musical Instrument Digital Interface. MIDI is an industry-standard protocol that enables musical instruments so equipped to communicate with each other. A synthesizer, for example, could be connected to the CC organ and played from any of its *keyboards*. The MIDI interface also allows a performance to be encoded on a $3\frac{1}{2}$" diskette and replayed using the Yamaha MIDI data filer

in the right-hand drawer of the *console*.

Mixture. A *stop* consisting of multiple *ranks* of pipes. Mixtures are used to simultaneously add harmonics of varying pitches, resulting in a more colorful and brilliant *ensemble* sound. Mixtures are usually scaled and voiced as *principals*.

Mutation. A stop that sounds a pitch other than a unison or octave (foundation tone). The pitches sounded by mutation stops (mostly fifths and thirds) occur naturally in the harmonic overtone series. The strengthening of a particular overtone causes the foundation tone to change or "mutate." Mutation stops are used to add distinctive *color* to foundation tone.

Orchestral. The name of the fifth (uppermost) *manual* of the CC organ and home to the stops of the *expressive* Orchestral *division*. The Orchestral division contains several stops intended to be played against an accompaniment on another manual. Some of its stops are reminiscent of the sound of orchestral instruments, such as Clarinet and Cor Anglais (English Horn).

Pedalboard, Pedal. The *keyboard* played by the feet, and the *division* of the organ that is home to that keyboard. Like many organs, the CC organ's pedalboard contains thirty-two keys, from bass (or low) CC to g^1 (middle G). The pitch center of the pedal division is generally considered to be 16-foot pitch, an octave below that of the *manual* divisions.

Piston or Thumb Piston. Small buttons located beneath each keyboard that, when pressed, recall a preselected combination of *stops*. See also *combination action* and *toe stud*.

Principal or Diapason. A type of *flue* pipe that produces what is often described as "basic organ tone." The principal stops are considered to be the "backbone" of the organ. The tone is characterized by a balance between fundamental (or foundation) tone and harmonic development.

Rank. A set of pipes matching in tone quality, one for each note on the keyboard. The pipes of a rank will vary in length, in order to provide the various pitches needed. The *speaking length* of an open *manual* 8-foot rank, for example, will vary from approximately eight feet to three inches, over the keyboard's five-octave range. While many manual ranks contain sixty-one pipes and pedal ranks thirty-two pipes, there are exceptions. Many ranks in the CC organ's Swell and Choir *divisions* contain sixty-eight pipes, in order to extend the range when 4-foot *couplers* are used. Occasionally ranks will have fewer pipes than expected, such as in some mixtures and occasional celeste ranks. See also, *straight stop*, *borrow*, *extension*, *voice*.

Reed. An organ pipe whose tone is generated by a thin, brass tongue (reed) vibrating against a small, open-faced, hollow tube (*shallot*). The resulting tone is then amplified by a resonator (often conical in shape), which comprises the top portion of the pipe.

Registration. The art of selecting appropriate *stops* for a given piece of music.

Regulating, Regulation. The process of refining the *voicing* of a *rank* of pipes at the installation site. It involves primarily adjusting the loudness and, to some extent, the speech and tonal characteristics of the pipes to fit the acoustic of the room and achieve a musically appropriate balance throughout the compass of the rank.

Reversible. A *piston* or *toe stud* that usually affects a single stop or coupler. Pressing the reversible once engages the associated stop or coupler; pressing it again disengages it. *Full organ* is also a reversible function.

Scale. In organ building, scale refers to the relationship between the diameter of a pipe and its *speaking length*. The wider the pipe (relative to its length), the stronger will be its fundamental tone. A narrower pipe (relative to its length), produces stronger harmonic development.

Shallot. A part of the sound-producing mechanism of a *reed* organ pipe. The shallot is a hollow tube with its lower end closed and the upper end open. A section of the wall of the shallot is cut away and finished off to a flat surface. The slit, or shallot opening, thus formed is covered by a thin brass tongue (reed) that is fixed to the upper end of the shallot.

Shutters. See *louvers*.

Sixteen-foot pitch. The foundation pitch or "center of gravity" for the *Pedal* division of the organ. See *16'*.

Solo. On the CC organ, the fourth *keyboard* from the bottom. The Solo keyboard is home to the stops of both the Solo and *Grand Solo* sections of the instrument. The Solo *division* is *enclosed* and contains several stops intended for solo use, against an accompaniment on another manual. On the CC organ, the Solo division also includes a *principal chorus*.

Speaking length. In a *flue* pipe, the speaking length is the distance from the mouth of the pipe to its top or, in other words, the length of the column of air that vibrates inside the pipe. A pipe's speaking length is shorter than its overall length, which also includes the length of its foot (the portion of the pipe below the mouth). A very high-pitched pipe may be about the size of a pencil in overall length, yet have a speaking length of three-quarters of an inch or less.

Stop. "Stop" is a word that can have various meanings, depending on context. It is sometimes used as a shortened version of *drawknob* (or *stopknob*). It is also used synonymously with *voice*.

Straight stop. A *stop* that plays its own, discrete rank(s) of pipes is said to be a straight stop, as opposed to one that is *borrowed* from another division or *extended* from another stop.

String. A type of *flue* pipe of narrow *scale*, producing a tone relatively weak in fundamental, but with strong harmonic development. The harmonic content is somewhat similar to that of a bowed string.

Swell. The name of the third of the CC organ's five *keyboards*, and the home keyboard for the stops in that *division*. The Swell division is *expressive*, or *enclosed*, and, in the CC organ, is nearly equal in strength to the *Great* division. The Swell takes its name from its ability to "swell" (increase) in volume.

Swell box. Another name for *expression box*. Also see *enclosure*.

Swell pedal(s). A commonly used name for *expression pedal(s)*.

Swell shades. See *louvers*.

Thumb piston. See *piston*.

Toe stud. A small knob or lever, located just above the *pedalboard* and designed to be pressed with the feet. Toe studs function either as *pistons* to recall a preset combination of *stops*, or as *reversibles*.

Tonal design. The art of determining what *stops* are to be included in an organ, and specifying precisely how each stop is to be *scaled* and constructed. Tonal design is usually the domain of the tonal director, who supervises *voicing* in the factory and *tonal finishing* at the job site. Often, several different voicers and tonal finishing teams work on one instrument. It is the tonal director's job to coordinate all of these efforts for a musically integrated result.

Tonal families. Organ sound is often divided into four broad categories: *Diapason* (or *Principal*); *Flute*; *String*; and *Reed*. Those four basic families are sometimes further divided, as in Table 2 of Chapter 10. Echo Diapasons are soft Diapasons. Flutes may be subdivided into "open" or "stopped," depending on whether the top of the pipe is capped (which lowers its pitch one octave) or left open. *Hybrids* share some of the characteristics of two tonal families. "Chorus" reeds include trumpets, trombones and tubas, and are often added to the *ensemble* for brilliance and power. "Color"

reeds produce softer reed qualities such as French Horn, Clarinet, and English Horn (Cor Anglais). The color reeds are usually used for playing a solo melodic line, accompanied by a contrasting *registration* on a different keyboard.

Tonal finishing. The process of directing the *regulation* of each pipe in relation to the other pipes in its *rank*, and each rank in relation to other ranks in its *tonal family*, its division, and the entire *ensemble* of the instrument. Tonal finishing may be compared to the work of a conductor who balances the color and dynamics of instruments in an orchestra. Tonal finishing is a team effort, involving a "voicer," who physically works with the pipes, and a "finisher" making musical and acoustical judgments at the console. Most voicers are skilled in both roles. Most finishers have basic voicing skills or knowledge of the voicing process. In some cases, voicer and finisher trade roles during the day to gain a complete perspective of the instrument. The finisher is usually the primary decision maker, but in some cases, the voicer determines the objective, and the finisher directs the voicer in matching pipes to samples preselected by the voicer at the console at the start of the finishing session.

Tone. The quality or character of musical sound.

Touch- (or Velocity-) sensitive keyboard. A *keyboard*, similar to that of a piano, from which the volume of sound produced is dependent upon the speed or energy with which the key is depressed. Organs with electro-pneumatic action have no need for such keyboards. The only reason for including one would be to enable an organist to use variations of touch to control the volume of some electronic instrument that might be connected to the organ through a *MIDI* interface.

Tremulant. A mechanical device that causes the *wind* pressure in a *windchest* to increase and decrease (pulse) at a steady rate, producing a vibrato (undulating) effect.

Voice. A discrete tonal color. "Voice" is often used interchangeably with *stop*. Most organ voices consist of a single *rank* of pipes, but *mixtures* are compound stops that are comprised of multiple ranks. The CC organ has 103 voices, but because of its several mixture stops contains 130 ranks.

Voicing. The skillful production of tone, involving setting the timbre and speech characteristics of pipes by adjusting the variable elements at the mouth of a *flue* pipe or the several components that comprise a *reed* pipe. Many skilled organ technicians are capable of executing basic voicing procedures, however, a "voicer" is a specialist, thoroughly versed in all aspects of the art and capable of obtaining a uniform result throughout the entire compass of a *rank* of pipes.

Wind. Air under pressure. Wind pressure is measured by the amount of displacement of a column of water in a special gauge that is temporarily applied to a windchest.

Windchest. An airtight box on which the pipes of an organ are placed *rank* by rank. The windchest contains valves that open to admit wind into the pipes, and close to stop the air flow. The CC organ uses Pitman-style windchests that operate electro-pneumatically (electro-magnets controlling leather pneumatic pouches that open and close valves).

INDEX

Boldface locators indicate a more extensive treatment of topic. Locators followed by an asterisk (*) indicate photographs or other illustrations. Locators followed by *n* indicate endnotes. CC stands for Conference Center.

PHOTO CREDITS

Jeffrey D. Allred: 44. © 2008 Jeffrey D. Allred, *Deseret News*. (Use courtesy of *Deseret News*.)

Welden C. Andersen: Jacket back cover bottom, 111, 126. (Use courtesy of Intellectual Reserve, Inc.)

Lamont Anderson: 17, 18, 38, 39 bottom, 57, 116 left and right, 118, 137, 149 top left and right, 151 right and bottom, 152 right.

Wendell Ballantyne: 139.

Scott Bleak: 73, 76.

Drake Busath: Jacket back flap. (Use courtesy of Busath Photography.)

Busath Photography: 28. (Use courtesy of Busath Photography.)

Jed A. Clark: 163. (Use courtesy of Intellectual Reserve, Inc.)

Daughters of the Utah Pioneers: 6. (Use courtesy of Daughters of the Utah Pioneers.)

Jim Harland: 77 right, 105 bottom, 106, 117, 121 top, 123 all but far right, 124 all, 125 right, 148 bottom right, 151 top left.

Intellectual Reserve, Inc.: Jacket front cover, Jacket back cover top, 2, 9, 12, 14, 35, 39 top, 45 top, 53. (Use courtesy of Intellectual Reserve, Inc.)

Janice Massatt: 140 left.

Kenneth Mays: 19, 45 lower.

Louis Patterson: 77 bottom, 103 left and right, 107 bottom, 110, 123 far right, 125 left, 146 all, 148 all except bottom right, 149 lower three, 152 left, 154 all. (Use courtesy of Schoenstein & Co.)

Schoenstein & Co.: 46, 115, 121 lower, 131, 140 right. (Use courtesy of Schoenstein & Co.)

Joe Smithberger: 77 top left. (Use courtesy of A.R. Schopp's Sons, Inc.)

Ed Thompson: 29.